# JESUIT HIGHER EDUCATION IN A SECULAR AGE

# JESUIT HIGHER EDUCATION in a SECULAR AGE

## A Response to Charles Taylor and the Crisis of Fullness

### Daniel S. Hendrickson, SJ

GEORGETOWN UNIVERSITY PRESS / WASHINGTON, DC

The publisher is not responsible for third-party websites or their content. URL links were active at time of publication.

Library of Congress Cataloging-in-Publication Data

Names: Hendrickson, Daniel Scott, author.
Title: Jesuit higher education in a secular age: a response to Charles Taylor and the crisis of fullness / Daniel Scott Hendrickson.
Description: Washington, DC: Georgetown University Press, 2022. | Includes bibliographical references and index.
Identifiers: LCCN 2021022861 | ISBN 9781647122331 (hardcover) | ISBN 9781647122348 (ebook)
Subjects: LCSH: Taylor, Charles, 1931– Secular age. | Jesuits–Education (Higher) | Jesuit universities and colleges. | Education–Philosophy. | Secularism. | Religion and culture.
Classification: LCC LC493.H457 2022 | DDC 378/.071–dc23

LC record available at https://lccn.loc.gov/2021022861

∞ This paper meets the requirements of ANSI/NISO Z39.48–1992 (Permanence of Paper).

23 22     9 8 7 6 5 4 3 2

Printed in the United States of America

Cover design by Brad Norr
Interior design by BookComp, Inc.

*I dedicate this book to the inspiring mission of Jesuit higher education and to my many mentors and colleagues who daily live its tradition honorably and creatively, transform the lives of students, and strive for a bright future.*

# CONTENTS

# JESUIT HIGHER EDUCATION AND THE RESTORATION OF ENCHANTMENT

The philosopher Charles Taylor argues in *A Secular Age* that secular cultures are losing the capacity to experience genuine "fullness."[1] He developed this concept of human flourishing from studies in philosophy and anthropology, corresponding to existential senses of meaning and purpose. Taylor returns consistently to fullness through dimensions of "contact" with a transcendent reality. He characterizes these intersections of contact as phenomenal experiences that translate as a way of relating, both morally and ethically.

Through my ongoing engagement with Taylor's interpretation of contemporary Western culture, his two general descriptions of fullness, and his "ontic" or philosophical commitment to a transcendent source, I developed three specific ways of sharing with students and others what I call "pedagogies of fullness": study, solidarity, and grace. These are my terms for higher education strategies emerging from the Renaissance humanist tradition of Jesuit education. They facilitate human, relational contacts that make fullness, and, hence, meaning and purpose, possible.

By networking multiple understandings of individual experience (study); immersing students in contexts of otherness, or alterity (solidarity); and validating inexplicable and phenomenal moments of consolation, gratitude, and wonder (grace), I argue that Jesuit higher education has the opportunity to restore fullness in our increasingly and more resolutely secular age. Moreover, as Taylor characterizes Western individuals as independent and invulnerable, my three pedagogies of fullness open up interdependence and vulnerability as relational possibilities to ourselves, others, and an Other. These correspond to my hopeful, philosophical way of envisioning both the self and the social. This way of seeing and envisioning, part of what is more broadly often referred to as a "Jesuit imaginary" views people and social milieus as inter-related, and interrelational. They, and we, transform each other.

As these pedagogies and this imaginary emerge organically from the precepts of Jesuit higher education and work together to cultivate Taylor's fullness, they offer possibilities for various interpretations of this book as a whole. For instance, it is possible to evaluate them as laying out a challenge to Jesuit higher education in the twenty-first century to better realize the origins and history of its own tradition. A Jesuit university, then, can be assessed in relation to how well it knows and lives the fundamental tenets of its origins, as well as how well it recognizes and responds to contemporary problematic cultural conditions.

Moreover, for Jesuit universities where any or all aspects of these peda-gogies are already in practice, I intend this book to endorse their fine work. I offer this book as a bridge between Jesuit higher education's reality and Tay-lor's existential and cultural concerns. Taylor's parlance of porous and buffered selves, his social imaginary, fullness, and more, give Ignatian and Jesuit terms a contemporary philosophical backdrop against which we can view them.

Finally, I argue that higher education participates quite widely in what I refer to as a "crisis of fullness." Whether higher education is symptomatic of present-day expressions of fragmentation, superficiality, and instrumen-tality, or whether it is a source of them, I explain why I believe Taylor's con-ception of fullness is both visionary and vulnerable, and why the specific arena of Jesuit higher education can and should remedy such problems and facilitate Taylor's relational possibilities.

Although all things Jesuit are fundamentally Roman Catholic, discussing the intellectual tradition, the history and culture, and the pertinent authori-tative documents of the Church—essential aspects of any Catholic univer-sity—are beyond this book's scope. Instead, this is a work of philosophy, history, and education research intended to undergird other efforts with my study and theory.

Chapter 1, "The Search for Fullness in a Secular Age," proposes study, sol-idarity, and grace as three Jesuit higher educational strategies that function as contemporary remedies for Taylor's identification of a crisis of fullness. It also sets up later Renaissance humanist, Jesuit, and higher education ele-ments, given that each pedagogy amplifies a relational dynamic cultivating conditions that are needed to realize Taylor's visionary potential. Within the context of the self, among others, and with an Other, these relations also cor-respond philosophically to epistemic, moral-ethical, and metaphysical possi-bilities. In their explicitly relational qualities, my concept of the pedagogies of study, solidarity, and grace establishes for students of Jesuit higher education ways of knowing and living that can propel them, and all of us, into the future.

Chapter 2, "Developing Taylor's Conception of Fullness," explains further how contemporary thinkers display yearnings for his fullness in their own works. After considering possible hermeneutic, Heideggerian, existential, and epistemic semblances of fullness, I return to the concept itself and extend it to the Christian idea of agape. Aspects of agape reinforce a religious sensibility of fullness but also introduce a strong moral-ethical correlation. I conclude by recognizing a correspondence between personal instances of fullness and social relating, thereby forecasting a particular imaginary, that is, a Jesuit imaginary.

Chapter 3, "Charles Taylor in Educational Discourse," has two objectives: first, to show how educational theorists use Taylor creatively, confidently, and consistently; and second, to demonstrate ways the academy currently discusses and debates *A Secular Age*. Chapter 4, "Renaissance Humanistic Backgrounds of Jesuit Educational Thought," returns to the genesis of Renaissance humanism in my own observations and through the life and work of the educational theorist and teacher Pier Paolo Vergerio. It prepares the reader for the longest chapter, 5, "The Tradition of Jesuit Education," where various inspirations and ideals converge, each of which influences our current educational tradition. A rapid process of growth, the development of educational documents, a global dissemination of the tradition, the propagation of strident humanist essentials, the deployment of a hopeful anthropology, and the sharing of a discerning spirituality of the Jesuit order all shaped a tradition well equipped to deal with the existential crisis of a secular age that Taylor describes.

In chapter 6, "Higher Education in a Secular Age," I propose a higher educational context through which I have discussed pedagogies of fullness in the Jesuit university. This context exposes current higher education problems quite similar to Taylor's personal concerns of fullness. Initially referred to as *malaises*, these problems reveal contemporary trends of institutional fragmentation, superficial subjectivity, and instrumental epistemics that are recognized and grieved for by historians, philosophers, and other scholars. Given that these problems represent commonplace orientations of the university in general, readers might also recognize in them expressions that compromise the existential realities of fullness that they notice in students' lives. The concluding chapter, 7, "Forming a Learned Imagination," sets the pedagogies of study, solidarity, and grace as goals. They lead us to a collective and individual imagination formed by a Jesuit perspective, one that is now able to engage and integrate self, society, and our world.

This is a more hopeful picture than one we have often been given of students and universities today. How students of Jesuit higher learning envision themselves, others, and the world already represents an operative Jesuit imaginary. It is a social context that is widely communal, and presently holds the promise of always moving closer to genuine fullness. And if you read Taylor as I do, experiencing something of fullness in our lives is to once again be enchanted.

## NOTE

1. Charles Taylor, *A Secular Age* (Cambridge, MA: Belknap Press of Harvard University Press, 2007).

# CHAPTER ONE

# THE SEARCH FOR FULLNESS
# IN A SECULAR AGE

The philosopher Charles Taylor's *A Secular Age* was the motivating force of this book.[1] It not only inspired me, but it also launched scholarly discussions from many camps in the academy. In an age of academic disciplines, and with corresponding concerns about a lack of dialogue between departments on university campuses, it is remarkable to see literary critics, historians, philosophers, political theorists, scientists, sociologists, and theologians conversing so eagerly about a single publication. In New York, Chicago, and New Haven, conferences immediately convened after the 2007 publication of the book. More recently—in journals like *Faith and Philosophy, Inquiry,* and *New Blackfriars;* and in books such as *Rethinking Secularism* (2011), *The Joy of Secularism* (2011), and, in particular, *Varieties of Secularism in a Secular Age* (2010)—scholars with many interests have devoted serious attention to *A Secular Age.* In all its nine hundred magisterial and prize winning pages, Taylor explains that the northern Atlantic societies of the global community—those nations framing the upper quadrant of the Atlantic Ocean, such as Western European, Scandinavian, and North American states—are less religious than ever. In the course of world history, this is "sudden," the result of a five-hundred-year process of secularization that he and now I address.

Taylor is not traditionally categorized as a philosopher, given that he accepts support and entertains challenges from thinkers both within and beyond his own particular discipline. I am willing to do likewise, for three reasons. The first is that the disciplinary silos within the academy could and should be more conversant with one another. Special interests and pointed inquiries within disciplines lead to historic insights in their respective fields of study, but remarkable achievements are also discovered in collaboration. Recent discussions about the state of higher education understand a current crisis of university culture through, in part, fragmented academic communities. The situation is not uncomplicated, but some regret how inquiries lead to ends of their own through means of their own. Moreover, some perspectives—for example, scientific ones—gain influence and prestige in proportions that stifle and silence others. As a result, not only are interests and inquiries dealt with in isolation from others, but some are disregarded. Taylor, a philosopher with communitarian sensibilities, allows for a more open dialogue, whereby historians, scientists, sociologists, and theologians, for example, participate meaningfully in a conversation he frames.

He prefigured key backgrounds for *A Secular Age* in a 1996 lecture, "A Catholic Modernity." It was given at a Catholic institution, the University of Dayton, when he received a prestigious award, and it was later published by Oxford University Press.[2] "The remarkable fact that academic culture in the Western world breathes an atmosphere of unbelief," he describes, "has cultivated . . . a habit of masking religious interest."[3] He concedes, "Yes, [some of us] do a lot of that, obviously too much. The reasons are many, including ones to do with the advantages . . . of conformity."[4] Some such advantages, according to him, regard reputation, tenure, and promotion.

In his speech Taylor publicly identifies himself as a Roman Catholic, and, subsequently, the talk grounds him in important ways. First, his gesture toward unbelief, in the decisively rational context of the university, is simply a good entrée into *A Secular Age* and his explanation of the five-hundred-year process leading us to the less-religious place the academy finds itself today.

Even though in many ways Taylor is a philosopher, he is also a historian of ideas. He thinks across millennia. If there was any doubt about his faith perspective after his "Catholic Modernity" address, or if it is unfamiliar to readers who know him exclusively through his more scholarly, but religiously muted, publications—such as *Sources of the Self: The Making of the Modern Identity* (1989) and *The Ethics of Authenticity* (1991)—Taylor's recent *A Secular Age* is a full and wider manifestation of a profound religious identity in his life and work.

To expand on this first point, I believe Taylor wants us to recognize the geocultural and sociocultural spread of Western secularism that began to unfold in the sixteenth century, around the time of the Protestant Reformation. We must recognize it, he insists, in comparison with the once-enduring Christian reality dominating the history of these places before 1500, and also in comparison with the rest of the global community today: Hindu India, the Muslim Middle East, Catholic Latin America, Buddhist Asia, and so on. Perhaps the suddenness of secularism is more evident. Whether it is or is not, Taylor's main point is that the current stronghold dynamic of Western secularism by no means attests to a simple subtraction theory; that is, the West grew up and got smart. Becoming secular is not a matter of what is being let go or sloughed off. An understanding of secularism is incomplete if it only accounts for Enlightenment-era rationality and scientific achievement that mitigate and invalidate alternative perspectives of knowing. If Western secularism comes about quickly, it is also complicated, and many forces, Christianity included, are seriously complicit. The introductory remarks to Taylor's "Catholic Modernity" essay, then, establish for us Taylor's religious interest and the *existential* version of secularism he focuses upon.

This leads to my second reason for following Taylor's lead, and for referencing these opening remarks. Taylor's talk is an indictment that the academy generally masks religious belief or, simply, breathes unbelief. Though he has quietly noted his own religious commitment throughout his career, in this particular address he directly embraces the reality. Recognizing nuance is ironic because it is such an important dynamic of *A Secular Age*. Nuance happens in Taylor's parsing of "secularism" as a term. The overarching nuance regards the version of secularity he wishes to discuss, "Secularity 3": the conditions of belief.[5] It narrows the discussion of secularism away from an analytical concern about religious creeds and their contents, and also away from questions about the nature of faith and belief, and simultaneously expands the discussion and frames an existential preoccupation. He wants to discuss secularism in the ways it affects our daily lives and how we understand our own selves and our emotional, intellectual, political, and social capacities and relations. Knowing his existential focus, and also its correspondent Secularity 3, is crucial for understanding better the lengthy narrative of Western culture he chronicles.

This existential focus engages my third reason for referencing Taylor's uncharacteristic religious transparency in his 1996 lecture. Readers of Taylor's work cannot now *not* appreciate the roles and meanings of specifically religious terms and motives in his writing. For instance, his deployment of the Greek term "agape" in *A Secular Age* is significant. It is a Christian word and should be interpreted as such. Agape, moreover, is expressly important to my book as a whole in its connection to Taylor's term "fullness," a fundamental construct in *A Secular Age*. In my understanding, fullness represents the thrust of Taylor's book and drives it. The term is a philosophical-anthropological construct that functions in tandem with the existential perspective of Taylor's Secularity 3. The cultural conditions of belief and the human experience of fullness together manifest important insights about a secular age. Taylor deploys agape to further expand our interpretation of fullness, and if he is right about the academy, dwelling in an overt religious construct creates something of a challenge for us.

## TAYLOR'S FULLNESS AS THE CONTEXT OF THIS BOOK

Taylor affirms that many people have a certain kind of experience when life seems purpose-filled, connected, driven, and genuine.[6] This phenomenal moment facilitates a profound sense of interior peace and a sense of wholeness. A personal instance as such "unsettles and breaks through our ordinary sense of being in the world, with its familiar objects, activities and points of reference, . . . when 'ordinary reality is abolished and something terrifyingly *other* shines through.'"[7] He discusses this on page 5; but 607 pages later, he keeps looking back over his shoulder to this epiphanic description of "fullness" and to Bede Griffiths, the person through whom it occurred. Griffiths was an Englishman who remembered a certain moment of fullness for the rest of his life. His experience of fullness recalls a dimming springtime evening in his school-age youth, one filled with birdsong and new blossoms, and around the boy, the friendly flight of a chirping lark. The combined elements of the external world, a calmed and confirmed disposition within Griffiths himself, and a poignant sense of meaning and purpose were sudden. It seized Griffiths, and in some way, it encompassed and enchanted him. He felt attentive to the world and his life in a way that was notable for its intensity and impression, but he also felt pulled beyond himself, or at least influenced by something he himself did not originate. For years Griffiths seems to have been wonderfully haunted by this moment.[8]

Never forgetting an experience that seemed existentially transformative, Griffiths later became a Benedictine monk, and he soon left the locale of his English monastery to spend his life in India, and eventually in an Indian ashram. From the subcontinent he, a Western-trained monastic, established a career comparing and articulating the affinities and symbolic contrasts among Christian, Hindu, and Muslim experiences of fullness.[9]

"What I want to do" in *A Secular Age*, Taylor insists, "is focus attention on the different kinds of lived experience involved in understanding your life in one way or the other."[10] His way of doing this stems from Griffiths's revelation and Taylor's prognosis that the experience of fullness—in particular, an expression of being enchanted by realities or a singular reality beyond us—will cease occurring for those of us who dwell in a secular age. His discussion about the kinds of experiences that we rarely or no longer enjoy exposes a concern. He worries that our Western and modern-era perspective will either misinterpret fullness as self-generated, or that our twenty-first-century sensibilities will prevent fullness from happening altogether. In a subsequent publication, moreover, Taylor speaks about fullness as a categorical term that attempts to capture and highlight an aspect of the human condition whereby each of us experiences life either as meaningful, genuine, and authentic or as capable of being such.[11]

Taylor wants to rescue fullness, resuscitating a part of our lives. In *A Secular Age*, he speaks and writes about being *disenchanted*, and indicates that he is interested in something that might be called *reenchantment*. The lament of modernity and its particular malaises—discussed in both *Sources of the Self* and *The Ethics of Authenticity*—are related. In accord with Taylor's diagnosis, I interpret the waning or simply *un*occurring experience of fullness on our individual campuses as steadily grieved in *A Secular Age*. This eclipse of fullness is the fundamental malady of the kind of disenchantment that disturbs Taylor so profoundly.

When Taylor arrives at his final chapter, he returns to fullness and Griffiths's epiphany. The sensibility it represents was familiar to the late Czech poet, activist, and political leader Václav Havel, who experienced profound fullness during imprisonment at the Heřmanice Correctional Institute in Ostrava, former Czechoslovakia, sometime between 1979 and 1984. He recorded this in his *Letters to Olga* (1984).[12] Taylor refers to epiphanies like Griffiths's and Havel's as "heightened moments of love"—a "satisfying" or "motivating intensity," according to Michael Warner[13]—that are not "dangerous" sensations of personal empowerment but, rather, similar to the transformation revolutionizing the life of Ignatius of Loyola, the late-medieval Spaniard and founder of the Society of Jesus, the Jesuits.[14] In his own writing, Ignatius indicates notable moments of interior or spiritual consolation, describing them as an awareness of connection, reconciliation, light, purpose, peace, and general confirmation.[15] But Taylor asserts that "we have to enlarge our palette of such points of contact with fullness, because we are too prone in our age to think of this contact in terms of 'experience'; and to think of experience as something subjective, distinct from the object experienced; as something to do with our feelings, distinct from changes in our being: dispositions, orientations, the bent of our lives."[16]

He considers less contemplative and ecstatic expressions that refer more immediately to the transformation of one's life, offering it as a genuine and persistent expression of moral, ethical relating.[17] Fullness invites us to conceive subjectivity as open to emotional, social, political, and spiritual possibilities. As fullness gains momentum in *A Secular Age*, he connects it to capacities for friendship, intimacy, dialogue, moral responsibility, social and political cooperation and action, prayer, and social justice. The ambit of fullness is particularly wide and distinctly relational. Later in this book, we will see how Taylor further expands fullness beyond potentially sensational epiphanies into a more balanced moral-ethical dynamic of love, represented by "agape."

"Study," "solidarity," and "grace" are terms I use to construct my specific vision of a Jesuit imaginary. They are distinct, yet they share a sensibility for dimensions of openness. Within the self, toward others, and to an Other: I refer to these strategies of instruction collectively as pedagogies because they are all specifically relational. Many avenues of associating and connecting qualify them, while educating us to engage with Taylor's sense of fullness. As the pedagogies build upon one another, we will see how the work of "study" explores and establishes a sense of self that moves respectfully, inquisitively, and adaptively into the contexts of difference that a student will experience as "solidarity." In turn, "study" and "solidarity" will condition a student to better welcome and readily value the inexplicable, phenomenal, and transformative dimensions of "grace."

I have set up the stratagems of study, solidarity, and grace to emerge organically out of the tradition of Jesuit education, while framing them for their ability to condition ways of relating. Focusing here upon subjective, social, and transcendent relations, the pedagogies of fullness can alleviate contemporary problems of strident meaninglessness. In their ability to *restore* relations, they make fullness possible. Further, agape, an expanded version of fullness described by Taylor as a kind of "stepping beyond," also functions in my model as *moving toward*. Study, solidarity, and grace move students of Jesuit higher learning toward themselves, others, and an Other.

## AN OVERVIEW OF EACH PEDAGOGY OF FULLNESS

Although the interplay of my pedagogies of fullness is not insignificant, it is necessary to appreciate each of them on their own, including better knowing the distinct spaces they each represent. Within the context of the self, in the alterity of people and places well beyond our own familiar milieus, and from the heavens, they each stand within especial geographies ripe and ready for exploration, understanding, and formation.

### The Pedagogy of Study: An Exploration Inward

Fundamentally, the pedagogy of study explores the vast domain of the self. As an educational method, it is a strategy of inquiring and experiencing, a way to spark students' multiple intellectual capacities by formulating, assessing, or immersing their (and our) thoughts, feelings, intuitions, and imaginations in an Ignatian educational context, often for the first time. This comprehensive focus on self-regarding insights and emotions, interests and impulses, confusions and conflicts, confidences and credence, and so on, but it does so in relation with typical student social realms. Family, friends, a campus and residence hall, a church community, a civic sector, a political sphere, an economic environment, and many other contexts exert social influence upon students, so they are a key part of my pedagogy. Study's ability to explore the self and value external influences around individuals makes it quite personally formative. Terence's adage *Humani nil a me alienum puto* ["Nothing human is foreign to me"] represents study classically and showcases a willful and inquisitive orientation that navigates the undulating landscape of the self.[18]

This brings us to the core document for Jesuit higher education, the *Ratio atque Institutio Studiorum Societatis Iesu* [*The Official Plan for Jesuit Education*] (1599), known as the *Ratio Studiorum*, which was written over the years by multiple educators. Various historical realities benchmark the *Ratio*, such as the Jesuits' 1548 opening of a school in Sicily for lay students, after which they almost immediately wrote the educational treatises that first formed the *Ratio*; the 1773 suppression of the Jesuit order and its nearly eight hundred schools around the world; the 1814 official restoration of the Jesuits and a simultaneous North American educational focus; and, by the middle of the twentieth century, a waning relevance of the treatise. Although the *Ratio* is generally viewed as bureaucratic and curricular, the educational theorist Robbie McClintock reveals a special sensitivity in it for a Renaissance humanist educational and modern philosophical expression of study championed by Michel de Montaigne.[19]

In his *Essays* (1580), Montaigne discusses study as an assaying, that is, a trying, testing, and exploring method of writing and reflecting that made him and his subjective turn in philosophy famous. In essence, study is a philosophical method that cultivates abilities of profound subjective self-awareness. In "Of Experience," Montaigne describes an inward gaze that will "study myself," revealing to himself wisdoms of many kinds. He explains that "my metaphysics ... my physics" will better inform him about his own life, the lives of others, and the world.[20] He indicates in "Of the Education of Children" that "my concepts and judgments can only fumble their way forward, swaying, stumbling, tripping over; even when I have advanced as far as I can, I never feel satisfied, for I have a troubled cloudy vision of lands beyond."[21] Obsessed with attaining certainty, and solely interested in rational capacity, René Descartes, conversely, established a now pervasive and strident modern philosophical orientation that is problematic. Study represents an alternative and more robust epistemic disposition. As an educational perspective, study is formative. Also, philosophically, it portends a different kind of subjectivity, which Taylor's describes as "porous," and that I will consider later in this book.

Shy, impudent, loquacious, reticent, wasteful, judicious—Montaigne names and wrestles with his many moods and behaviors and comes to know them intimately.[22] I view such a spectrum as just one way of manifesting the vital realities of student life, replete with a dynamism that Montaigne relishes. I "portray passing," he explains, and not stagnation in life, that is, fixity of perspectives and habits that resist challenges and possibilities.[23] In another essay he states, "my aim is to reveal my own self, which may be different tomorrow."[24] Montaigne's method—"a thorny undertaking . . . to penetrate . . . dark depths"—tunnels holistically into the dimensions of human experience to acquaint individuals with their many intellective capacities, facilitating an honest assessment of oneself as well as exercising the emotions, intuitions, and imaginations that rational perspective generally disregards.[25] As we will see below, John Stuart Mill discovered the force of these intellectual construals late in his life and recognized in them an existential value.

Increasing self-knowledge and engaging intellective abilities inclusively, the practice of Montaigne's study also honors the social dimensions of the self that I now place in a specifically Jesuit higher education context. Interacting with others, meeting new people, hearing new ideas, seeing different rituals, and navigating unconventional mores shape and expand students' personal horizons.[26] But with Montaigne, doing so also teaches us more about the beliefs and values we embrace and the sociocultural spheres with which we are already familiar, letting us confirm and validate our values and practices, or refashion them, or perhaps even form ones anew.[27]

Indeed, the pedagogy of study is an explicit educational necessity of Jesuit education, and with a nod to McClintock, it is an educational strategy for relating in our secular age.[28] Beyond the holistic portents of study and the wide epistemic range it permits, numerous other components of my theories merge in this pedagogy. The "pilgrim" orientation of the Jesuit perspective, for instance—a personal bent of searching, inquiring, and questioning—represents the discerning and examining aspects of Jesuit spirituality in the earliest life of the college student. Ignatius of Loyola represented a pilgrim disposition in his life and nourished a corresponding ethos in his organization. Carl Jung designates Ignatius's *Spiritual Exercises* (1548) as one of three worldly historical advances in the practices of self-knowing and imagining.[29] The practice of discernment assays moods and behaviors, and the meditations of the *Exercises* spur imaginations.

The imaginative thrust alone reflects the Renaissance humanist practice of scholarly, learned piety, or *pietas litterata*, and it also anticipates, in an age of industry, the desperate call for imagination we see in Alfred North Whitehead's assessment of higher education. Like Karl Jaspers, Jacques Maritain, John

Henry Newman, and José Ortega y Gasset (whom I discuss below), Whitehead engages university education, calling for "generalization" to govern it.[30]

My deeply personal realities of the pedagogy of study are related to the development of Taylor's theoretical imagination, where the intellect strives and gropes into new terrain or even obscurity. This searching and imagining, he insists, begins in mere hunches and intuitions and leads toward important discoveries. Similar to John Dewey's work, we appreciate the power of interest in each of our lives to propel how we learn and grow. Study pushes well beyond professional training and credentialing and represents the existential realities of formation and transformation. I incorporate this all into my pedagogy and extend it to a Jesuit milieu.

Like Whitehead and Dewey, I also anticipate learning, discerning, and inquiring—all expressions of the Jesuit pilgrim disposition—as personal habits showcasing life as a persistent adventure. Study cultivates students' abilities to keep thinking, feeling, and imaging far beyond their years on a Jesuit campus.

In all this, the humanities, a curricular bedrock of Jesuit higher education in every age, are recognized for their ability to evoke a particular way of knowing, and they undergird each of my pedagogies of fullness. Beginning here with the pedagogy of study, I appreciate the humanities for how they cultivate an existential sensitivity in line with Taylor's fullness. A philosophical-anthropological construct, fullness yearns for meaning and purpose, axes around which literature, art, philosophy, and theology easily revolve.

We can also embrace the pedagogy of study—a pilgrim adventure that wanders meaningfully through personal construals and experiences and deepens thoughts and feelings—in how it breaks down the rational buffers that suppress sentiments, distrust intuitions, and prevent imaginations. Students' intellectual capacities are better networked through the evidences, emotions, instincts, and images they dwell in, and such networking attests to an internal relating that honors Charles Taylor's thinking.

Here I am reminded of Adolfo Nicolás, the former superior general of the Jesuits, in his 2010 address "Depth, Universality, and Learned Ministry: Challenges to Jesuit Higher Education Today," when he described the thoughtless, efficient, and impulsive expressions of communicating today through new technologies.[31] He encouraged Jesuit higher education to espouse the tools of analysis, reflection, and discernment embedded within its own tradition in fresh pedagogical ways. He spoke precisely about the problem of superficiality that represented one of the three illnesses of higher education in a secular age. He described naive and careless uses of information technology, explaining that "when one can access so much information so quickly and so painlessly; when one can express and publish to the world one's reactions so immediately and so unthinkingly, ... when the latest opinion column ... or the newest viral video can be spread so quickly to people half a world away, shaping their perceptions and feelings, then the laborious, painstaking work of serious, critical thinking often gets short-circuited."[32]

After citing the problems of superficiality related to social media and information technology, he specifically outlined three challenges. The first regarded the urgent need today in education anywhere for cultivating profundity of thinking and imagining in and through mechanisms of instant messaging. Rightly, Nicolás's explicit concern was about instantaneous and insincere uses of social media, and he encouraged all of Jesuit higher education to find ways to prevent a short-circuiting of the deeper and strenuous dimensions of thinking and relating.

Finally, when we come to our discussion of the concept of agape as an expression of fullness, I will indicate three participatory and associative relations, two of which should be outlined here. The participatory aspect of agape represents a kind of stretching toward the divine, an active striving of an individual to a type of excellence that can be appreciated as an extension of the Greek influence of excellence (arête from the *Iliad* to Isocrates) as well as an expression of the originary conception of *"theiosis"* ("becoming divine"), a kind of growing and excelling through personal transformations. It is partly represented by the sense of Jesuit *"magis,"* the "greater," or the "better." Humanism is rife in personal virtues, and the discerning and evaluating capacities of study in Jesuit higher education represent just some of the ideals toward which these pedagogies of fullness lead.

Especially pertinent, however, is one of the associative actions of agape, the networking of internal intellective capacities. The visceral motivation of the Good Samaritan to help another is significant for a number of reasons, but the one of particular interest to Charles Taylor is a gut reaction. The Good Samaritan let himself be animated by an intellective source that propelled him into action. Taylor discusses all three agapic realities as instances of "stepping beyond." I recognize them as *moving toward*. Here, in both these, through study, a student can be encouraged to move, first, toward an excellence or an ideal, or God, even, as interpreted of the Good Samaritan story; and second, toward an integrated wholeness of self that Parker Palmer and Arthur Zajonc postulate in their work.[33]

## The Pedagogy of Solidarity: An Exploration toward Others

Complementing the first pedagogy that integrates the self, the pedagogy of solidarity relates to alterity, or otherness.[34] Solidarity pertains to the social contexts of students' lives and highlights other educative capacities. In this shift of focus, solidarity, or alterity, cultivates individuals' adaptability to new environments—the lives, cultures, customs, and concepts of others— and transforms the horizons of the self. Not only does it spark the numerous intellectual capacities of the pedagogy of study, prompting, for instance, original thoughts, different emotions, sudden intuitions, novel interests, and innovative imaginations—the activities that represent the inner experience of study—but this outer focus facilitates new relationships to other places, persons, and perspectives. Dimensions of flexibility and adjustment to difference let students assess and appropriate experiences of alterity/otherness in their lives and forge meaningful and respectful associations and affiliations with the sources of alterity.

With such a focus on otherness, and because of the possibility for genuine connections, Cicero's phrase *Non nobis solum nati sumus* ["We are not born for ourselves alone"] is illustrative. With the pedagogy of solidarity, the epistemic components of study broaden even more, but I augment a new philosophical reality—that of the moral-ethical—with the explicit relational influences that this pedagogy implies.

An early Jesuit teacher, Jerónimo Nadal, more commonly referred to in English as Jérôme Nadal, inspired essential components of my pedagogy of solidarity through the Jesuit mandate in part IV of the *Constitutions* (1558) to adapt to "times, places, and persons," with a concept of the whole world as "home" to the Jesuits. Part IV, according to the Jesuit historian George Ganss, SJ, softens the *Ratio*'s institutional rigidity and reveals how the Jesuits intended their detailed plan of education to respond to cultural contexts. The image of the world as home, furthermore, generally represents the global mission of the Jesuit organization, one of the first religious congregations in Roman Catholicism that did not bind its members to specific and cloistered residences or to traditional routines of institutional religious life.

In referencing home as a "highway" (rather than a house), Nadal not only recognizes the worldly disposition of the Jesuits but also, literally, their international presence. The hallmark expression of Jesuit life is being "missioned," or assigned to places and projects. The highway metaphor captures this activity of travel, physical movement, and being elsewhere well. But the action of the metaphor need not be literal. It also represents searching dispositions of inquiry, examination, growth, and possibility right where one is. Ignatius was hailed as a pilgrim not just for walking Europe, although he did, but also for the modern elements of reflection, discernment, and personal desire that he personally practiced and institutionally implemented. The *Constitutions* and the *Spiritual Exercises* together convey these pilgrim expressions of both movement and mind-set, that is, either *going* somewhere or *searching* from the vantage of anywhere.

I contend that our mandate to adapt—that is, to be flexible and friendly to differences and to feel at home in otherness, while respecting both what is home to others and to oneself—makes a fine staging ground for this second pedagogy. Ignatius adapted through his ability to appropriate his experiences in self-fulfilling and socially effective ways. He also expected his Jesuits to demonstrate capacity for emotional, intellectual, and spiritual malleability, as they would intimately engage the lives of others—proximate and afar, familiar and foreign—in personal or institutional ministry. The Jesuit novitiate, then, would stretch and test new Jesuits via three classic "experiments" that I consider in more depth later in the book: the long retreat, the hospital assignment, and a pilgrimage experience. These experiments assay aspirants' personal resources and assumptions, further equipping them for a complex and often messy world. Moreover, part IV is an authoritative educational document. Its directive for educational personnel and programs to acclimatize to "times, places, and persons" is a pedagogical force of its own.

Aligned with the practices of the Jesuits Matteo Ricci and Roberto de Nobili, my pedagogy of solidarity honors the multiple aspects of a healthy self-possession and the existential realities that inform a sense of self, while encouraging students to negotiate openly and respectfully how to be at home elsewhere. Ricci and de Nobili are paradigmatic figures imbued with the intellectual fervor of the Renaissance. Much of Ricci's relationship with the Ming Dynasty of China revolved around a sharing of ideas and instruments. Ricci himself was a linguist, a theologian, a mapmaker, and more. He shared and exchanged concepts and customs. As a seventeenth-century missionary, he indeed hoped to attract new membership into his own religious way of life, but we remember him for an accommodating, assimilating, and inquiring disposition that transformed his own existence, inasmuch as it transformed others. In China for the rest of his life, Ricci was never *not* a Jesuit, but he is noteworthy for becoming personally known and officially ranked in a regime that was highly guarded even from its own people.

Many precedents exist for the pedagogy of solidarity. The ancient Greek conception of arête is recognized as a personal striving toward virtuous ideals. Pedagogically, this becomes clear with Isocrates (436–338 BCE) and Cicero, who consider rhetoric in a sense a personal virtue that is wholly communal. The Jesuit pedagogues embraced this, and, through the influence of Desiderius Erasmus, developed the ideal of *eloquentia perfecta*, a direct reflection of the humanist expression of *Christianitas*.

In 1973, the superior general of the Jesuits, Pedro Arrupe, spoke about specific aspects of solidarity at the International Congress of Jesuit Alumni in Europe. The title of his address, "Men for Others," now referred to as "Men and Women for Others," charted, in many ways, a renewed educational investment in humanistic social and civic engagement of Jesuit education around the world.[35]

Arrupe made three points. The first two regard the pervasive and negative effects of capitalism in Western societies and how consumerism and mass production compromise and obfuscate important and essential elements of life, such as relationships. Arrupe discussed differences between those who benefit exponentially from capitalism and the many others who suffer from its effects. He thus asked his audience to be mindful of the world's poor, "the truly marginalized," both far afield and close to home.

After the first two points of his address demanded a cultural analysis and an awareness of others, he insisted in his third point that today, in the contemporary era, Jesuit education must form men and women to be agents of social change. "For if there is any substance on our reflections," he pondered aloud, "then this [kind of education] is the prolongation into the modern world of our humanist tradition as derived from the *Spiritual Exercises* of Saint Ignatius."[36]

True to the origins of Jesuit education—that is, its Ciceronian-inspired ideal of *eloquentia perfecta*, the virtue of *pietas*, and expressions of *Christianitas* (again, components I will consider more fully later)—Arrupe pushed Jesuit education back to the essentials of its tradition and asked it to face contemporary problems on those original terms. The driving question of his talk regarded the kinds of qualities and characteristics graduates of Jesuit education should take into the world, and its answer, in the end, rested in an ideal of justice. This specific objective, a renewed essential of Jesuit educational endeavors, also came under Arrupe's leadership to represent all the works of the Jesuits: "The mission of the Society of Jesus today is the service of faith, of which the promotion of justice is an absolute requirement. . . . In one form or another, this has always been the mission of the Society; but it gains new meaning and urgency in the light of needs and aspirations of the men and women of our time, and it is in that light that we examine it anew."[37]

With these words, articulated in "Decree 4" of the Thirty-Second General Congregation of the Society of Jesus (a convening of Jesuit representatives from around the world to assess the organization's leadership and priorities), Arrupe oriented the works and projects of the Jesuits toward explicitly contemporary issues.

In doing so, he also anticipated the crisis of Taylor's fullness. Millions of people around the world, Arrupe explained, "specific people with names and faces," suffer in countless ways, and such people, he insisted, "have a feeling that what is at stake here is the very meaning of [being human]."[38] His recognition, moreover, of the humanistic aspects of Jesuit higher education, along with its interest in forming socially just persons, shows how the individuating, isolating, and utilitarian prospects of fragmentation, professionalism, and rationalism frustrate the Jesuits' higher educational mission.

Arrupe's successor carried the mantle forward. In an address intentionally delivered at the twenty-fifth anniversary of the Thirty-Second General Congregation, Peter-Hans Kolvenbach cited the inspirational thrusts of Decree 4 as well as of Arrupe's 1973 talk. The ideal of justice and "the expression, 'men and women for others,'" Kolvenbach explained, galvanized and transformed Jesuit higher education, and must be again renewed.[39]

More explicitly than Arrupe, Kolvenbach took an opportunity to explain the origins and history of Jesuit education. He reminded American Jesuit higher educators of the holistic pedagogy of Jesuit education generally and the inherently connected issues of such an education to issues of justice and human flourishing. For four and a half centuries, he explained, "Jesuit education has sought to educate 'the whole person' intellectually and professionally, psychologically, morally, and spiritually."[40]

Globalization, however, unlike other paradigm shifts in modernity—such as the revolutions of religion, science, and industry—offered possibilities and problems of its own. Jesuit higher education, he challenged, must not only revitalize its efforts to educate holistically but must also do so in light of the particular forces of globalization that exploit, manipulate, or disregard peoples and nations: "Tomorrow's whole person must have . . . a well-educated solidarity," a relational objective that is learned not through concepts but "contact."[41] Intellectual and moral energies of students—their inquiries, imaginations, ideals, and actions—can be enlivened through personal and meaningful interaction in the lives of others, especially with those adversely affected by globalization. We will see, too, that "contact" is precisely what actualizes Taylor's fullness.

Kolvenbach wants students of Jesuit higher education to feel and think through the daily "gritty" circumstances of people in the world around them. Like Arrupe's query of what kinds of skills and sensitivities graduates of Jesuit education should manifest, Kolvenbach asserts at the end of his address that an assessment of Jesuit higher education directly pertains to "not what our students do, but who they become."[42] Such a formative interest, and the kinds of contacts Kolvenbach encourages, rebuff the lonesome perspective of fragmentation, the shallow and practical *training* of students, and the limitations of technical rationality. The cooperative, in-depth, and holistic possibilities of educating for solidarity allow the humanist ideals of this 450-year-old pedagogy to persist.

The late French philosopher and public intellectual Pierre Hadot (1922–2010) discusses the tradition of spiritual exercises in ancient philosophical ways of life and reminds us of a spiritual correlate to Kolvenbach's learned solidarity.[43] In Ignatius's *Spiritual Exercises,* the imaginative experience of the Trinitarian gaze generally impels practitioners into relationships with others, connections that are meaningful, reciprocal, and transformative of selves and societies.

Moreover, Nicolás, a leader who was worried about technological and communicative habits that sustained expressions of superficiality, also saw the social benefits of such tools. As he challenged Jesuit higher education to inspire deeper dimensions of thoughtfulness and circumspection with social media, the internet, and devices of communication, he looked for ways, first, to share such tools with those who did not have access to their powers and abilities and, second, to better network Jesuit higher education itself. Pointing to Madrid, Jogjakarta, Bogotá, Chennai, Jersey City, and Beirut as a few of the cities where Jesuit universities exist, he said, "My hope . . . is that we can move . . . to the establishment of operational consortia among our universities focused on responding together to some of the 'frontier challenges' of our world which have a supra-national or supra-continental character."[44] Like his predecessors Arrupe and Kolvenbach, he exuded a special sensitivity to globally existing poverties and oppressions.

Of the three challenges he voices, the first of which I discussed above in the context of the pedagogy of study, the other two are particularly social. First, he invites cooperative international alliances among Jesuit institutions themselves—places of higher education specifically but also other educational and ministerial venues of the Jesuits—to understand and alleviate worldwide issues of economic poverty, social injustice, and ecological deterioration. To this end, I appreciate Jonathan Cole's desire for departments and disciplines at major research universities to better collaborate on such global issues.[45]

Second, Nicolás pushed Jesuit universities to mitigate a disparity of knowledge distribution separating those who can afford technologies from others without such access. Nicolás's recent concern about trite networking and inconsequential associating reminds Jesuit higher education of the need in today's globalization for personal and substantive relating. All this, moreover, allows us to assess the dynamic of fragmentation in and around universities and resolve the a-relational footholds it all too often attains.

Later in the book, I also engage the communicative and dialogic roles of the university considered by Karl Jaspers and Jürgen Habermas. Given that these essential dynamics have the ability to represent a unified or holistic conception of the university—or stitch together a fragmented one—they also form an indispensable aspect of solidarity, particularly in its focus on dialogue.

In its global program of letter writing initiated at the end of the sixteenth century, the Jesuit order already set a reflective and descriptive communicative precedent for sharing and discussing foreign realities. Moreover, because real and meaningful conversation connects students to places, persons, and perspectives, I eventually further augment and extend Alasdair MacIntyre's and Anthony Kronman's insights about the need to ask serious questions about oneself and others. Though their encouragement for discursive existential query informs this pedagogy of study, it also represents the bridges that a pedagogy of solidarity builds. As a basic practice conversant with existential realities, dialogue represents the kind of contact Kolvenbach wants. Even the Spanish philosopher José Ortega y Gasset's insistence for students of higher education to dwell within the vital ideas of culture helps here.[46] Students of solidarity must engage the vital ideas of their own and other cultures.

Finally, as an aspect of fullness, a pedagogy of solidarity enacts the moral-ethical dynamic of what we will see as Taylor's agape. The second associative dimension, a stepping beyond familiar persons and places into less familiar realms—a moving toward others—gives us a wider kinship. Again, Taylor speaks of stronger and expanded senses of community. Moreover, in moving toward alterity to forge solidarity, the communal, social, political, and religious associations of porous selves are all the more possible. The first pedagogy of fullness focuses upon the self. This pedagogy of fullness relates that self to others.

## The Pedagogy of Grace: An Exploration Toward the Transcendent Other

Essentially, my theory of a pedagogy of grace cultivates an orientation to a transcendent Other, or at least invites this transcendental orientation. As the first pedagogy of fullness cultivates the inner construals of individuals and the second facilitates meaningful associations with other people, places, and perspectives, a pedagogy of grace relies upon the dynamics of study and solidarity to facilitate an openness to unusual dimensions of revelation and signification.

The ancient Roman poet Horace (65–27 BCE), in his famous command, "carpe diem"—that is, *Carpe diem, quam minimun credula postero* ["harvest today without thinking of tomorrow"]—in my estimate offers a classic insight about this pedagogy. In "seizing the day," he encourages us to be attentive to the activities and opportunities at hand and aware of the present. In a sense, he lets individuals be seized by such realities. Horace's focus on the present does not disregard the intentional work of study and the deliberate associations of solidarity, but offers an alternative intentionality, or expressions that are *less* intentional, or even unintentional. It can even be said that the educative work of study and solidarity both help cultivate the conditions of this third pedagogy, a disposition not of suspicion or fear of the unexpected, but of ready, or *already*, openness.

The pedagogy of grace represents what is not planned, or what is unprepared, or surprising. It is a pedagogy that cultivates an availability—or appreciates in students the kind of openness cultivated by study and solidarity—whether for inexplicable and phenomenal moments of wonder, awe, inspiration, gratitude, consolation, or confirmation. They are experiences that I regard highly and even prescribe at various junctures in this book.

As a pedagogy of fullness, grace is in many ways what Taylor first expresses as fullness through Bede Griffiths, and then Václav Havel, and so quickly references through Friedrich von Schiller's conception of "play," an impulse recognizing a beauty beyond us. In the pages that follow, I engage Hubert Dreyfus and Sean Dorrance Kelly, René Arcilla, and John McDowell philosophically as they encounter the dimension of the beyond, suggesting that a revelation from elsewhere—what Martin Heidegger considers a "whooshing" of some kind—has a meaningful impact on us.[47]

Such external significations defy to some degree the autonomy, individuality, relevancy, and willfulness of rational individuals who, according to an influential reading of a strand of knowing linking Immanuel Kant to René Descartes, credit themselves as wholly inventive or creating meaning and purpose. Endorsing Schiller's play and assuring its external origins—persons are played rather than being the instigators of play—I incorporate Hans-George Gadamer's interpretive gestures that articulate and honor such experiences. With Taylor in *A Secular Age*, this receptivity to transcendence culminates in the poetry of the Jesuit Gerard Manley Hopkins.[48]

Contemporary indications of fullness—play, whooshing, and presentness; that is, what I build my pedagogy of grace upon as I engage Gadamer's hermeneutic—Dreyfus's and Kelly's Heideggerian articulation, Arcilla's existential explanation, and even McDowell's epistemic expressions of yearning, lean into the ontic commitment Taylor insists upon, a philosophical precedent that authenticates external sources of life and being and permits a relating to a supreme alterity, or an Other. To the internal and external porosities of study and solidarity, then, grace offers yet another way to relate.

Such openness is fundamental to Ignatius's *Spiritual Exercises*. His personal experience of praying, as I discuss below, is open to the reality of a transcendent Other, and recognizes the world itself as graced by such an Other. In comparing the *Exercises* and the *Ratio Studiorum*, Claude Pavur describes a disposition of openness in both of the documents as "radical."[49] The treatises were recognized for both the ontic commitments they offer and senses of relating they facilitate. Finally, in their addresses about the Jesuit university, the three Jesuit leaders manifest the same orientation, an expression of knowing that is, furthermore, represented by Taylor's "theoretical imagination."

From Taylor—as with the first two pedagogies—we can also see the agapic reality of this third one. Just as agape, a Christian-specific term, represents a stretching toward God while demonstrating aspects of responding and relating to God, it also characterizes a sharing in the life of God. This religious ability, one I offer after considering the insights of Anders Nygren and Gene Outka, allows one to believe in God's love and in turn to love like God. As a pedagogy of fullness, grace represents the possibility of such a relationship, an openness to another source beyond ourselves, for what is good in life.

If we continue to reflect upon each of the pedagogies of fullness to better realize this third pedagogy, I call our attention to a leading philosophical expression at work in them. The first pedagogy of study, in its efforts to cultivate through personal capacities and experiences a wider knowing, exudes epistemological sensitivity. The second pedagogy of solidarity—one that builds upon the work of study in relating to alterity and connecting to new persons, places, and perspectives—amplifies a moral-ethical interest. Here, in our third pedagogy, grace represents a metaphysical aptitude, a propensity of ultimate "porosity" (to use Taylor's term), whereby another kind of openness is possible.

I show how the porous subject emerges in special regard with this pedagogy, a self who in Taylor's estimate resists or elides what seems to be the first or highest of many buffers of a secular age. As each of the pedagogies withstands exaggerated expressions of autonomy, individuality, and relevancy, the pedagogy of grace nourishes dimensions of openness along the lines of inquiry and experience. Inquiry pushes the searching, exploring, and questioning of reality to a new realm or a different domain, and experience lets the self acknowledge, appreciate, or allow the connections to such spheres of influence. The pedagogy of grace encourages an extraordinary awareness, and as it is metaphysical, it is also phenomenal.

In further comparison with the first and second pedagogies, I recognize the pedagogy of grace for its ability to resist the traps of fragmentation, superficiality, and strident rationality. Study delves into the deeply personal nature of interests and imaginations, insights and intuitions, and helps to alleviate, as I discuss below, the problem of a superficial subjectivity. In its ambit of intellective capacities, it also mitigates the expressions of instrumentality. It allocates a more expansive way of knowing, and relating, than a strictly rationalistic perspective. Finally, in refusing to fracture a network of knowing, study is holistic of the self. Solidarity, by virtue of its connections and associations, likewise prevents the dynamics of fragmentation and isolation. It manifests an interest in cooperation and collaboration that can be institutionally implemented. In adapting and accommodating to alterity, and in being openly communicative and intentionally dialogic, it too can be evaluated for how it draws upon the depths of subjectivity and how it must oppose instrumentality. Grace—in its openness to revelation, to the personal nature of phenomenal awareness, and to a kind of knowing that permits a metaphysical possibility—also resists expressions of fragmentation, superficiality, and instrumentality. By definition, openness is not isolating, an epiphany is not shallow, and a metaphysical possibility is not pragmatic, economic, or efficient.

Finally, as a pedagogy of fullness, grace—more patently than the other pedagogies, but not exclusively—facilitates conditions of belief in a secular age. As I engage below, the pedagogies each build upon the work of the one before. The broad knowing of study and the wide relating of solidarity dwell, to expand Kolvenbach's metaphor, in the "gritty reality" of self and society to assay, adapt, and relate students in higher educative ways. And inasmuch as all three pedagogies vitiate the dynamics of fragmentation, superficiality, and instrumentality, other conditions—such as wholeness, depth, and vision, of selves *and* of universities—become possible, cultivating aspects of relating that connote Taylor's fullness.

But I offer the pedagogy of grace as best framing particular conditions of belief that Taylor assesses in a secular milieu. By his admission, we first and fundamentally appreciate the crisis of fullness in a secular age by reference to a transcendent source, a reality upon which the pedagogy of grace relies.[50] In pointing students more intentionally to themselves and others, the pedagogies of study and solidarity open new possibilities of knowing and relating. In orienting students *less intentionally* to a revelatory source of wonder, awe, and inspiration and sensations of gratitude, consolation, and confirmation, and letting them be seized by any of these, we help them begin to experience the essential components of fullness in an age that distrusts, denies, or denigrates the meanings and purposes they proffer. The pedagogy of grace, then, on another level of relating, addresses Taylor's existential desire for meaning and purpose. In cooperation with the strategies of study and solidarity, these three pedagogies of fullness in Jesuit higher education—really, modalities of enchantment—condition ways of relating. As the cultivation of various contacts forms students, it lets them better imagine more fully relational lives.

## NOTES

1. Charles Taylor, *A Secular Age* (Cambridge, MA: Belknap Press of Harvard University Press, 2007).
2. Charles Taylor, "A Catholic Modernity," in *A Catholic Modernity? Charles Taylor's Marianist Award Lecture, with Responses by William M. Shea, Rosemary Luling Haughton, George Marsden, and Jean Bethke Elshtain,* ed. James L. Heft (Oxford: Oxford University Press, 1999), 13.
3. Taylor, "Catholic Modernity," 118.
4. Taylor.
5. Taylor, *Secular Age,* 20.
6. Taylor, 5.
7. Taylor.
8. Taylor.
9. Griffiths became a Catholic pioneer in interreligious dialogue. I appreciated some of his dialogical accomplishments while studying for my master of divinity degree at the Jesuit School of Theology of Santa Clara University in Berkeley.
10. Taylor, *Secular Age,* 5.
11. Charles Taylor, "Afterword: *Apologia pro Libro suo,*" in *Varieties of Secularism in a Secular Age,* ed. Michael Warner, Jonathan VanAntwerpen, and Craig Calhoun (Cambridge, MA: Harvard University Press, 2010), 315.
12. Taylor, *Secular Age,* 728–29.
13. Warner, VanAntwerpen, and Calhoun, *Varieties of Secularism,* 11, 317.
14. Taylor, *Secular Age,* 729–30.
15. David L. Fleming, ed., *The Spiritual Exercises of Saint Ignatius: A Literal Translation and a Contemporary Reading* (Saint Louis: Institute of Jesuit Sources, 1991), 206–7 [§316].
16. Taylor, *Secular Age,* 729–30.
17. Taylor, 729.
18. David T. Hansen, *The Teacher and the World: A Study of Cosmopolitanism as Education* (New York: Routledge, 2011), 52. An educational theorist, Hansen discusses Terence's proverb as illuminative of his cosmopolitan education. See also Robert McClintock, "Toward a Place for Study in a World of Instruction," *Teachers College Record* 73, no. 2 (1971): 176. McClintock recognizes an ethos of the *Ratio* that is not characterized by "instruction," per se, but as a persistent encouragement for students to "study." He approaches an early-modern, globally and historically prominent plan of education with fresh insight.
19. I took direct inspiration for this first pedagogy from McClintock's interpretation of the *Ratio Studiorum,* and I will gradually develop the relationship.
20. Michel de Montaigne, "Of Experience," in *The Complete Essays of Montaigne,* trans. Donald M. Frame (Palo Alto, CA: Stanford University Press 1948), 821.
21. Michel de Montaigne, "On Educating Children," in *The Essays: A Selection,* trans. M. A. Screech (New York: Penguin, 2004), 38. Hansen demonstrates appreciation for

Montaigne in his recent work and cites this same effective description of Montaigne's philosophical method. See Hansen, *Teacher*, 53.

22. Michele de Montaigne, "Of the Inconstancy of Our Actions," in *The Complete Works: Essay, Travel Journal, Letters*, trans. M.A. Screech (New York: Penguin Classics, 1991), 242.

23. Montaigne, "Of Repentance," in *Complete Works*, 611.

24. Montaigne, "Of the Education of Children," in *Essays*, 41.

25. Montaigne, "Of Practice," in *Essays*, 424.

26. Montaigne, "Of the Education of Children," in *Complete Works*, 112.

27. Montaigne, "Of Cannibals," in *Complete Works*, 150–52.

28. Tyson Lewis, "A Case for Study: Agamben's Critique of Scheffler's Theory of Potentiality," *Philosophy of Education Society Yearbook* (in press); Tyson Lewis, *The Appearance of Education: Studying, Stupidity, and Impotentiality in the Work of Giorgio Agamben* (New York: Routledge, in press); Mathias Decuypere, Jan Masschelein, Maarten Simons, and Joris Vlieghe, eds., *Curating the European University: Exposition and Public Debate* (Leuven University Press of Leuven, 2011). Lewis and Masschelein and colleagues appreciate and discuss the role of study in education and represent a renewed interest in its educative value. Also, given the style of Montaigne's method of study and his assessment of the specific pedagogical practices of his own educational experience, warping Montaigne's study into a specific pedagogy will be ironic and counterintuitive to some of his readers.

29. Kenneth L. Becker, *Unlikely Companions: C. G. Jung on the Spiritual Exercises of Ignatius of Loyola—An Exposition and Critique Based on Jung's Lectures and Writings* (Leominster, UK: Gracewing, 2001).

30. Alfred North Whitehead, *The Aims of Education and Other Essays* (New York: Free Press, 1967), 25.

31. Adolfo Nicolás, "Depth, Universality, and Learned Ministry: Challenges to Jesuit Higher Education Today," Conference Address, Universidad Iberoamericana, Mexico City, April 2010.

32. Nicolás, 2.

33. Parker Palmer and Arthur Zajonc's book, *The Heart of Higher Education: A Call to Renewal* (San Francisco: Jossey-Bass 2010), also represents the tenets of what I identify as the pedagogy of study.

34. Peter-Hans Kolvenbach's call for a well-educated "solidarity," to be considered later in the book, is a direct inspiration for this pedagogy of fullness. See Peter-Hans Kolvenbach, "The Service of Faith and the Promotion of Justice in American Jesuit Higher Education," Conference Address, Commitment Justice in Jesuit Higher Education conference, Santa Clara University, Santa Clara, CA, October 2000, www.loyola.edu/yotc/father_kolvenbach.html#txxv.

35. Pedro Arrupe, "Men for Others: Education for Social Justice and Social Action Today," Conference Address, Tenth International Congress of Jesuit Alumni of Europe, Valencia, July 1973, http://onlineministries.creighton.edu/CollaborativeMinistry/men-for-others.html.

36. Arrupe.

37. John W. Padberg, SJ, ed., *Documents of the 31st and 32nd General Congregations of the Society of Jesus* (Saint Louis: Institute of Jesuit Sources, 1977), 411.

38. Padberg, 417.

39. Kolvenbach, "Service of Faith."

40. Kolvenbach.

41. Kolvenbach.
42. Kolvenbach.
43. Pierre Hadot, *The Present Alone Is Our Happiness: Conversations with Jeannie Carlier and Arnold I. Davidson*, trans. Marc Djaballah (Palo Alto, CA: Stanford University Press, 2009).
44. Nicolás, "Depth," 8.
45. Jonathan R. Cole, *The Great American University: Its Rise to Preeminence, Its Indispensable National Role, Why It Must Be Protected* (New York: PublicAffairs, 2009), 490.
46. José Ortega y Gasset, *Mission of the University*, ed. and trans. Howard Lee Nostrand (New Brunswick, NJ: Transaction, 1991).
47. Hubert Dreyfus and Sean Dorrance Kelly, *All Things Shining: Reading the Western Classics to Find Meaning in a Secular Age* (New York: Free Press, 2011), 201, 205.
48. Hans-Georg Gadamer, *Truth and Method* (New York: Continuum, 2004), 112.
49. Claude Pavur, "The Curriculum Carries the Mission: The *Ratio Studiorum*, the Making of Jesuit Education, and the Making of the Society of Jesus," *New Jesuit Review* 2, no. 5 (2010).
50. Taylor, *Secular Age*, 13–16, 143–45.

# CHAPTER TWO

# DEVELOPING TAYLOR'S CONCEPTION OF FULLNESS

To better explain Charles Taylor's meaning of "fullness," allow me to begin with the words of a preeminent twentieth-century Jesuit priest and philosopher, Bernard Lonergan, who articulates the correlation between one's cognitive aptitudes and our place in the world: "In the midst of . . . widespread disorientation, [our] problem of self-knowledge ceases to be simply the individual concern inculcated by the ancient sage. It takes on the dimensions of a social crisis. It can be read as the historical issue of the twentieth century. If in that balance human intelligence and reasonableness, human responsibility and freedom, are to prevail, then they must be summoned from the dim and confused realm of latent factors and they must burst forth in . . . full flower."[1]

In an intellective way, Lonergan represents a dimension of Taylor's fullness, which he refers to as "insight." Lonergan's interest in the self-transformation of individuals ("conversions"), his anthropology's metaphysical and religious commitment ("transcendental knowing"), and his recognition of certain malaises of modern-era thinking and living—framed as a widespread kind of disorientation—all exude likenesses to Taylor's own terms and concerns.

What I value in Lonergan's work, however, is his appreciation and inclusion of the interpersonal, or social, implications of all this, an aspect that arises from my long-term philosophical interest in Taylor's career. We have generally discussed Taylor's fullness from the perspective of subjective relating, but I see Lonergan's hand-in-hand correlation between subjective knowing and the social domain of our lives as having a shared affinity with Taylor's communitarian commitments.

Taylor's conception of fullness begins in a nearly ecstatic experience of religious epiphany—a consoling moment of grace that is not self-empowering but transformative toward personal and social goods. Through the lives of first Bede Griffiths and then Václav Havel, I showcase particular theories about fullness through individual experience and metaphysical influence, thereby recognizing how fullness expands beyond a private dimension into a more explicitly moral-ethical one. It is this moral-ethical realm that attests to the transformations of both the social domain and the self through the "stepping-beyond" aspects that Taylor himself explains when he turns to the involvement of agape in our lives.

In what I see as participatory and associative characteristics of agape, Taylor represents as personal acts of goodness, a cohesion of one's own capacities and aptitudes, and the wider expressions of kinship. Taylor's stepping beyond—that is, getting beyond self-stagnation, rational perspective, and the familiarity of family and friends—can be regarded as moving toward one's latent or undeployed capacities, and thereby toward other sources of knowing and valuing, other kinds of people, and God. As an expression of fullness, then, agape brings one closer to self, others, and an Other.

In discussing both the phenomenal features of fullness and its moral-ethical, agapic aspects, it is helpful also to consider various thinkers' renditions of it, both for what they elucidate and in what I feel they confirm of Taylor's interest. Also, by mitigating the strident influences of secularism, nihilism, or materialism in our culture, some of these thinkers suggest specific virtues of knowing, acting, and relating that they feel restore feelings or recognitions in our lives of personal and social integrity.

Finally, and again, I end with Lonergan. This important Jesuit philosopher effectively builds a bridge between the realms of the self and the social. Also, because Lonergan is critical of modernity, he encourages us to recognize an essential correlation between the transformations of the self and corresponding effects upon social and communal realities. In doing so, we are better able to appreciate the broader implications of Taylor's fullness.

## CONTEMPORARY YEARNINGS

Looking, then, at the philosophical underpinnings of fullness, including its arc through a range of philosophers and chronologies, will both ground it in a notable discourse and showcase its sense of relevance and interest. Further, in my reading, and seemingly edging up to Taylor as closely as possible, likeminded contemporary philosophers share an appreciation for fullness in their work. These thinkers are reticent to embrace what I find to be an essential philosophical commitment of Taylor's, which he illustrates with religious terminology. These foundations, current renderings, and a metaphysical characterizations help sharpen Taylor's sense of fullness, including exposing its important social implications.

## Play and the Hermeneutic

Taylor's first reference to "fullness" as a term in *A Secular Age* cites J. C. Friedrich von Schiller's *Letters upon the Aesthetic Education of Man* (1794). Schiller's concept of "play" is a philosophical construct that has received great attention from the educational theorists Johann Heinrich Pestalozzi, Friedrich Froebel, and later philosophers of education.[2]

Schiller's own thinking is greatly informed by the philosophy of Immanuel Kant, an outlook that Taylor and other like-minded readers interpret and describe as the flourishing culmination of autonomous rationality and contemporary expressions of exaggerated individuality. Despite this, Schiller, in his second letter in *Aesthetic Education*, seems concerned about the dominance around him of instrumental rationality, a prevailing epistemic orientation that is characteristic of modern individuals. Schiller thus explains, "The very spirit of philosophical inquiry itself robs the imagination of one promise after another, and ... frontiers ... are narrowed ... as the limits of science are enlarged."[3] This assessment—or critique, if you will—is also poetically expressed. Taylor enjoys referencing Schiller's poem *The Gods of Greece* (1788) in much of his writing, and it is worth reviewing here:

> WHILST the smiling earth ye governed still,
> And with rapture's soft and guiding hand
> Led the happy nations at your will,
> Beauteous beings from the fable-land!
> Whilst your blissful worship smiled around,
> Ah! how different was it in that day!
> When the people still thy temples crowned,
> Venus Amathusia!
>
> When the magic veil of poesy
> Still round truth entwined its loving chain,—
> Through creation poured life's fulness free,
> Things then felt, which ne'er can feel again.
> Then to press her 'gainst the breast of love,
> They on Nature nobler power bestowed,
> All, to eyes enlightened from above,
> Of a god the traces showed.

There, where now, as we 're by sages told,
    Whirls on high a soulless fiery ball,
Helios guided then his car of gold,
    In his silent majesty, o'er all.
Oreads then these heights around us filled,
    Then a dryad dwelt in yonder tree,
From the urn of loving naiads rilled
    Silver streamlets foamingly.

Yonder Laurel once imploring wound,
    Tantal's daughter slumbers in this stone;
From yon rush rose Syrinx' mournful sound,
    From this thicket Philomela's moan.
Yonder brook Demeter's tears received,
    That she wept for her Persephone,
From this hill, of her loved friend bereaved,
    Cried Cythera, fruitlessly!

To Deucalion's race from realms of air
    Then the great Immortals still came down;
And to vanquish Pyrrha's daughter fair,
    Then a shepherd's staff took Leto's son.
Then 'tween heroes, deities, and men
    Was a beauteous bond by Eros twined,
And with deities and heroes then
    Knelt in Cyprus' Isle mankind.

Gloomy sternness and denial sad
    Ne'er were in your service blest descried;
Each heart throbbed then with emotions glad,
    For the happy were with you allied.
Nothing then was holy, save the fair;
    Of no rapture was the god ashamed,
When the modest Muse was blushing there,
    When their sway the Graces claimed!

Palace-like, then smiled your temples all,
    Ye were honored in the hero-sport
At the isthmus' crown-clad festival,
    And the goal the thundering chariots sought.

Beauteous dances that a spirit breathed
    Circled round your altars bright and fair;
Round your brows the crown of triumph wreathed,
    Garlands graced your fragrant hair.

Thyrsus-swingers' loud Evoë then,
    And the panther-team that shone afar,
Welcomed him who rapture brought to men;
    Fauns and Satyrs reeled before his car!
Round him sprang the Mænads' raving crew,
    While their dances showed his wine's great worth,
And the host's full cheeks of tawny hue
    Pointed to the cup with mirth.

In those days before the bed of death
    Stood no ghastly form. Then took away
From the lips a kiss the parting breath,
    And a genius quenched his torch's ray.
Even Orcus' rigid judgment scales
    By a mortal's offspring once were held,
And the Thracian's spirit-breathing wails
    E'en the angry Furies quelled.

Once again within Elysium's grove
    Met the happy shade his joys so dear;
Lover faithful found his faithful love,
    And his path regained the charioteer;
Linus' lute gave back each wonted strain,
    Admet clasped Alcestis to his heart,
And Orestes found his friend again,
    Philoctetes found his dart.

Nobler prizes then the wrestler crowned,
    Who the arduous path of virtue pressed;
Glorious workers then of deeds renowned
    Clambered up to join the spirits blest.
All the band of silent gods the while
    Bowed to him who summoned back the dead;
From Olympus' height the twin-stars' smile
    O'er the waves the pilot led.

Beauteous world, where art thou gone? O, thou,
    Nature's blooming youth, return once more!
Ah, but in song's fairy region now
    Lives thy fabled trace so dear of yore!
Cold and perished, sorrow now the plains,
    Not one godhead greets my longing sight;
Ah, the shadow only now remains
    Of yon living image bright![4]

In this poem, Schiller bemoans the modern aesthetic sensibility, which is contaminated by a technological worldview. Poetry, he explains, now "slavishly obeys the laws of gravity / A nature shorn of the divine."[5]

Later, from letters 15 and 16 in Schiller's work, we gain a clearer perspective of what he is up to with the concept of play and why Taylor engages with him. Schiller discusses two important instincts at work in human life; a sensuous instinct, and a rational one.[6] Play emerges as a third instinct, but it is an impulse that is only possible through the combination of the first two. The play instinct, "a new impulsion," Schiller says, facilitates a dimension of knowing or understanding that is less limited than what is known or understood through the independent functioning of our sensuous and rational capacities.[7] In combination, the natural functioning of our feelings and our reasoning seems to lose a bit of its staunch Kantian autonomy. The aesthetic sensibility of play is particularly receptive of expressions of beauty that are beyond us. This sensibility is what Taylor is interested in—an ability or capacity to appreciate or know external realities and to be changed by them. This external dimension is significant because Taylor remains ever convinced that modern epistemology relies too much upon what individuals come to know rationally and independently, and that such knowing is isolated from other influences within our lives and also is disconnected from sources around, or beyond, us.[8]

The philosopher Hans-Georg Gadamer takes up Schiller similarly and indicates that he reacts appropriately to a pervasive scientific orientation of modernity. In *Truth and Method* (1960), Gadamer explains that Schiller's interest in play is actually a wake-up call in a mechanically understood world to better appreciate beauty, although Gadamer also says that Schiller's articulation of it is too subjective; that is, in a certain sense it is too Kantian.[9] To pull the instinct of play beyond the parameters of wholly personal experience, Gadamer encourages us to recognize the distinction between one who experiences beauty and beauty itself: "The 'subject' of the experience . . . is not the subjectivity of the person who experiences it but the [beautiful object] itself. This is the point at which the mode of being of play becomes significant.

For play has its own essence, independent of the consciousness of those who play."[10] Gadamer explains that Schiller's play instinct "brings to light what is otherwise constantly hidden and withdrawn."[11] I include in my construct the fact that play—per Gadamer's rendering—happens *to* us. It stands over and above subjectivity. Persons are played, rather than being the instigators of play.

I position Gadamer's interest in this as hermeneutical. Though he expresses an interest in correcting Schiller, or even just improving what Schiller was trying to do with play, Gadamer wants to explain how works, particularly textual ones, inform us. In this we can consider the written words that are in front of us as laden with meaning, but with Gadamer we can also be mindful of the text of the world. Either way, both are external, imbued with meanings and purposes that we glean from them. The interpretations we render depend upon our own particular thoughts, sentiments, and intuitions, but such processes and responses are informed by the external realities of texts. The correlation between interpretation and the external is significant to Gadamer. Just as he is concerned about a world that is too mechanically or scientifically understood from a modern perspective, he also shows a yearning to break into the inner realm of modern individuals with meanings and purposes of external origins. Rather than further substantiating Gadamer with descriptions of his own, I turn to Rainer Maria Rilke, whom Taylor clearly admires, and Rilke's words that Gadamer uses to introduce his own magnum opus, *Truth and Method*:

> Catch only what you've thrown yourself, all is
> mere skill and little gain;
> but when you're suddenly the catcher of a ball
> thrown by an eternal partner
> with accurate and measured swing
> towards you, to your center, in an arch
> from the great bridgebuilding of God:
> why catching then becomes a power—
> not yours, a world's.[12]

Again, Taylor himself knows Rilke well, and deploys him with ease in his writings. Eventually, he faults some of Rilke's works—as he does pointedly in *The Ethics of Authenticity*—for an inability or lack of willingness to distinguish personal sentiments from objective realities that exist beyond us and our sentiments.[13] That Rilke's poetry does not more consistently, and committedly, appreciate the external sources of our lives (as this uncharacteristic precursor to Gadamer does so effectively) compels Taylor to turn at the end of *A Secular*

*Age* to a poet who does. In the final pages, the British Jesuit and Victorian poet Gerard Manley Hopkins becomes Taylor's shining, innovative example of ontic commitment.

In combining Schiller's and Gadamer's insights, I note that the subject—an individual person—becomes aware of *already being in relation to* powers, forces, and realms that exceed his or her own personal capabilities of comprehension and deliberation, *and* that this person now appreciates multiple capacities for knowing. The philosophical tradition framed by modern epistemology is pronouncedly uncomfortable with such external influences. That Schiller's play impulsion and the dynamic of Gadamerian hermeneutics point to something beyond subjective experience is a true violation of Enlightenment rationality. I would argue that Schiller and Gadamer seem to anticipate Taylor's fullness construct, inasmuch as they too break individuality open. In doing so, they endorse the concerns Taylor expresses about modernity.

## Heideggerian Whooshing

To better appreciate Taylor's own portrayal of modernity, the "malaises" he laments in many of his works would suffice, but so does the description of modernity that is portrayed in Dreyfus and Kelly's *All Things Shining*.[14] This book, like Taylor's, discusses the general culture we live in. I contend that it also demonstrates a yearning for fullness.

Although Dreyfus and Kelly disagree with some of Taylor's fundamental philosophical commitments, *A Secular Age* inspired them. Dreyfus and Kelly approached Taylor about the idea for their project at the New School in New York, during a conference dealing with Taylor's work, and Taylor endorsed it. Above, I quoted Taylor's definition of fullness, saying that it is a moment "when 'ordinary reality is abolished and something terrifyingly *other* shines through.'"[15] This is the shining in which Dreyfus and Kelly dwell. It is an illumination of a reality beyond us, or even a kind of sheening or excelling that is called out of us.

As Taylor does in *A Secular Age* and elsewhere in his writings, Dreyfus and Kelly explain that meaninglessness and a lack of individual purpose exist today like never before in our history. In the context of higher education, Anthony Kronman of Yale University constructs a similar argument in his book *Education's End: Why Our Colleges and Universities Have Given Up on the Meaning of Life* (2007), where he likewise speaks about us and our time as empty, flattened, disenchanted, and in crisis.[16] He recoils at the "characteristically American emphasis on the importance of 'useful' knowledge," and he also hopes to cultivate a different sensibility.[17]

In *All Things Shining*, Dreyfus and Kelly say that a nihilism of the present era leaves us with the distasteful prospect that nothing in the world matters.[18] Taylor himself refers to this as the Peggy Lee principle, recalling the famous song by Peggy Lee, who asks, "Is that all there is?"[19] Dreyfus and Kelly call this a particular American mood that is characterized by addiction, depression, consumerism, terrorism, and tennis academies.[20] They use the acclaimed late novelist David Foster Wallace to make their point and, just like Taylor, bring us to realize that we cannot, by our own individual resources, manufacture the meanings and purposes of our lives. As they worry about a cultural melancholy, they also worry about relativism.

To spell this out philosophically, Dreyfus and Kelly discuss the history of Enlightenment-era philosophy. They consider the father of modern philosophy to be René Descartes, who insisted that we can do this; that is, we can manufacture meaning and purpose from our own personal resources. According to them, Descartes interpreted the world as a taxonomy of subjects and objects sufficient unto themselves and interactive in limited ways.[21] Subjectivity, then, is more alone than as previously depicted, and as a source unto itself is a locus of truth and certainty. Certainty, that is, *self-achieved* certainty in turn empowers our choices. The condition of subjectivity in Cartesian perspective is thus inflated *willfully*: "Human subjects at their best are completely detached, self-contained, and, far from being passive, have a will-power so great that it rivals God's."[22] However, the mechanistic worldview that Descartes's philosophy details, the corresponding scientific certainty it demands, and his resulting doctrinaire regard for factual evidence gain far too much momentum for their comfort—a modern force that Schiller feared— Dreyfus and Kelly maintain that Descartes's sense of personal autonomy is the real culprit behind modern meaninglessness.

Starting with Descartes, then, but also following a particular philosophical thread through the Enlightenment, they reach Friedrich Nietzsche to show us how philosophers of the Enlightenment have convinced us that meaning and purpose must be solely constructed from individual willfulness.[23] The Nietzschean insight that we can become the overman, a god, is a spectacularly self-aggrandized perspective emerging out of Enlightenment rationality.[24]

Dreyfus and Kelly are quite sure that Taylor's ways forward in *A Secular Age*, the itineraries to new belief he explores at the end of the book, are not helpful. Taylor is a serious religious thinker. Roman Catholicism represents a faith perspective that operates in his life along intelligent, passionate, and practical strands. His fascination with and practice of Buddhism, moreover, stand by its side closely and comfortably. But for Dreyfus and Kelly, these transcendental-striped orientations are not relevant or appropriate for dealing with the problems of our secular age, and they say so up front.[25] They are, however, concerned about the meaningless destinations a secular age offers. They ask an interesting question, and one that Taylor entertains in his own way: "What if we haven't lost the sacred, shining gods, but have simply lost touch with the meanings they offer?"[26]

It is clear that modernity discourages Dreyfus and Kelly. They agree with Taylor that it is a source of individualism, consumerism, and relativism—"isms" preventing us from recognizing realities that facilitate meaning and purpose more profoundly. They explain that "our focus on ourselves as isolated, autonomous agents has had the effect of banishing the gods—that is to say, covering up or blocking our sensitivity to what is sacred in the world."[27] They end evocatively, saying: "The gods are calling us but we have ceased to listen. They are calling us to cultivate [poiesis, or a poietic, 'bringing into being'] sensitivity."[28] As such, they insist that meanings of ourselves and the world around us are not self-generated but are generated for the self, and that we can cultivate the skills to find them and be meaningfully affected by them. What is key here, however, is the sensitivity they aspire to restore, a capacity, I argue, similar to Taylor's fullness. It does not demand Taylor's metaphysical commitment, but it is telling, especially as an antidotal expression to a modernity that Dreyfus, Kelly, and Taylor similarly grieve.

The "whooshing up" that Dreyfus and Kelly prescribe—the flashes of excellence not all that different from the conceptions of ancient Greek arête—are objectified and externalized, so to speak, in the ancient Greek conception of "physis," an etymological origin to our modern conception of physics: "The word *physis* in Homeric times wasn't the name of some ultimate *constituent* of the universe; it was the name for the way the most real things in the world present themselves to us."[29] Dreyfus and Kelly yearn for fullness, for a moment that "offers what autonomy cannot: a sense of participating in something that transcends."[30]

Dreyfus and Kelly's discussion becomes more practical and pointed in a recent follow-up article to their book, where they describe physical agility and artistic genius in our lives as specific examples of being called by the gods: "When human beings are acting at their best—in great feats of athleticism or in the composition of the finest poetry, in the activities of life in the everyday world or heroism on the battlefield in feats of war—people often say that they were not themselves responsible for what they did, . . . as if it was drawn out of them."[31] They proclaim that, in the ancient context, "the Homeric gods shined. They manifested what mattered in its best light and they drew people to perform heroic and passionate deeds."[32] Bringing such gods back into our consciousness—that is, becoming sensitized to Homeric polytheism—is

Dreyfus and Kelly's remedy to modernity's problems; but unlike Taylor, their cure needs neither metaphysics nor theology.[33] A Homeric polytheism, in their account, "retains a phenomenologically rich account of the sacred, and a similarly rich understanding of human existence in its midst."[34]

Such polytheistic sensitizing is possible in our contemporary lives, they insist, through the dispositions of wonder and gratitude: "We ... need, in particular, to cultivate the practices of opening ourselves to being overwhelmed by the power of moods and nature, and at the same time learn the practice of cultivating ourselves so that our routines are transformed into rituals that bring things out at their shining best."[35] In Dreyfus and Kelly's reading of history, moreover, ancient wonder and gratitude are prefigured generation by generation. In the caring and patriotic attitude of Athens and its citizens, Homer is echoed by the ancient Greek poet Aeschylus. Later, it occurs through Jesus's agapic loving. Dante Alighieri exudes religious bliss. Martin Luther celebrates joyfulness. Descartes himself articulates a sense of rational tranquillity, positive and productive moods in our lives that are then thwarted by the modern temperaments of gripping indecision, endless waiting, and anxiety to which T. S. Eliot, Samuel Beckett, and W. H. Auden so powerfully attest.[36]

Taylor responds to Dreyfus and Kelly, explaining that they have invented a form of polytheism that is "interstitial."[37] He turns to Martin Heidegger for backup, explaining that Dreyfus and Kelly offer a shallow polytheism devoid of the meaningful practices and moral and epistemic commitments manifested by ancient polytheists that were definitely present in Homeric expressions. Instead, they remain at a simpler Heideggerian level of basic experience, the place of "interface between *Dasien* [a being in the world] and world."[38] Genuine Homeric polytheism indeed evoked wonder and gratitude; it motivated creativity, valiance, and beauty, but it also provoked fear and dread and demanded ritualistic sacrifice to specific, and living, gods. Although Taylor appreciates their modernity-influenced concern for a muted, if not deadened, human sensitivity, he seems discouraged by the flimsy polytheism they articulate.[39]

This, in fact, is worth dwelling on for a moment. Is the metaphysical commitment of Taylor's fullness wholly necessary? Philosophically, it is. Taylor labors too persistently in *A Secular Age* to instantiate our ability to experience mystical realities that are external to subjectivity. However, from a practical, day-to-day perspective, I think Taylor would be excited to see anyone even edging toward the possibility of fullness, and doing so in the midst of somewhere between naturalism and supernaturalism. In this, there seems to be a metaphysical willingness or interest. The edging is itself a dimension of Taylor's fullness. It reveals a yearning—or, better yet, an openness and connectedness—that reflects the porous self Taylor discusses, a concept of subjectivity I will eventually describe more fully. I myself appreciate the middle ground. Though I endorse Taylor's metaphysics, his ontic commitment, I do not want to undermine those who either resist it or ponder alternative descriptions. Porosity can be appreciated from many angles, and the way of life fullness portends does indeed seem to represent an enriched subjectivity. Even some of the relational connections of fullness named above are better than none.

## An Epistemic Caution

To emphasize the philosophical problems of modernity and to endorse Dreyfus and Kelly's critique, I turn momentarily to John McDowell, or at least to Taylor's appreciation of McDowell. Previously in this chapter, I cited Heidegger's idea of *Dasien* as part of Taylor's critique of Dreyfus and Kelly's polytheism. Taylor indicates that they offer us a shallow and insubstantial variant of genuine Homeric polytheism. His reference to *Dasien* demonstrates an interaction between a knowing subject and an external world devoid of values, commitments, and influences operative in both domains. It is an explanation of Taylor's that echoes his elucidation of modern epistemology through his reading and appreciation of McDowell's *Mind and World* (1994).

In the article "Foundationalism and the Inner-Outer Distinction," Taylor applauds the philosophical insights professed in McDowell's hugely influential work, indicating "massive agreement with the main line of his thinking."[40] Taylor is wary of a rigid dichotomy between a knowing subject and the external world. Dreyfus was an interlocutor with Taylor, and is cited. And even then, through Dreyfus, Taylor points to Heidegger's *Dasien* construct with concern. Naming Heidegger, and including Maurice Merleau-Ponty, Taylor explains that both thinkers articulate what it means to be *Dasien*, and how "these accounts are rather rich, detailed, and multifaceted."[41] Heidegger and Merleau-Ponty "portray human conceptual thinking as embedded in an ordinary way of living and moving around in the world, and dealing with things, which is in an important sense pre-conceptual; what Dreyfus calls 'everyday coping.'"[42] Such *dealing* and *coping*, however, become problematic for Taylor because they signify a misleading relationship between the "inner" construal of a subject interacting with an external world. One problem is that an inside/outside distinction seems valid. Such a division "portrays our understanding of the world as taking place in a zone, surrounded by . . . a world, which is thus seen as playing the role of Outside to its Inside."[43]

Taylor's concern is that "what goes on in the inner zone is meant to be in some way at least partly modeled on what exists outside."[44] Such an image of knowing—which is "too powerfully embedded in our beliefs and (scientific, technical, freedom-oriented) way of life"[45]—leaves us with an impression of a "self-enclosed subject, out of contact with the transcendent world."[46] But Taylor, and even Dreyfus and Kelly in a certain light, want such a contact. In Taylor's assessment, this epistemic perspective, foundationalism, augments forms of relativism that Taylor wants to avoid; but it also limits the power of knowing, a constraint he is trying to dismantle in various ways, which are related to the wider capacities of fullness, his own phenomenological-existential construct.

## Modern Presentness

The educational philosopher René Arcilla discusses a particular philosophical-anthropological capacity in *Mediumism: A Philosophical Reconstruction of Modernism for Existential Learning* (2010), his recent work that is not wholly unlike Taylor's. However, Arcilla is more hopeful about modernity. Unlike Dreyfus, Kelly, McDowell, and Taylor, modernity for Arcilla is ripe with meaning and purpose. It is in this context that Arcilla articulates the possibility of an essential human capacity that resembles the phenomenological aspects of Taylor's fullness.

For Arcilla, modernity is particularly meaningful in its artistic expression. As Dreyfus and Kelly want to recultivate a forgotten poiesis, Arcilla appreciates an existing one. Modern works of art, through their medium of uncertainty and ambiguity, spark, or instantiate, the human condition of estrangement. "Strangerhood" is a natural reality of human life that Arcilla wants all of us to acknowledge; embracing it helps us face the fact that, as human persons, "we are always travelers passing through" a domain that we inhabit only temporarily and conditionally.[47] As modernity is meaningful, it also has a dark side. Elements of it can make us feel easily at home, or too easily identifiable. He takes up the role of modern aesthetics—or at least the artistic—in a pedagogical dimension, developing what he terms as "existential learning," an instructive process that prevents us from identifying ourselves with and in the trappings of modernity.

The critique that Arcilla offers of modernity focuses not upon the epistemic commitments of Cartesian-Kantian rationality but upon twentieth-century industry and capital gain. Prescient contemporary issues of consumerism, the cultivation of superficial self-identities, and the influences of mass media and mass production represent modernity's problems. Arcilla demonstrates existential sympathies in Marxist tones. If Schiller's play was a wake-up call in a suddenly mechanically structured world, Arcilla's existential learning—"awake now"—is likewise an alarm.[48] We may be estranged, but we should not allow ourselves to be alienated. Arcilla prompts us to recognize how and why we should evade being at home, so to speak, in a world that is always foreign, and he encourages us to forge ahead more freely and, thus, more responsibly.

The affinities I detect between Arcilla and Taylor come through, again, as a certain appreciation of fullness. Like Taylor, Arcilla demonstrates a keen interest in substantiating external, objective influences that affect us as knowing subjects. He also validates a corresponding transformative moment of recognition—one that is caused, not self-generated—and he stresses the necessity for an appropriate—in Arcilla's rendering, virtuous—response.

In *Mediumism* Arcilla argues that works of modern art can affect us existentially—the spark or instantiation discussed above—by making us aware of a philosophical-anthropological dynamic in our lives—also, again, estrangement.[49] In such a process, a particular experience of understanding—not something arbitrary and impulsive, but purposeful—happens:[50] "Conviction in a work's aesthetic identity and quality: this, then, springs from an experience of presentness. In its grip, we are fully present to the work, and 'get' all its features as a whole."[51]

This moment, "presentness," a kind of *wakefulness*, is described by Arcilla as being instantaneous and convincing, meaningful and beautiful.[52] More so, "this experience is patently an ideal state of being for us . . . 'grace.' . . . Its value is to be distinguished from [a] more mundane, incomplete, inconclusive counterpart."[53] Furthermore, much earlier in his work Arcilla foreshadows the experience of presentness, explaining that "there is a moment in the process of understanding, and an inner realm of ourselves" that is not unlike Griffiths's solitary moment.[54] Also, in Arcilla's description, a moment as such "is irreducibly solitary; . . . the sole and the common, solitude and community, isolation and communication, are components, not opposites. Each requires cultivation."[55] Below, we will see how Taylor expands his notion of fullness beyond a sense of personal empowerment. Here, however, in *Mediumism*, Arcilla explains that presentness is not just a dynamic between artwork and a viewer but also one of persons—you and me—who dwell in a "questionable" world that "elicits understanding."[56] Like Taylor, Arcilla is determined to break individuality open.

As we will appreciate an expanded version of fullness in Taylor's own rendering further along in this chapter, we will also wrestle with Taylor's admission that his account of fullness "has a religious or metaphysical ring" to it and his willingness to conceptualize fullness more generally.[57] Fullness, he emphasizes, is not a moment of Kantian cognition but a general philosophical-anthropological construct that fundamentally accounts for senses of and strivings for meaning and purpose in our lives.[58] Arcilla's presentness is much different, but when Taylor says that "we need a conversation between a host of different positions" for what fullness is, I appreciate the many affinities between Taylor's and Arcilla's conceptions.[59]

To be a bit more pointed about such resemblances, both fullness and presentness are contextualized not as theological or metaphysical but as philosophical-anthropological. This is despite Arcilla's characterization of presentness as "grace" and Taylor's unquestionable metaphysical commitments. To each, both are fundamental human realities. Also, in the experiences they facilitate, both are phenomenological; that is, each provides an awareness of some kind. Furthermore, there are *gripping* or *seizing* realities to these moments, and Taylor and Arcilla both offer grasping descriptors. Taylor in particular is articulate about a qualitative aspect of time in such moments, an experience that is suspended from ordinary, prosaic measurements of minutes and seconds, for instance—a distinction Arcilla also makes by distinguishing presentness from the mundane. To continue, they each testify to revelations and significations that happen outside or external to subjectivity, disclosures that rely upon human capacities that can appreciate them. And finally, each augments a moral dimension.

To understand Arcilla's ethical correlate, consider his description of the "present," an external source that initiates within us a condition of presentness. He instructs that it is freely generous and loving, and that it compels from us similar kinds of responses.[60] The present transforms us, and we can participate in it or espouse its qualities. He explains that it "entails accepting certain practical commitments," which emulate the generosity and love of the present.[61] When he intimates that "I am apt to feel awe at its miraculous, inexplicably spontaneous genesis as generosity," he also seems to anticipate Dreyfus and Kelly and their yearnings, in a secular age, for wonder and gratitude. Arcilla's two specific virtues are gratitude and generosity.[62]

It would be unfair to conflate Arcilla's and Taylor's existential concerns and, for that matter, Arcilla's and Dreyfus and Kelly's virtues. Influences from Jean-Paul Sartre and Stanley Cavell, assisted by articulations of freedom in Michael Oakeshott's work, are only the tip of Arcilla's existential iceberg. But given the likenesses between the combined reality of works of art, presentness, and an ensuing existential learning, I am indeed impelled to keep pushing Arcilla into the realm of Taylor's fullness. Arcilla reads modernity differently, but he seems to share in the existential concerns of Dreyfus and Kelly's recovery of ancient whooshing as well as Taylor's religiously enchanted fullness.[63]

## Holistic Epistemics

Understanding Taylor's fullness—as we did above through Schiller's concept of play, and then through Gadamer's refinement of it—is essential, I think, for rightly appreciating and maintaining the particular existential orientation that Taylor establishes. It is the "conditions" of belief in which he is interested, and the way we live our lives. For him, play reinforces the phenomenological aspect of fullness. Yet there is a temptation to engage fullness merely in epistemic language, at least in my own negotiations of Taylor's fullness. Steering around the pitfalls of Enlightenment epistemology is important for Taylor. Its traps force either/or, right/wrong, and true/false certainties that replicate dogmatic perspectives to which modern epistemologists reacted in their Enlightenment inspirations. Taylor offers pages of explanation in many of his works about the problems and limitations of the Cartesian-Kantian strand of knowing. In the end, their abilities to empower human subjects through their own internal capacities have, according to Taylor, narrowed reasoning aptitudes to facts, evidence, and explicit rules and have furthermore translated into modern moral-ethical theories of utility and duty. As modern thinkers hoped to wake human knowing from a dogmatic slumber, rationality seems to have inaugurated a catatonic dogmatism of its own.

Stephen Toulmin offers a helpful overview of this, considering a specific time in Western history to pinpoint a paradigm shift in philosophy—a subjective turn—that occurred through two philosophers, Michel de Montaigne and René Descartes. It is worth noting Toulmin's comparison of these two philosophers, for as thinkers at the cusp of modernity, both are recognized as "individualists."[64]

In Montaigne's *Essays* (1580) and in Descartes's *Discourse on Method* (1637) and *Meditations on First Philosophy* (1641), both thinkers proffer modern philosophical methods of "self-examination."[65] However, Toulmin maps the ways by which they take radically different paths and how they philosophically produce dramatically divergent results. Montaigne's "aim was to set aside pretense and attitudinizing, self-aggrandizement or ostentatious self-reproach, and to provide an unvarnished picture of his experience of life, and attitudes of mind."[66] His writings reflect a philosophical skepticism that is reflected through his thoughts, feelings, and impulses of human living, in particular. Though Montaigne is not recognized as a universalizing or synthesizing thinker, his writings portend that his own daily experiences inform all of us about what it means to be human.[67] Alternatively, with Descartes—whose method established a rigid form of rationality[68]—and also inaugurated a relentless "quest for certainty" in philosophy[69]—Toulmin discovers "a taste of 'solipsism,'" that is, a more radically personal epistemic perspective that dwells within specific insights and truths of individuals themselves.[70] Moreover, of the two, Montaigne's method showcases various sources of knowing (sensing, intuiting, thinking, wondering) that are operative within the human experience, whereas Descartes solely spotlights and celebrates scientific rationality.

These new self-reflective methods in philosophy were developed quickly, Toulmin explains, in a fifty-year interim between the 1580 publication of Montaigne's *Essays* and Descartes's publications in the late 1630s.[71] As seventeenth-century philosophy advances, Montaigne fades, and Toulmin suggests that, in following Descartes, Western philosophy took a wrong turn. Now, in the twenty-first century, we are paying the price. Modernity, he feels, has run its course. Toulmin says that philosophy "can cling to the discredited research program of a purely theoretical (i.e., 'modern') philosophy, which will end by driving it out of business; it can look for new and less exclusively theoretical ways of working, and develop the methods needed for a more practical ('*post*-modern') agenda; or it can return to its pre-seventeenth-century traditions, and try to recover the lost ('*pre*-modern') topics that were sidetracked by Descartes, but can be usefully taken up for the future."[72]

Taylor does not entirely agree with Toulmin's prognosis. For instance, Taylor persistently welcomes the special gifts of modernity, such as new and powerful formulations of personal rights and human dignities. Expressions of democratic governance and perspective, too, are generally nonnegotiable. Like Toulmin, however, Taylor also clearly feels that we are paying some sort of price. The lack of fullness represents an existential cost. But Taylor flirts with an epistemic correlate to fullness, and it is most evident in a talk he gave at Fordham University in June 2009.

At Fordham's Rose Hill campus in the Bronx, Taylor returned to the critique of modern rationality he often exercises, and he reminded his audience that human reason is more than Cartesian rationality, the methodic, self-certain, mind-dominating, scientific way of knowing that characterizes mainstream epistemology today. Again, in this, he is like Toulmin. The Enlightenment perspective employs an epistemic bias and has suppressed or discredited what Taylor calls "theoretical imagination." Human reasoning, he explains, has "a creative component; it can and must generate new ways of conceiving the reality it is trying to understand."[73] With this, he explains that "there is no standard answer, no sure method"—an orientation Montaigne would endorse. The work of reason functions through attempts to articulate what emerge in our lives "as barely definable hunches, or inchoate insights."[74] This, possibly, is where Taylor diverges from Toulmin and, thus, Montaigne. He continues, explaining that "these uninformed insights draw us strongly; we are willing to engage our attention very deeply in them. We have an as yet unfounded and nonetheless powerful and anticipatory confidence in them."[75]

Taylor more than once cites the decisively modern achievements of the natural sciences, whose "explanations recur to factors which are not defined by their meanings for us, but simply by their efficient causal relations."[76] If he laments the dominance of Cartesian-Kantian epistemologies, he does not totally discount them. But he insists that the very possibility of the emergence of hard scientific truth partly comes about through the hunches and fumbling of theoretical reason to begin with, an expression of reason that modern perspectives do not fully appreciate.[77] Gesturing to Kant's *Religion Within the Limits of Reason Alone* (1793), Taylor instructs that "the vicissitudes of the appeal to 'reason alone' force us to depart" too radically from other sources of knowing in our lives.[78] Moreover, when reason functions in such lonely scientific isolation, it loses its ability to properly engage other realities, such as "ethics, political theory, social science, history, literature, philosophy, aesthetics"—all crucial matters of human life.[79]

Taylor stays on course. Reason, he insists, "is something we don't only do alone, but also inescapably involves dialogical collaboration and exchange."[80] Does Montaigne account for this? Taylor does not seem to think so, at least in *A Secular Age*, where he is instructive of Montaigne's radical individuality. He only cites Montaigne three times, and in his most engaged discussion of him, he seems to fault Montaigne for the self-enclosed method of reflection he offers.[81] Taylor is more telling in *Sources*, however. There, he indicates that Montaigne's method has indeed affected the modernity we live within by endorsing an intense individuality, a contemporary orientation that Taylor tries to rebuff.[82] He suggests that Montaigne's conception of subjectivity actually overdistinguishes persons from one another as radically unique entities and thereby resists showing what is common and shared among us. But worse, understandings of one's self are not enhanced by social and worldly influences but are garnered by looking deeper and deeper within.[83] Finally, Taylor also thinks that Montaigne's subjectivity is devoid of "spiritual aspirations," yearnings that seem fundamental to his fullness construct.[84]

As Taylor argues that the powers of reason attest to many sources within us, a dynamic indeed creditable to Montaigne, learning and knowing also happen in a community of others. This, a social dimension, is also for Taylor an attractive element of the integrating function at work in Schiller's play.

Inasmuch as modern individual selves are fragmented and divided in their own natural capacities, so too is society. Conversely, Schiller cites the extraordinary accomplishments of ancient Greeks, such as their ways of thinking, expressing, and living. The more persons function in and through the "totality of [individual] being," the better are the societies we inhabit.[85] I would like to return to this social dimension—featured at the beginning of this chapter—in my closing thoughts.

As Toulmin shares certain concerns about modernity, he also helps us recognize how Taylor salvages components of it. Taylor does not discount the Enlightenment outright. Some of its achievements are essential for good living. Moreover, Taylor even rescues modern epistemology, at least partially. He remains sharply critical, but he indicates a faith dimension at work within the unsubstantiated intellectual hunches and gropings that evolved into world-altering scientific achievements. In all this, he lets us better appreciate his conception of fullness from an intellective vantage. He stresses personal avenues of knowing that modern epistemology either discounts or refuses to acknowledge, and he gives us an account of knowing that is not individualistic but is informed by others.

## AGAPE

It is through the concept of "agape," however, that Taylor is most expansive of fullness. We began the chapter with a general assessment of what fullness initially means to Taylor and proceeded to evaluate how others—Schiller and Gadamer, Dreyfus and Kelly, and Arcilla—represent it or seem to yearn for it in some way. With Toulmin, we have also negotiated a number of readings of modernity that generally support Taylor's concerns. Though Arcilla views modernity with special pedagogical regard, the critique he does offer is not entirely unrelated. Through agape, we will see a decisive metaphysical commitment of fullness and, for this commitment, note a moral-ethical correlate. This commitment, I contend, is necessary, and without it Schiller and Gadamer, Dreyfus and Kelly, and Arcilla remain vulnerable to some of the very concerns they condemn.

In the final chapter of *A Secular Age*, Taylor calls for broader conceptions of fullness and immediately focuses a spotlight upon agape. Taylor has been strategic, however, by referencing agape along the way. In *A Secular Age* it is an important word in Taylor's lexicon well before chapter 20. Also, in *Sources of the Self*—a work widely discussed in educational theory—agape is a principal concept. Interestingly, in *Sources*, it is referenced much less than in *A Secular*

*Age*, and it is not even indexed. However, the construct is used intentionally and even tactically, and its role in supporting the main argument of *Sources* is evident. I contend that it is fundamental to the text and, metaphysically and religiously, represents the moral source of human living for which Taylor argues. If I am right to latch on to the expression of fullness in *A Secular Age*, to make sense of the work through its existential and phenomenal capacity, I make sense of *Sources* through agape.

Most basically, agape is Greek for love, but ancient Greek works in literature and philosophy do not seem to use the specific term all that much. Internet searches yield conjectures, at best. One source suggests the possibility that the ancient Greek poet Homer employs derivatives of the word in the *Odyssey*, in books V and VII.[86] The agapic expression is referenced as a religious and devotional love shown for the goddess Isis by foreign Egyptian dockhands working in the Athenian port city Piraeus.

Anders Nygren's seminal work, *Agape and Eros* (1953), and Gene Outka's own extended study, *Agape: An Ethical Analysis* (1972), articulate a linguistic affinity between agape and eros—both are Greek terms for love—but stress significant conceptual differences between the two. Nygren and Outka each look seriously at eros and admit that it has a complicated philosophical history. They tend to agree that "the Eros motif... reaches its height in Plato, at whose hands it is also cast into its classical" and divergent depictions of erotic impulse and epistemic desire.[87] Nygren reminds us that, beyond Plato, Aristotle and Neoplatonic thinkers also render specific meanings of their own.[88]

Agape, Nygren explains, is essentially and specifically Christian:[89] "The history of the Christian idea of love begins with an entirely new and peculiarly Christian fundamental motif of religion and ethics—the agape motif," which, furthermore, attests to conceptual differences in its own historical development.[90] That is, even within its own specific context, the term charts an evolutionary process. To make sense of its Christian origins, Nygren turns not to Greek philosophical discourse but to Jewish perspective, and he highlights Christianity's dramatic novelty in religious and ethical perspectives. Though informed by both Greek and Jewish thought and practice, Christianity—especially through agapic love—is featured as fundamentally innovative.

For instance, "in Christianity... [love] is universal in its scope. In Judaism love is exclusive and particularistic: it is directed to one's 'neighbour' in the original and more restricted sense of the word, and it is directed to 'neighbours only.'"[91] In Christian disposition, this agapic love—defined by the New Testament commandment to love God and all others equally—is unanimously and freely expressed.[92] The love of the Christian God is unconditional, and, in the realm of ethics and morality, Christians are encouraged to emulate it. The *neighbor*, per Taylor's own discussion (as I discuss below), is not really just a neighbor but also anyone. As the ambit of fullness is wide, so too with agape.

Christian references to agape are abundant. The Septuagint, the ancient Greek translation of the Hebrew Bible, refers to agape as God's unconditional love for people of the created world. The ancient literature that follows the Septuagint in the New Testament form—in the genres of letters and Gospel texts—bespeaks the dynamic of agape in a similar fashion, as the love of God, but it also describes agape as loving *like* God. It becomes something that we too can do. It is the Christian God's love for us, and it is also our actions of charity. A supranatural locus is maintained, and the charitable acts that ensue are understood as being motivated by and expressive of the originary external source. Nygren summarizes a scriptural evolution of the term beginning in the Gospel writings, advancing through the epistles of Paul the Apostle, and culminating in letters by writers who were specifically influenced by the Gospel of John. As such, agape had "its roots in the new and specifically Christian way of fellowship with God, as this is depicted in the Gospels. It finds its highest expression in Paul . . . [and] the supreme formal statement is reached in the Johannine 'God is Agape.'"[93]

In *Sources*, Taylor describes the presence of agape in philosophical thought across its own history.[94] From Greek antiquity, he compares agape with the transformative effect, morally and epistemologically, of seeing the Platonic Good. The early medieval philosopher Augustine's (354–430) understanding of Plato (c. 424–28 BCE)—which the Neoplatonic philosopher Plotinus (c. 204–70) informed—recognizes cosmic emanation as agape. Later Platonic thinkers of Renaissance humanism—namely, Marsilio Ficino and Giovanni Pico della Mirandola—also articulate a metaphysical source of love that is recognized as agapic. As an antecedent to agape, we have already considered how Jewish thought represents ways of participating in God's love of his chosen people. Universal justice obligated in the philosophy of Kant—per Outka, "the 'agape-commitment' is very [much] like a concept of the categorical imperative"—is referenced by Taylor as a secularized variant of agape.[95] And, of course, Taylor himself also details the Christian scriptural understandings of agape.

Along the lines of philosophical resemblance, let me briefly feature once again Nygren and Outka. Outka discusses a version of justice, equalitarian justice, in agapic affinity. Unlike distributive or retributive expressions, for instance, "equalitarian justice . . . overlaps significantly with agape. The account by a number of philosophers is often linked to [articulations of] universal human rights. [The Plato scholar Gregory] Vlastos provides one such account. He offers a rationale for equalitarian justice without appealing directly to theological or metaphysical doctrines. Points of normative overlap with agape are plain enough."[96]

It is Nietzsche, however, who seems most helpful—at least to Nygren. He explains that Nietzsche's articulation of Christianity as a "transvaluation of all ancient values" is especially pointed. Of Greek and Roman antiquity, Judaism, and "indeed the entire pre-Christian and non-Christian world, . . . [this] 'transvaluation' is seen, above all, in the central Christian motif, the agape motif."[97]

In *A Secular Age*, many of the same philosophical similarities are maintained or rearticulated. "Agape" as a term is much more developed. In my reading, I recognize two instructive expressions of agape, one that reveals a *participatory* aspect and another that testifies to an *associative* character, both of which demonstrate agape as a "stepping beyond."[98] Before discussing the "stepping beyond" aspects of agape in *A Secular Age*, I turn once again to *Sources*.

I mentioned above that agape is characterized religiously and metaphysically as well as morally and ethically. These portrayals may seem unrelated to one another, or at least at home in spheres of their own. The first points upward or outward in one direction, to the domain of the supernatural; and in another direction, the other gestures toward the natural realities of human life. This distinction, however, is precisely what Taylor wants to argue against in *Sources*. The metaphysical and the ethical are connected, and the first becomes a source for the second.

In *Sources*, that source—ultimately explainable, according to Taylor, "by reference to a cosmic reality, the order of things"—is called a "constitutive good," or, with Plato, simply the "Good."[99] Taylor continues, emphasizing that it "is a moral source . . . [in that] it is a something the love of which empowers us to do and be good."[100] Taylor moves beyond Plato to Jewish and Christian conceptions of the Good to explain the role of God in this. Our love for God and God's love for us—that is, God's agape—is what empowers moral-ethical living.[101] As discussed above, Dreyfus, Kelly, McDowell, and Taylor are concerned about autonomous and individualist epistemologies that are internally narrowed and socially uninfluenced; in *Sources*, Taylor is similarly worried about self-relative moral and ethical explanations. He asks, "What happens when, as in modern humanist views, we no longer have anything like a constitutive good external to [us]?"[102] In *Sources*, Taylor does not want to simplify this philosophical problem too easily, and he thereby suggests that we recognize the role of constitutive goods in our lives and begin the difficult task of articulating what, how, and where that role impels us. This "articulacy," he suggests, helps us stumble closer to recognizing sources of goodness.

The fusion of the two expressions of fullness is not insignificant. As Taylor first discusses fullness in epiphanic terms and then desires to expand the idea of fullness beyond the sphere of personal experience and insight, he deploys the notion of agape. As with the first rendering of fullness, agape is specifically religious. But in its moral-ethical dimension, agape is visceral and connecting.

We can return, now, to the stepping-beyond characteristics of agape that I glean from *A Secular Age* in expressions that I name participatory and associative. First, the participatory aspect: Whereas Nygren and Outka cite the Christian commandment to love both God and neighbor and develop their discussion of agape from this conflated concept of loving, Taylor turns to the well-known parable of the Good Samaritan and the agapic ethic it reveals.[103] His reading of this famous story is influenced by the educational theorist and social activist Ivan Illich. Illich is a figure from whom Taylor takes great inspiration. The lesson of the parable, ultimately, is about the "neighbor" who is anyone, anywhere, and the charitable response Christians should unconditionally offer neighbors.

In loving others unconditionally—as demonstrated by the Samaritan stranger—exercising agape is an expression of moral goodness. It attests to the transformation of oneself in terms of moral growth. After all, it would have been uncommon for the foreign Samaritan to engage a Jewish local so freely, let alone charitably, and vice versa. Also, it manifests the kind of good recognized of the Christian God, an unconditional goodness that individuals themselves are to emulate. Being morally good as such is a way of participating in an activity of the Christian supreme being. Taylor explains that Greek philosophers—and, in particular, the Platonic thinkers of the Renaissance—articulated a concept "of 'theiosis,' a 'becoming divine,' which was part of human destiny, ... the demand to go beyond merely human flourishing."[104] This is one part of the stepping-beyond character of agape, in what I call the "participatory aspect." Individuals can participate in divine action. For Taylor, moral goodness, as expressed in gestures of care and concern for another— any another, unconditionally—is a movement away from the context of the natural contentment of ordinary life toward "becoming partakers in the life of [the divine]."[105]

Stated more succinctly, we participate in and emulate the source of moral goodness for which Taylor argues in *Sources*. The good that impels us is the good that we in turn manifest. In such a process, transformation happens. Would the actions of the Good Samaritan be meaningless and inconsequential to the Good Samaritan himself? We ourselves become better persons through the goodness we manifest. And, clearly, there are recipients of the goodness—the traveler, for instance, who is assisted by the Samaritan, and hearers and readers of the story from one generation to the next are likewise transformed. The point of the participatory aspect highlights the moral growth of which any of us are capable.

Now the associative character: Taylor instructs that the subjective turn of modern philosophy and its pronounced rational character have made possible new modes of moral and ethical expression.[106] With the abolition in modern thought of metaphysics and the rise of its replacement, empirical science, people no longer appeal to supernatural, transcendental sources to make sense of themselves and the world. Modern individuals are able to appreciate facts and evidences that can be rationally confirmed, and rationality is thereby esteemed. What is irrational, conversely—such as perspectives of belief or intuitions and impulses not related to facts and evidences—are less appreciated. He thus explains that "in no case, is a paradigm bodily emotion seen as *criterial* for right action—as in the case of New Testament agape."[107] His point is not that rationality is unimportant, but that other factors—gut and emotional ones—figure into an ethical response. Moreover, he explains that the nature of agape "can't ever be understood simply in terms of a set of rules, but rather as the extension of a certain kind of relation, spreading outward, in a network."[108] Taylor says that agape "moves outward from the guts," instructing that "the New Testament word for 'taking pity' . . . places [this ethical] response in the bowels."[109]

With regard to the two-dimensional associative quality of agape, I see functioning in *A Secular* Age, on one hand, agape networks across the various aspects of our lives: mind, heart, gut. On the other hand—as demonstrated between the foreign Samaritan's manifestation of myriad differences (ethnic, social status, religious) and the local individual he helps—agape takes us "beyond the bounds of any already existing solidarity."[110] In our lives, agape is holistic across a range of intellectual, emotional, and intuitional responses; and it connects us to others much different from ourselves. The connection to others is a moral expression that reveals a stepping beyond the bounds of a familiar community toward the context of a less familiar supercommunity: "The paradigmatic stepping beyond of agape . . . is not motivated by a preexisting community or solidarity" but by the possibilities for radically wide kinship.[111] Moreover, the gut-impulsive feature of agape counters the categorical rules, inherent obligations, and rationally determined end results of modern ethical theory.

In summary, agape takes us beyond a confined rational context and limited social loyalties. The associative dimension of agape networks across, first, the complex interior of our own lives (being thereby inclusive of emotional and intuitional data, and the gut response); second, well beyond who is already friendly and familiar; and third, in its participatory dimension, agape participates in a moral source external to us. It is perhaps better to speak of them, then, as "moving toward." The dimensions of agape move us closer toward ourselves, others, and an Other.

Working backward through this final articulation, Taylor thinks that something of a moral source can seize any one of us—and this comprehensively, that is, holistic of mind and body—and Taylor insists that we can respond in the unconditional way through which it seizes us to begin with. The three *moving toward*—understood through Platonic-like *theiosis*, internal and external sources of knowing, and a wider sense of community—are realities of the fullness he strives for at the end of *A Secular Age*. Fullness is thereby articulated along the particular moral-ethical dimensions of the term "agape." The dilemma of fullness that arises in a secular age portends an existential crisis that is not bereft of concerns about actual relationships and daily behaviors. Fullness is not lonesome, simply facilitating senses of meaning and purpose for individuals. It is also social. With Taylor, the stakes for modernity gain momentum.

## THE SELF AND THE SOCIAL

The Canadian philosopher Bernard Lonergan—the author of *Insight: A Study of Human Understanding* (1958), among other works, including "Topics in Education: The Cincinnati Lectures of 1959 in the Philosophy of Education" —is not easy to read.[112] Somewhere he even admits as much. He provides a helpful abridgment of *Insight*, his defining work, in the article "Cognitional Structure."[113] The gist of the article, and, thus, of *Insight*, is that human knowing is like an impressive, albeit complex, potent system that empowers human experience with a strong, ready-built, ready-to-use set of components that can exact nothing shy of brilliance. The attainment or achievement of knowledge is a salient feature of his anthropology. In all this, Lonergan appreciates and maintains an Enlightenment epistemic perspective that celebrates Kant, in particular. So much more clearly than Kant, however, Lonergan also insists that we can know God, and much of *Insight* is devoted to showing how and why such insights are both possible and necessary.

Lonergan explains that being a human person "is something independent of the merely accidental, and so one is pronounced 'human' whether or not one is awake or asleep, a genius or a moron, a saint or a sinner, young or old, sober or drunk, well or ill, sane or crazy."[114] The hope, however, is to represent how individuals grow, emerge, and tend toward authentic and genuine dimensions of the human condition. Ramping up his investment in our natural capacities, he explains that "there is a contemporary, concrete, dynamic, maximal view that endeavors to envisage the range of human potentiality and to distinguish authentic from unauthentic realization of that potential."[115] He continues, instructing that "authenticity never is some pure, serene, secure possession; it is always precarious, ever a withdrawal from unauthenticity, ever a danger of slipping back into unauthenticity."[116]

A full appreciation of Lonergan recognizes his challenge to keep *knowing*. Inquiry, exploration, analysis: these are just some of the kinds of virtue he would celebrate, an employment of human natural capacities that enrich the human experience. In this, I hold John Dewey's concept of growth—"an ability, a power; and by potentiality potency, force"—in *Democracy and Education* (1916) in similar regard.[117] For Lonergan and Dewey, such a capacity must be nourished and maintained throughout life. Lonergan charts moments of growth—that is, insights—through significant personal transformations. He describes such transformations as conversions. Insights, thus, catalyze conversions. Lonergan categorizes such transformations as intellectual, moral, and religious. In *Insight*, Lonergan "labored to create the instrument of the mind" to represent a process of transformation; and "insight," his fundamental concept, signifies a moment of flourishing in the process.[118] Insights are moments that benchmark human flourishing. He explains that "deep within us all, emergent when the noise of other appetites is stilled, there is a drive to know, understand, to see why, to discover the reason, to find the cause, to explain."[119] But there is even more. For Lonergan, the individual is never *not* socially situated. The personal transformation that may occur—"a succession of enlargements of consciousness"—relates with, responds to, and reflects a world of others.[120] Dewey, again, also says something similar about the social dimension of life, and in fact he does so in a more pointed way: "A being connected with other beings cannot perform his own activities without taking the activities of others into account. For they are the indispensable conditions of the realization of his tendencies."[121]

I have articulated a fundamental concept of *A Secular Age*, one that also signifies a moment of human flourishing. Taylor never quotes Lonergan in *A Secular Age*—nor elsewhere to my knowledge (nor does he cite Dewey)—yet there are striking affinities in much of Taylor's work with Lonergan's (and Dewey's) work.[122] Taylor's fullness, articulated above through Griffiths's and Havel's epiphanic experiences, expanded by the Christian moral-ethical expressions of agape, and even recognized in the theoretical imaginings that would know and welcome Taylor's metaphysically oriented construct, all manifest a philosophical-anthropological reality of the human condition that has been thwarted, or suppressed, in a secular age. The kind of crisis it portends is an existential one of meaning and purpose. And though a crisis as such may be a lonely reality in an individual's life, it is also a cultural phenomenon. In a sense, there are many lonely crises, or, rather, there is a social crisis.

Some scholars reject fullness outright. Most, however, appreciate it, and even if they correct it in some way or give it a different name, many feel that Taylor is onto something with fullness and his desire to restore it. The Dewey scholar Philip Kitcher is especially excited, and he even offers an assessment of the religious dimension of fullness that is both honest and balanced. His consideration of the religious is significant not so much for the personal benefits it offers individuals but for the communal and social aspects it allows.

## NOTES

1. Mark D. Morelli and Elizabeth A. Morelli, eds., *The Lonergan Reader* (Toronto: University of Toronto Press, 2002), 35.
2. Morelli and Morelli, 6. For a brief but instructive description of "play" per Pestalozzi's and Froebel's renderings in educational theory, see Martha C. Nussbaum, *Not for Profit: Why Democracy Needs the Humanities* (Princeton, NJ: Princeton University Press, 2010), 59–60.
3. J. C. Friedrich von Schiller, *Letters Upon the Aesthetic Education of Man*, "Letter II," www.fordham.edu/halsall/mod/schiller-education.asp.
4. Translation by Edgar Alfred Bowring, in *Poems of Places: An Anthology in 31 Volumes*, ed. Henry Wadsworth Longfellow (Boston: James R. Osgood, 1876–79; Bartleby.com, 2020, www.bartleby.com/270/).
5. Charles Taylor, *A Secular Age* (Cambridge, MA: Belknap Press of Harvard University Press, 2007), 316–17.
6. Schiller, "Letter VII."
7. Schiller, "Letter XIV."
8. Taylor's more recent work articulates the importance of social connectedness to specific ways of knowing, such as in language formation and communication: Charles Taylor, *The Language Animal: The Full Shape of the Human Linguistic Capacity* (Cambridge, MA: Belknap Press of Harvard University Press, 2016).
9. Hans-Georg Gadamer, *Truth and Method* (New York: Continuum, 2004), 55, 102.
10. Gadamer, 103.
11. Gadamer, 112.
12. Gadamer, v.
13. Charles Taylor, *The Ethics of Authenticity* (Cambridge, MA: Harvard University Press, 1991), 84.
14. Hubert Dreyfus and Sean Dorrance Kelly, *All Things Shining: Reading the Western Classics to Find Meaning in Secular Age* (New York: Free Press 2011), 71.
15. Taylor, *Secular Age*, 5.
16. Anthony Kronman, *Education's End: Why Our Colleges and Universities Have Given Up on the Meaning of Life* (New Haven, CT: Yale University Press, 2007), 229, 235.
17. Kronman, 114.

18. Dreyfus and Kelly, *All Things Shining*, 71.
19. Taylor, *Secular Age*, 311, 507.
20. Taylor, 24–25.
21. Taylor, 137.
22. Taylor.
23. Taylor, 48.
24. Taylor, 56.
25. Taylor, 21.
26. Taylor, 89.
27. Taylor, 221.
28. Taylor.
29. Taylor, 200.
30. Taylor, 205.
31. Hubert Dreyfus and Sean Dorrance Kelly, "Saving the Sacred from the Axial Revolution," *Inquiry* 54, no. 2 (April 2011): 200.
32. Dreyfus and Kelly, 197.
33. Dreyfus and Kelly.
34. Dreyfus and Kelly, 195.
35. Dreyfus and Kelly, 197.
36. Dreyfus and Kelly, 201–2.
37. Charles Taylor, "Recovering the Sacred," *Inquiry* 54, no. 2 (April 2011): 118–19.
38. Taylor, 119.
39. Loius Dupré's study of similar poets and philosophers, and their appreciations of a tran-scendent reality, is instructive: Louis Dupré, *The Quest of the Absolute: Birth and Decline of European Romanticism* (Notre Dame, IN: University of Notre Dame Press, 2013).
40. Charles Taylor, "Foundationalism and the Inner-Outer Distinction," in *Reading Mc-Dowell: On Mind and World* (New York: Routledge, 2002), 106.
41. Taylor, 110.
42. Taylor, 111.
43. Taylor, 106.
44. Taylor.
45. Taylor, 107.
46. Taylor, 115.
47. René V. Arcilla, *Mediumism: A Philosophical Reconstruction of Modernism for Existential Learning* (Albany: State University of New York Press, 2010), 43.
48. Arcilla, 82.
49. Arcilla, 48.
50. Arcilla, 22.
51. Arcilla, 51.
52. Arcilla, 52.
53. Arcilla.
54. Arcilla, 18.
55. Arcilla.
56. Arcilla, 22.
57. Charles Taylor, "Afterword: *Apologia pro Libro suo*," in *Varieties of Secularism in a Secu-lar Age*, ed. Michael Warner, Jonathan VanAntwerpen, and Craig Calhoun (Cambridge, MA: Harvard University Press, 2010), 315–16.

58. Although critical of Kant's general epistemological argument and its role in Western secular perspective, a fuller appreciation is warranted, particularly regarding the notions of the "sublime" and "respect" and discussions about the moral law, human nature, and the duties of respect in his *Third Critique* and the *Metaphysics of Morals*; see Immanuel Kant, *Critique of Judgement*, trans. James Creed Meredith and ed. Nicholas Walker (Oxford: Oxford University Press, 2007); and Immanuel Kant, *Doctrine of Virtue: Part II of the Metaphysics of Morals*, trans. Mary J. Gregor (Philadelphia: University of Pennsylvania Press, 1971).

59. Taylor, "Afterword," 317.

60. Arcilla, *Mediumism*, 60.

61. Arcilla.

62. Arcilla.

63. It is also worth noting the affinities and differences between Taylor's conception of fullness and a similar experience described by the French philosopher Pierre Hadot. Hadot also speaks of a sense of "presence"; see Pierre Hadot, *The Present Alone Is Our Happiness: Conversations with Jeannie Carlier and Arnold I. Davidson*, trans. Marc Djaballah (Palo Alto, CA: Stanford University Press, 2009), 5–6.

64. Stephen Toulmin, *Cosmopolis: The Hidden Agenda of Modernity* (Chicago: University of Chicago Press, 1992), 41.

65. Toulmin.

66. Toulmin, 37.

67. Toulmin, 41.

68. Toulmin, ix.

69. Toulmin, 44.

70. Toulmin, 41.

71. Toulmin, 44.

72. Toulmin, 11.

73. Charles Taylor, "What Exactly Is Reason?" (lecture), Fordham University, New York, June 16, 2009. This lecture was later published; see Charles Taylor, "Reason, Faith, and Meaning," *Faith and Philosophy* 28, no. 1 (January 2011): 5–18.

74. Taylor.

75. Taylor.

76. Taylor, 10.

77. Taylor, 6.

78. Taylor, 5.

79. Taylor, 7.

80. Taylor, "What Exactly Is Reason?"

81. Taylor, *Secular Age*, 539.

82. Charles Taylor, *Sources of the Self* (Cambridge, MA: Harvard University Press, 1989), 181.

83. Taylor, 182.

84. Taylor, 180.

85. Schiller, "Letter VI."

86. "The Multilingual Archive," www.multilingualarchive.com.

87. Anders Nygren, *Agape and Eros*, trans. Philip S. Watson (London: SPCK, 1957), 57.

88. Nygren, 57.

89. Nygren, 48.

90. Nygren, 53.

91. Nygren, 63.

92. Nygren, 61.

93. Nygren, 57.

94. Taylor, *Sources*, 143 (on Plato, Augustine, and Neoplatonic thinking), 250 (on Ficino and Pico), 269 (on Jewish teachings), and 367 (on Kant).

95. Gene Outka, *Agape: An Ethical Analysis* (New Haven, CT: Yale University Press, 1972), 201.

96. Outka, 202.

97. Nygren, *Agape and Eros*, 200.

98. Taylor, *Secular Age*, 246.

99. Taylor, 92–93.

100. Taylor, 93.

101. Taylor.

102. Taylor, *Sources*, 93.

103. Luke 10:25–37.

104. Taylor, *Secular Age*, 224.

105. Taylor.

106. Taylor, 257.

107. Taylor, 615.

108. Taylor, 282.

109. Taylor, 741: "The New Testament word for 'taking pity,' *splangnizesthai*, places the response in the bowels."

110. Taylor, 246.

111. Taylor.

112. Bernard Lonergan, "Topics in Education: The Cincinnati Lectures of 1959 in the Philosophy of Education," in *The Collected Writing of Bernard Lonergan: Volume 10, Topics in Education*, ed. Robert M. Doran and Frederick E. Crowe (Toronto: University of Toronto Press, 2005).

113. Bernard Lonergan, "Cognitional Structure," in *Collected Works of Bernard Lonergan: Volume 4, Collection*, ed. Robert M. Doran and Frederick E. Crowe (Toronto: University of Toronto Press, 1988).

114. Bernard Lonergan, "The Response of the Jesuit, as Priest and Apostle, in the Modern World," *Studies in the Spirituality of Jesuits* 2, no. 3 (September 1970): 89.

115. Lonergan, 89.

116. Lonergan.

117. John Dewey, *Democracy and Education: An Introduction to the Philosophy of Education* (New York: Free Press, 1944), 41.

118. Frederick Crowe, *Method in Theology: An Organon for Our Time* (Milwaukee: Marquette University Press, 1980), 23.

119. Morelli and Morelli, *Lonergan Reader*, 48.

120. Morelli and Morelli, 277.

121. Dewey, *Democracy*, 12.

122. To better appreciate a comparison between Taylor and Lonergan, see Brian J. Braman, *Meaning and Authenticity: Bernard Lonergan and Charles Taylor on the Drama of Authentic Human Existence* (Toronto: University of Toronto Press, 2008).

# CHAPTER THREE

# CHARLES TAYLOR IN EDUCATIONAL DISCOURSE

In the final chapter of *A Secular Age*, "Conversions," Charles Taylor describes the life story and conceptual contributions of an educational theorist, Ivan Illich, explaining that Illich's "story is quite close to the one I have been trying to tell in these pages. Indeed, I have learned a lot from him."[1] Voiced at the end of a notably long narrative, the parallel between himself and a noncanonical theorist in the field of educational philosophy is interesting, to be sure, but not insignificant. As he moves through art, poetry, epistemology, history, political theory, and a host of other scholarly disciplines and interests, Taylor offers meaningful implications for the philosophy of education.

Illich's suspicion of bureaucratic structures and his distaste for dogmatic perspectives instantly manifest affinities with Taylor's critique of instrumental reason. Taylor describes a religious correlate of instrumental rationality, "excarnation," a concept that he himself fashions and deploys throughout *A Secular Age*. It represents overt, privileged, and even prejudiced expressions of rationality within the realms of faith and religion.

In my estimate, many of Taylor's concerns lend themselves to enduring inquiries in educational theory, and also new ones. Taylor describes his "buffered subject," for example, through myriad a-relational positions. Democratic participation, dialogic engagement, moral responsibility, and meaningfulness all diminish, in Taylor's account. As he suggests in *A Secular Age*, an alternative "porous" disposition deserves serious consideration. The porous self represents—through the permeations and gateways it connotes—dimensions of openness and connection that enrich or enhance emotional expression, personal intimacy, holistic knowing, social contact, political engagement, religious involvement, and spiritual capacity—all of which are outcomes and objectives of my pedagogies of fullness.

I begin this chapter, then, with my analysis of Taylor as cited and discussed in the scholarship of educational theory. Philosophers of education reference Taylor both meaningfully and frequently in the leading journals of educational theory. *A Secular Age* has also received attention in the field, and most of Taylor's other works—major publications as well as essays—are consistently cited or named as important references. In the philosophy of education, contemporary scholars read his work and continue to engage in dialogue with it.

Because of the steady regularity with which these scholars reference Taylor, as well as the variety of works and topics with which they wrestle, it is possible to see snapshots, or themes, through which to gain a sense of the educational scholarship on him. These topics—recognition, the good life, instrumentality, and hypergoods—in many ways overlap. They also network to fundamental notions in Taylor's work not discussed here. The references to Taylor by educational theorists are abundant, and as such these tropes seem to form, I think, four interesting parlors of discourse. I am also eager, naturally, to speak about their relevance to my theories, including pointing out other categories that demonstrate Taylor's presence in educational theory.

The second section of this chapter reveals how *A Secular Age* itself is being discussed generally. It is because of his wide variety of scholarly interest that I find Taylor's Templeton Prize receipt remarks so telling: "I sense in this prize awarded to me a recognition not only of my work but of this collective effort. This awakens powerful, if somewhat confused emotions: joy, pride, and a sense of inadequacy mingle together. But above all I feel the great satisfaction of knowing that this whole area of work will acquire a higher saliency through the award of this prize."[2]

These remarks indicate a range of sentiments. The prize is described as the world's highest paying award bestowed to any individual. Founded in 1972 by a financial investor and philanthropist, it recognizes contributions that explore, articulate, demonstrate, or expand the spiritual dimension of human life. Not necessarily imparted to members of particular spiritual traditions or professors of specific religious beliefs, the prize has been awarded to representatives of Buddhist, Christian, Hindu, Islamic, and Jewish faiths; to those with life commitments in philanthropy, philosophy, science, and theology; and to women and men who work as artists, clerics, humanists, and social reformers.

Taylor's remarks let us recognize that, indeed, *A Secular Age* is being shared around the academy, and that this "collective" effort is welcome and necessary. Following Taylor's lead, philosophers of education can appreciate the cares and concerns of other scholars about *A Secular Age*, and they can enhance the discourse with perspectives of their own. Educational theorists have a long and informed relationship with Taylor's works, both major and minor. They are well equipped to approach, dwell within, and move beyond *A Secular Age.*

As you have seen, Taylor's sense of fullness captivates me. It comes from his own lexicon, one I find powerful in its use of language to describe an orientation to life, whether he refers to excarnation, the buffered self, a porous individual, or this sense of fullness that compels mine, all of which has generated such a notable amount of scholarship. Scholarly discussions around fullness are notable, and they demonstrate a surge of sustained interest in the term leading to my own particular desire to engage with it as a university leader.

## CHARLES TAYLOR IN EDUCATIONAL THEORY

Charles Taylor's widely influential discussion on multiculturalism, "The Politics of Recognition," is alone a significant point of reference for educational thinkers. Turning to it, as well as other key areas of focus in his career—the good life; ways of knowing and responding to the world around us, particularly regarding the problems of an "instrumental" perspective; and the values and ideals that form our lives, referred to by Taylor as hypergoods—elucidates four themes in Taylor's body of work that engage and inspire philosophers of education.

### The Politics of Recognition

The philosopher Charles Bingham's engagement of Taylor focuses on one of the best-known essays, "The Politics of Recognition."[3] Of interest to Bingham is how Taylor frames the need to recognize individuals and groups in and through the profound distinctions of personal and corporate identity—such as gender, race, and sexuality, to name a few. Bingham explains that "our identity is partly shaped by recognition or its absence, often by *misrecognition* of others, and so a person or a group of people can suffer real damage, real distortion, as the people or society *mirror back to them* a confining or demeaning or contemptible picture of themselves."[4] Bingham quotes Taylor to remind his own readers of its influence and staying power in many disciplines of thought, and he also celebrates its perseverance through pointed philosophical critiques.

Bingham suggests that the endurance of Taylor's insight reflects a special "folk" status—the "folk paradigm"—it has achieved.[5] As such, Taylor's description of recognition "has become so commonsensical that it seems generally accepted without any appeal to further clarification."[6] Moreover, Bingham details a direct correlation between it and matters of justice, suggesting that misrecognition and injustice equally reflect "cultural domination (being acquired to assimilate), nonrecognition (being rendered invisible), and disrespect (being routinely maligned)."[7] In postcolonial theory, political science, psychoanalysis, and moral philosophy, through the works of Franz Fanon, Nancy Fraser, Jessica Benjamin, and Taylor himself, "the general folk understanding of recognition still holds."[8] Bingham explains that poststructuralists inspired by Michel Foucault and Kelly Oliver, as well as Fraser, have unsuccessfully tried to dislodge Taylor's recognitive assumption from its philosophical prominence.

Educational theorists themselves, however, offer compelling critical nuances. Stimulated by Emmanuel Levinas's thought, some of their concerns revolve around a dynamic of projection that is implicit in Taylor's version of recognition. Bingham describes this as a dimension of "passive empathy" that occurs through significant missed opportunities. Educational thinkers like Sharon Todd, Megan Boler, and Deborah Britzman, he explains, each demonstrate that Taylor's version of recognition employs assimilative assumptions that regard others in one's own terms, a concern that is central in Kwame Anthony Appiah's book *Cosmopolitanism: Ethics in a World of Strangers*. Todd, Boler, and Britzman also suggest that Taylor's recognition prolongs or even impedes a sense of political solidarity and that it simply remains momentary and undeveloped. Through the interesting strategies of guilt and listening, a "pedagogy of discomfort," and the dynamics of "after-recognition," Todd, Boler, and Britzman engage significant weaknesses of Taylor's recognition and suggest correctives that they feel attest to an educational impact that is more genuinely multicultural.[9]

Therefore, Bingham is important to my argument for a couple of reasons. Working so closely within the pedagogical dimensions of identity and recognition reminds us of a need to appreciate a wide spectrum of the many *identifiers* of persons and groups and the corresponding conceptions of human flourishing that can be articulated. How any of us understand and embrace our own sense of identity, as well as recognize and respond to those around us, are directly related to my pedagogies of study and solidarity. Study dives deeply into our lives, and solidarity, or alterity, pushes us beyond. Moreover, Taylor's "Politics of Recognition" appreciates what fullness is to individuals and groups, and how it influences conceptions of self and social imaginaries. Educators interested in pedagogies of fullness must also welcome diverse instances through which an actual experience of fullness might come about.

Lawrence Blum, too, thinks that Taylor's essay on recognition is canonical.[10] Again, for issues related to personal and group identity in and across significant personal, social, and religious contexts and combinations, Blum suggests that Taylor identifies recognition as a good in and of itself. Recognition is not only an important construct for thinkers to deal with in its own right but is also a prism through which wide discussion from numerous disciplines must occur. Blum's concern with Taylor's account, however, is twofold. He critiques specific limitations of Taylor's essay, and then he names significant implications of such critiques for educational practice. As with each of the pedagogies of fullness, he reminds us of the personal, intimate nature of Taylor's sense of fullness in the lives of individuals, as well as its naming by Taylor as a philosophical-anthropological construct that is representative of the human condition.

Summarizing Taylor's essay, Blum explains that philosophical liberalism fundamentally names, preserves, and protects the equal dignity of all human persons, but that its mission to do so wrestles with two competing realities: the commonality and universality of persons on one hand; and on the other hand, the way persons are unique and different. The tension is similar to one created by Taylor's philosophical-anthropological construct, fullness, and the humanly conditional or Christian-specific representation it garners. In Blum's case, the universalizing tendency articulates rights that must be exactly the same for everyone, while the other, a personal and contextual sensitivity, hopes to honor myriad life-orienting distinctions of individuals and groups. The concern for difference, Blum explains, "has two related but distinct substrands: one focuses on differences among individuals, the other on differences among groups."[11] An overarching concern of Blum's is to reveal how Taylor's "Politics of Recognition" compromises the first of these, that of individual distinction.

To do this, Blum uses an actual classroom example. He details the experience of a Haitian American student whom a teacher singled out to ask to represent a Black, or African American, perspective on an issue.[12] Taylor, Blum instructs, recognizes the importance of racial distinction but misses the ethnocultural differences within races. In doing this, Taylor not only fails to nuance the complexities of racial groups but also fails to articulate an important aspect of individuality. Educators, he insists, must be acutely sensitive to this. Teachers should avoid representational designations that Taylor might facilitate, or, in the least, fail to prevent. Blum insists that anyone—and teachers in particular—should also be more sensitive along these lines.

Blum persists, extending his concern for individuality in Taylor's essay to another educative issue: "Although Taylor explicitly focuses his theory of the dialogical formation of identity on individuals, . . . he does not . . . articulate individuality and its recognition as a value distinct from recognition of group-based identities."[13] Blum's diagnosis of Taylor's overemphasis on group identity corresponds to a debate in teaching. Through subject-centered teaching, teachers become less intentional about the individual situations of their students and more concentrated, instead, upon specific subjects, such as mathematics or history. "My point," Blum stresses, "is that *both* individuality (as an educational value) and recognition of group-based identities are student-centered values," and that Taylor's essay does not assist such a concern.[14] It would be my own point, however, to once again suggest the interplay here of both a pedagogy of study and of solidarity.

For Blum, Taylor's essay misses the mark on the sense of equality. He concedes that Taylor well protects a material or political expression of equality, one that regards opportunities. In education, material equality regards resources, such as facilities, supplies, and good teachers. Taylor does not develop recognitional equity, however. As an equity of individuals—in the educational context, how students are treated as equals—is important; so too is an equity of ethnocultural distinction. Blum argues that, just as we might facilitate an equity of resources to individual persons, equity must also be culturally, socially, or ethnically sensitive to particular groups: "It is worth being reminded that students want to be recognised in their appropriate group-based distinctness, but *also* recognised as equals to their fellows."[15] It is one thing to offer good teaching to all students, and another for teachers to treat a Haitian American student as an equal among others.

Finally, Julia Resnik's engagement of Taylor's recognition is not decisively less theoretical, but it is more notably practical.[16] Her application of Taylor contextualizes recognition in culturally and religiously specific ways. Before explaining her particular application of Taylor, however, Resnik reminds us that, generally, societies today are increasingly multicultural and that schools must adjust appropriately. Taylor, she explains, has played an undoubtedly important role in the formulation of educational policies worldwide that have indeed made adjustments, and for this she is grateful. Detailing the essence of Taylor's recognition, she says that "because the identity of the individual is construed in a dialogical manner through recognition or misrecognition of his group of origin by the larger society, absence of recognition, or misrecognition . . . could be harmful" and, moreover, regarded as oppressive.[17] This insight, however, is inspired not by Taylor's main essay on the topic but by Taylor's earlier, longer, and more comprehensive project, *Sources of the Self* (1989).[18]

Because Resnik strongly appreciates Taylor, like Blum, she also points to criticisms of his principle of recognition. Though a total reworking of Taylor's principle is not her concern, she does agree with Susan Wolf—also a contributing writer in the Amy Gutmann edition, which features Taylor's essay—that Taylor fails to represent an important existential dimension of recognition, one that better honors the particular real-life situations of individuals. The daily circumstances of life, however, and the driving existential perspective of *A Secular Age*, must come as a relief to Resnik. If Resnik is well targeted with her concerns about "The Politics of Recognition," Taylor's *A Secular Age* can be noted for its difference in tone and philosophical texture. If his form of recognition is not quite corrected, his conditions of belief, that is, his Secularity 3, establishes the existential regard for which she yearns, as well as special regard, I think, for a pedagogy of grace. Recall that Taylor's discussion of secularism focuses not upon religious creeds and their contents, or the analytical questions about the nature of faith and belief, but represents, instead, an existential preoccupation. Taylor wants to discuss secularism in the ways it informs and even transforms our daily lives, shaping how we understand our own selves and our emotional, intellectual, political, and social capacities and relations.

## The Good Life

Hanan Alexander's thinking offers patent similarities to Taylor in many ways. One article, in particular, characterizes the context of modernity and the ethical theories it has generated, and it also helps to establish my next category of scholarship, the good life.[19] Like Taylor in *A Secular Age*, his description of the Enlightenment celebrates the successful creation of modern liberal democracies, and at the same time laments a strident burgeoning of deontological and utilitarian moral theories and practices.[20] Alexander feels that substantial political achievement is recognized in its ability to establish environments wherein "conflicting visions of the good" can live shoulder to shoulder in a shared civic locale.[21] Political failure, however, emerges out of this. If an open society of liberal democratic living allows for contrasting and even competing visions of the good, Alexander finds that its citizens are not able to develop and instill correspondent conceptions of the good within their own lives. His concern resembles Taylor's modern malaises, or Hubert Dreyfus and Sean Kelly's contemporary American melancholy, as diagnosed in *All Things Shining* (2011). Alexander articulates this as an educational problem, explaining that "parents and teachers have too often become inarticulate and insecure about what to say to children concerning how best to live their lives; consequently, the children of these confusing and uncertain times have been searching elsewhere for responses to perennial existential questions."[22]

Alexander's educative solution to the problem comes through the cultivation of "intelligent spirituality" through which individuals are able to imagine "visions of the good life that integrate subjective, collective, and objective orientations to goodness."[23] Described in *Sources of the Self*, René Arcilla is likewise interested in Taylor's "moral orientation."[24] Alexander explains that these personal, shared, and independent orientations refer to conceptions of the good life that arise within three contexts, one of individual persons themselves, one of communal "solidarity and belonging," and one of religious belief and practice.[25] These important milieus correspond with the pedagogies of study, solidarity, and grace, and they function not in isolation from one another but in dynamic interrelation. Alexander turns to Taylor to demonstrate how these contexts are indeed related and interactive. His research indicates that Taylor's discussion in *The Ethics of Authenticity* (1991) of a person's sense of individuality—conceptions and understandings of one's uniqueness, a sense of one's own authenticity—is inseparable from so much that is beyond the self, such as a community of others that is wholly necessary for substantiating a sense of personal individuality to begin with.[26]

As Alexander proceeds, he argues that conceptions of the good life are essential to democratic living. Citing an essay in *Philosophy and the Human Sciences: Philosophical Papers, Volume 2* (1985), "Moral Education and Liberal Democracy," as well as referencing *Sources of the Self*, Alexander explains that moral education must "cultivate moral agency, which is linked inextricably with cultivating a capacity for democratic citizenship."[27] The "capacity to influence one's own destiny . . . is . . . a matter of choice, intent, and purpose, and lies at the very heart of the democratic ethos."[28] Schools, moreover, cannot solely bear the burden of this educative task. Families and communities must help.

Alexander turns to Taylor's work, *Hegel* (1975), to describe the kind of balance needed among the duties, loyalties, traditions, and narratives that are present on one hand in such contexts, and the autonomy, critique, and dialogue offered by the other hand.[29] The contrasts are represented by Ferdinand Tönnies's descriptions of *Gemeinschaft* and *Gesellschaft* communities as well as Émile Durkheim's corresponding descriptors, *mechanical* and *organic*.[30] Alexander instructs that Taylor achieves a similar comparison in *Hegel*. Taylor there speaks of *Sittlichkeit* and *Moralität* communities, ones that are more systematic and prescriptive of duties and loyalties and, conversely, others that are more dynamic and freely discerning of goods and values.[31] Alexander is significant here not only in his concern for meaning and purpose. His "intelligent spirituality" is akin to Taylor's epiphanic sense of fullness, and my own pedagogy of grace. In addition, as Alexander is focused upon the ways students are imaginative in their own capacities in future social and political engagements, he showcases a regard for the pedagogy of solidarity, or alterity—that of reaching out, or stepping beyond.

In a different project, Karl Hostetler's concern with the good life is articulated through language of the *common good*.[32] In his research he explains that moments of crisis, like the September 11, 2001, terrorist attacks on the United States, often convey notions not of Western-style individualism but of community and solidarity. Crises call to mind the common good. Communitarian notions, he believes, should "play a larger, more constant role in American schools and life."[33] As soon as he proclaims this, however, he recognizes a serious and persistent debate in educational philosophy about what the common good is and, beyond that, how to bring it about. He surfaces a contentious regard about the possibility of the common good in the context of genuine democracy.

To wade through the various issues, Hostetler leans on Taylor. For example, Iris Marion Young suggests that a democratic society—and, by implication, the schools within such societies—must dismiss a notion of the common good.[34] The element of "difference" must instead be respected. Common good ideology stifles the possibility of true democratic equality by homogenizing rather than distinguishing the needs of individuals. Hostetler disagrees through Taylor's *The Ethics of Authenticity*, where Taylor explains that "mere difference can't itself be the ground of equal value. If men and women . . . are equal, it is not because they are different, but because overriding the difference are some properties, common or complementary, which are of value."[35] Taylor's point is that equality emerges in the sharing that is recognized of such valued properties, prompting Hostetler to pronounce that Young's primary esteem for difference cannot provide and preserve the kind of democratic equality she celebrates.

Citing an essay by Taylor, "Explanation and Practical Reason," in Martha Nussbaum and Amartya Sen's compilation *Quality of Life* (1993), Hostetler explains Taylor's insight regarding the notable extent to which moral beliefs are common among people of diverse situations and that knowledge of this is actually shared and assumed across expressions of difference.[36] Hostetler does not want to minimize moral dilemmas that occur between sociocultural divides; but in using Taylor, he wants to suggest the possibility of deliberation about and resolution of such moral dilemmas. That is, Hostetler wants to recognize the prospect of a common good perspective.

Hostetler considers *Sources of the Self* in three brief but not insignificant glances. The first two are about conceptions of the good people might share.

The third reference, however, echoes Taylor's caution about the kinds of destruction that can happen when high ideals are pursued. He then wagers for us a communitarian challenge: to be especially careful, deliberate, and hopeful in seeking shared ideals.

Although Hostetler's communitarian sensitivities help to illuminate Taylor's similar sympathies, I find Hostetler significant for showing us the dangerous predicament that inaccurate or inappropriate understandings of Taylor's fullness might invite. Again, Taylor stresses that fullness is not a surge of personal empowerment in one's life but an opportunity for genuine expressions of transformation—the likes of which are prompted and guided through the pedagogies of fullness.

Paul Smeyers and Nicholas Burbules provide yet another example of research about the common good and education in regard to Taylor.[37] These philosophers of education voice their "intuition" that education is an initiation into life practices. They describe eighteenth-century civility, for example, and a pressing concern—for better and worse—in Enlightenment-era education to introduce and form students in the "knowledge, sentiments, and valued activities and practices of civilized life."[38] They then discuss an oppositional Romantic response through Jean-Jacques Rousseau. Establishing themselves upon a Wittgensteinian foundation—Ludwig Wittgenstein's "form of life"— they contend that education is indeed a form of practice, but they maintain that they can evade generally conservative agendas, such as blind endorsements of tradition. To do so, they turn to essays in Taylor's *Human Agency and Language: Philosophical Papers, Volume 1* (1985).

Using Taylor, Smeyers and Burbules explain that practices in societies are generally accompanied by descriptions and explanations, or a sense of narration.[39] Their interest in regarding education as life practice celebrates the ways by which practitioners in education—students and teachers—can better recognize and understand the practices they already exercise in daily life. Also, students and teachers can anticipate practices worthy of cultivation. Smeyers and Burbules suggest that any of us might tend toward such practices already. Furthermore, these descriptions and explanations exude "strong evaluations," that is, intuitions about what in life is right or wrong, better or worse, higher or lower, and so forth.[40] Smeyers and Burbules cite Taylor's concept of strong evaluations in his essay "What Is Human Agency?" from *Human Agency and Language: Philosophical Papers, Volume 1*.[41] The same concept is prominently featured in *Sources of the Self*. Strong evaluations not only represent ideals about the good life that can be critically and reflectively assessed but, as with a pedagogy of study, also offer personal insights regarding issues of individual selves and identities.

## Instrumental Rationality

As Taylor and many like-minded colleagues concentrate specifically upon ethical theories of the Enlightenment, Mark Mason grieves a burgeoning post-modern moral relativism that seems to evade giving genuine moral responsibility to others. Mason, furthermore, describes a new category of scholarship in educational philosophy that carries Taylor into the realm of education, manifesting interests and sensitivities related to the pedagogies of fullness.

Reminiscent of Taylor's *The Ethics of Authenticity*, Mason's article, "The Ethics of Integrity," hopes to cultivate in education an acute postmodern sense of moral responsibility.[42] Though Mason enjoys the insights of Seyla Benhabib, Anthony Giddons, Maxine Greene, and others, references to Taylor are not insignificant or superficial. Mason well explains concepts important in *The Ethics of Authenticity*, such as the "disembedded" self and instrumental rationality. Six years before the publication of *A Secular Age*, Mason even seems to anticipate Taylor's magnanimous 2007 publication. In important ways, the disembedded self is Taylor's "buffered" subject. Moreover—and somewhat ironically—Mason's research works seriously with Zygmunt Bauman's discussion of disenchanted societies and ensuing moral crises related to them. Readers of *A Secular Age* are keenly sensitized to Taylor's own deployment of the concepts and ideas that represent the dynamics, or lack thereof, of enchantment.

Taylor's disembedded self, Mason explains, purports "an increasingly atomistic and strongly individualistic outlook on the world that involves a consequent withdrawal from public life and a minimal sense of moral responsibility to others."[43] It corresponds, he continues, to a rise in instrumental rationality, "a kind of rationality that calculates the most economical or efficient means to a given end with scant regard for the human or other moral consequences."[44] Again, these fundamental concepts that drive the essay are from Taylor, and they let Mason draw a correlation between personal identity and moral responsibility. A disconnected and lonesome sense of self—with, moreover, an instrumental orientation toward anyone and everything—cultivates a fragmented, fragile, and ephemeral self-identity.[45] This sense of identity is the locus with which Mason wants education to deal: "A key challenge facing teachers . . . is the development of a more deeply founded sense of identity in their students as a means to a more strongly developed sense of moral responsibility."[46] It is Mason's ethics of integrity that offers a foundation upon which this works. As the particular pedagogies of solidarity and grace represent, a significant component of such an ethics rests on Taylor's challenge for us to discover moral sources not within our lives but beyond them.[47] For Mason, the moral demands that come to us beyond the context of the self are fundamentally Levinasian: a "sense of unbridled responsibility to the Other."[48]

Toward the end of the article, Mason deals explicitly with Taylor's discussion of authentic personhood and his own development of personal integrity. As with other educational theorists, Mason endorses Taylor's insight that the authenticity of self is ultimately social—it relies upon and responds to our relationships with others.[49] In fact, with Taylor, authenticity is not at all possible without others to which it responds. Mason thereby insists that education—through what I propose as a pedagogy of solidarity, or of alterity—must expose our *embeddedness* with each other, draw from it a profound sense of shared dignity, and create out of it an unavoidable sense of responsibility for one another. The ensuing ethics of integrity, Mason explains, is wholly consistent with Taylor's ethics of authenticity.

Clarence Joldersma's research invites Taylor into the realm of environmental concern, although Joldersma is not the only educational philosopher to focus upon timely environmental issues.[50] He maintains that teaching students to care for and better appreciate the natural world need not instill negative feelings about scientific engagement. Education, he insists, should maintain robust scientific interest, and can do so without an instrumental orientation. Joldersma relies upon Martin Heidegger to represent a hermeneutic approach to science that understands science differently: as "social practice, . . . [whereby] science so construed can disclose the planet as Earth . . . that is fragile and for which we are responsible."[51] To build his argument, Joldersma uses "Heidegger, Language, and Ecology," an article by Taylor from his own 1995 collection of essays, *Philosophical Arguments* (1995).[52]

However, Joldersma seeks help from Taylor a bit more substantially earlier in his essay. As Joldersma wrestles with Heideggerian disclosure with regard to the natural world, he employs an epistemic perspective that validates the truth and reality of things in objective and external qualities. He demonstrates an interest in the "ontic commitment" of *A Secular Age*, a philosophical acknowledgment that validates the impact upon us as knowing subjects of external and even ulterior realities around us. We might also call to mind Arcilla's *Mediumism* (2010) and Dreyfus and Kelly's *All Things Shining*, and their pushes to open and expand subjectivity to other influences. Joldersma cites *Sources of the Self* to instruct that the meaningfulness and validity of many things are not self-originating and self-relative.[53]

Later in the essay, Joldersma labors to deflate the instrumental nature of science. He takes inspiration from Taylor's *A Secular Age* to argue how we are able to "understand science primarily as a set of embodied social *practices* rather than as an abstract process of developing and justifying theories."[54] Taylor is helpful both in his disregard for an instrumental perspective that he feels characterizes much of the Western, post-Enlightenment perspective on life but also for his insistence that blaming science for this is injudicious and simplistic.

Joldersma's most interesting reference to Taylor comes in his conclusion, however. Like other educational theorists, he adapts "one of Taylor's felicitous phrases"—the "social imaginary"—to announce that simply, but urgently, "students, teachers, and others need a 'global imaginary'" that accounts for imminent environmental crises.[55] The Jesuit imaginary that is influenced and shaped by the pedagogies of fullness also bespeaks this global imaginary, for its important sensitivity to urgent environmental concerns as well as broader implications of living and leading in and of a global community.

Paul Theobald's article also appreciates Taylor's concern about an instrumental orientation in our lives.[56] Theobald describes a difference between a dominant and prevailing "standards-based" system of education, and, alternatively, one that is "place-based." His main concern is to validate and promote a movement within curriculum theory that revolves around the concept of community, a central interest of Taylor's. More theoretically, "place-based curriculum and instruction capitalizes on the crucial role of context in human learning."[57] For Theobald, context—and more specifically, our ideas about community—corresponds to political ideology. Theobald thus argues that educational systems within communities reflect political theories and structures of government in significant ways. He feels strongly that educational systems must orient themselves "to the welfare of human communities," even when the theories and structures of politics and governments within which they operate are inimical or neglectful of such interests.[58] This is where Taylor comes in.

Referencing *Philosophical Arguments*, Theobald describes Taylor's distinction between two foundational patterns of philosophical thought in American society, the L-stream and the M-stream. Respectively, they correspond to the philosophers John Locke and Charles de Secondat Montesquieu. As Descartes's role in *A Secular Age* is as principal antagonist of modern epistemology, Locke is next in line. For Taylor, however, Locke's political theory makes him doubly guilty for the extreme senses of individuality and instrumentality that ensue in a secular age. Locke, Theobald explains, interprets the relationship between persons and their governments in instrumental and economic terms. In fact, the economic dimension of human life eclipses or precedes the political aspect. The conception of human persons as essentially economical and, therefore, prepolitical, facilitates a comprehensive focus upon the self across much of Locke's philosophy, a thought system that has been a pre-vailing stream of influence in the American way of life. Theobald asks, "In a society defined by an aggregation of individuals freely pursuing their own economic self-interests, governed by those contractually bound to ensure the freedom to do so, what role should education play?"[59]

It is Taylor who shows us, he contends, a different choice: the Montes-quieu option. Though the American political system has embraced essential components of Montesquieu's political philosophy—such as a "beloved trin-ity" of governmental branches as well as the checking and balancing functions they each attained—it was early on regarded as quasi-monarchical and, thus, less democratic.[60] Yet Montesquieu's philosophy exudes a flavor of demo-cratic inquiry and cooperation. In turn, its sense of community facilitates not a spirit of economic competition but of general solidarity. It is through Locke, Theobald implies, that we adapt and harness an instrumental per-spective on American life, whereas through Montesquieu we might be more cooperative and less competitive with one another. Gesturing toward *Sources of the Self,* Theobald further endorses Taylor as helpful for educational the-orists. Taylor—as well as Robert Bellah, Alasdair MacIntyre, Michael Sandel, Robert Putnam, and others—represents in his communitarian sensitivities a "Montesquieu-Jefferson-Tocqueville tradition," which American education has generally failed to embrace.[61]

## Hypergoods

Insisting that "good teaching requires self-cultivation rather than self-sacrifice," Chris Higgins's main concern is to show us the strong correlation between the life of teaching and a teacher's values and ideals.[62] Furthermore, his research explains that such a concern is better dealt with not by "the psychologists who study teacher motivation or the sociologists who study institutional life, but to philosophers concerned with professional ethics."[63] A modern, Enlightenment-influenced variant of ethics that pulsates through many of us, however, is tainted by its obsession with particular duties or specific actions that, as stated, is a philosophical calamity that Taylor counters through his agape construct. Higgins's work helpfully positions a final snapshot of an area of scholarship in educational theory that is substantiated by Taylor.

Higgins reminds his readers that other perspectives preceded deonto-logical and utilitarian expressions in ethics, and that "metaethical interven-tions" by Alasdair MacIntyre, Bernard Williams, Taylor, and others recall for us important ancient articulations of human flourishing.[64] You might also recall Taylor's interest in agape, a metaphysical-moral-ethical construct that is fundamental to *Sources of the Self* and an important expression of both Taylor's fullness and my pedagogies of fullness. Higgins uses Taylor to reorient the ethical perspective and to apply such a perspective to an ethics of teaching.

In Higgins's article, Taylor's *Sources of the Self* is never all that far away. Higgins first turns to it to explain that the ethical concepts that frame any of our lives are notions that are "culture-wide or even epochal in scope."[65] It is Taylor who instructs that our ideals—ones that represent visions of human flourishing—"are embedded in thick languages," and as such they are not necessarily the private ideals of individual persons.[66] Citing Gary Fenstermacher, David Hansen, Richard Stanley Peters, and other philosophers of education invested in ethical discourse, Higgins discusses this to counteract the fears of those who are concerned about the projection of a teacher's personal ideals upon his or her students. The discussion stems from an earlier stated concern of Higgins to rightly distinguish between moral education and educational ethics, the first being a smaller aspect of the larger domain of the latter.

When Higgins turns again to Taylor and *Sources of the Self*, it is to deal with a principal issue of his essay: altruism. In educational ethics, he argues, modern altruism is an inappropriate ascetic ideal, and Taylor's widely known conceptions of *narrative* and *hypergoods* help us distinguish it as problematic. When we tell others about ourselves, the "existential narratives" we articulate represent the preexisting realities of family, culture, and history, as well as a quality of searching and striving, or, in Taylor's language, "quest."[67] The narratives of our lives—the stories of our identities—expose, then, the particular ideals or estimable goods that each of us seeks. These hypergoods—for instance, friendship, justice, and authenticity—"provide the very framework for ranking our other goods and orienting our lives."[68]

From Taylor, Higgins suggests that modern altruism falls in on itself. An altruistic perspective in educational ethics—the particular asceticism Higgins combats—might offer a certain vision of human flourishing, but it eliminates the conception of a self in relation to the ideal that is trying to be honored. Though subjectivity and self-identity are essential aspects of Taylor's fullness, conceptions of the self, it will be shown, are fundamental to the enterprise of Jesuit education, a morally and socially conscious tradition of education that also counters altruistic prospect. If Taylor is right about the fundamental relation between self-identity and hypergoods in our lives, Higgins insists that an altruistic ideal in education or anywhere is not really possible.

Calling to mind the important construals of a pedagogy of study, David Dewhurst's research focuses upon the role of emotions in education.[69] He agrees with Peters and Israel Scheffler that philosophical perspective must diminish a dichotomy between cognition and emotion. He echoes a concern in philosophy that recognizes the persistence of an unproductive duality that inappropriately and inaccurately qualifies human emotion as irrational and illogical. Taylor's "theoretical imagination" helps contextualize Dewhurst, as do the conversations about play by J. C. Friedrich von Schiller and Hans-Georg Gadamer, presentness by Arcilla, and agape and fullness by Taylor. Recall, too, Taylor's "excarnation," a word signifying exclusive rational standpoint.

In the realm of education, then—and here more pointedly—we must validate emotional responses. They are a significant aspect of human cognition, both in what they offer and in what they receive. In what sentiments reflect, then, they are an important source of knowledge. But it is also stressed that knowledge can act upon them, letting us recognize them as they arise, harness them when necessary, and even direct them toward fruitful achievements. And, as emotions might lead any of us toward important insights in our lives, to an important degree they already reflect for us some of our significant beliefs and values.

Quoting from *Human Agency and Language: Philosophical Papers, Volume 1*, "The Concept of a Person," Dewhurst introduces Taylor as a philosopher among a certain set of thinkers endorsing a cognitive orientation of emotions. Dewhurst's principal concern in this article, however, is not to reassert such an endorsement. Though he maintains a cognitive orientation, he here tempers the perspective. In doing this, he also uses Taylor. Like language, the realm of emotion also has expressive limits.[70] If educators invest in the rationality of the emotions, Dewhurst uses Taylor to caution against a full buy-out. Emotions may indeed reflect a cognitive dimension, but Taylor explains that it is better to interpret a gestalt quality of emotions and to admit, for instance, that emotionally influenced perspectives in our lives may *and* may not reflect or attain rational justification. Furthermore, Dewhurst turns to *The Ethics of Authenticity* to remind us how our lives are constituted by the world around us. This, in fact, seems to be Dewhurst's more interesting application of Taylor. His understanding of Taylor regards the rich complex of an individual's life, a horizon of influence in and through which any of us— or any of our students—is functioning and being formed. Such persuasions anticipate the internalized conditions of modernity that Taylor bemoans in *A Secular Age*. Dewhurst uses Taylor to argue that emotional responses that arise from within our depths may actually correspond to an external reality that one does not wholly understand, or even an uncertain horizon toward which one might tend.

Robert Bullough, Clifford Mayes, and Robert Patterson also employ Taylor's horizons of significance.[71] Though these scholars reference *Sources of the Self* in the bibliography of their article "Teaching as Prophecy," they do not explicitly discuss or engage Taylor or his concepts.[72] In responding to critical reviews of their article, however, they draw significantly from *The Ethics of Authenticity*. Their rejoinder affirms many of the concerns expressed by their critics. Bullough, Mayes, and Patterson use Taylor to show their affinity with such concerns—"Test teachers. Test students. Punish. Reward . . . enhance competition. Forget citizenship and public life"[73]—but also to remind their readers that Taylor rightly positions these issues and, moreover, represents the significant problems with teacher education that they themselves want to combat: a loss of meaning, an eclipse of ends, and a loss of freedom: "Taylor seeks to recover the ethic ensconced in authenticity, an ethic that recognizes self-identity formation as necessarily taking place against horizons of significance and through discourse. It is this ethic that is lost in teacher education's celebration of instrumental reason, made evident in the reduction of education to training."[74]

The current discussion about teacher education, they insist, manifests an obsession with specific techniques and skills that corresponds to dehumanizing statistical results, and lends credence to the compelling objectives of the pedagogies of fullness, including the Renaissance humanist commitments of Jesuit education. The authors admit that technical skill in teaching is not unimportant, but not at the expense of a teacher's own sense of herself or himself as well as individual attentiveness to students:[75] "The image of teacher as prophet challenges . . . [a] tendency toward disassociation because teacher prophets necessarily call forth, using Taylor's terms, horizons of significance against which and through which self-formation takes place," and this in the context of both teachers and students.[76]

Finally, Pamela Moss's interest in Taylor regards her invitation to educational researchers to better engage in dialogue with one another.[77] She helps to validate the array of voices within the field of educational theory demonstrated in these pages as well as the voices from many other fields of inquiry that are featured. Because the dialogic aspect is a category of interest that could stand alone, her affinity with Taylor's horizons of significance, the final category here considered, is revealed in how she challenges researchers to know the biases such horizons host. She invites them to better explore alternative horizons.

Moss stands squarely within Gadamerian hermeneutics. She hopes to convince educational theorists to employ Gadamer's formulation of critical dialogue. Critically reviewing research from different spheres within the field—namely, those representing competing interests—will foster, she insists, a better understanding of divergent perspectives in others' work as well new insights about their own.

References to Taylor's essay "Understanding the Other: A Gadamerian View on Conceptual Schemes" function as an important source for endorsing both Gadamer and herself.[78] For example, she cites Taylor to counteract indictments in educational philosophy that Gadamer is relativistic.[79] She also uses Taylor to encourage researchers to pinpoint issues of discord, the moments in scholarly discourse where another's data "interpellate, challenge, offer a notional alternative to" what they themselves have discovered and understood.[80] Finally, Moss points out Taylor's distinction between "the knower and the known" to remind any researcher of the influential role that preconceptions play, as well as of the social, political, and cultural biases that shape the interpretive results any of us glean from our research.

## Conclusion

Although the specific topics—recognition, the good life, instrumentality, and hypergoods—and the broader themes from which they emerge are imperfect in representing the tremendous interest in Charles Taylor among educational theorists, they show a pattern of engagement and offer instances of shared discourse. As indicated above, the representation of concepts from Taylor is impressive, and the implications for educational theory are expansive. From the notions of recognition, personal identity, narrative, dialogue, quest, and strong evaluations, to name a few, educational theorists turn to Taylor to discuss and debate teacher ethics, student- and subject-based teaching, environmental education, educating values, standardization and testing, educational policy, and more. Likewise, they also showcase overlapping interests in the three pedagogies of fullness, study, solidarity/alterity, and grace.

If space permitted, it would be rewarding to manifest other issues that other scholars of education glean from Taylor's work, including further manifestations of my pedagogies of fullness. Connections to the roles and influences of imagination,[81] tradition,[82] religiosity,[83] specialized communal contexts,[84] and cosmopolitanism[85] in education represent some of these other discourses.

But it must also be stated, once again, how the scholars discussed in the pages above demonstrate affinities with *A Secular Age* and, more particularly, with Taylor's fullness. It is this sense of fullness that inspires my corresponding pedagogies, both in their ability to represent the fundamental interests of Jesuit higher learning and the framing and focus in our lives of a Jesuit imaginary. Let us turn now to the academy-wide conversations about the book and their explicit evaluation of fullness.

## *A SECULAR AGE* IN SCHOLARSHIP

A book of essays generated by a conference at Yale University shortly after the publication of *A Secular Age*, titled *Varieties of Secularism in a Secular Age* (2010), is remarkable for its representation of the academy. Michael Warner, Jonathon VanAntwerpen, and Craig Calhoun agree that Taylor's contribution is historic, and that is it quite complicated.[86] The editors offer a compelling introduction that provides both a road map of the lengthy work and an evaluation of notable reviews released in prestigious and popular publications, reviews that they feel generally underappreciate the complexities of *A Secular Age*. Warner, VanAntwerpen, and Calhoun elucidate gross simplifications or unfair misinterpretations of Taylor, citing, for example, John Patrick Diggins, Peter Gordon, and Bruce Robbins.[87] The University of Chicago and New School University also hosted conferences on Taylor in 2007 or early 2008. The dedicated issue of *Social Research: An International Quarterly of the Social Sciences* from the New School forms a book of its own. Voices in all these publications and conferences represent the wide spectrum of the academy and likewise inspire further consideration of *A Secular Age*.

José Casanova leads the charge in challenging Taylor to better define his discussion of secularism.[88] Casanova thinks that the term is Eurocentric and thereby limited in applicability. Globally conscious, he is convinced that scholars of religion need to speak more pointedly of different secularisms in play around the world, and that a plurality of secularisms also applies to the specific Western context of Taylor's study.

It is necessary to represent secularism at work in different cultural contexts and arising out of varying political, social, and religious motives. Casanova likewise wonders if invested scholars should discuss a newer reality of postsecularism, a sociocultural dynamic—"much in vogue, and repeated often enough."[89] In this way secularism, according to Robert Bellah, has already run its course in some societies and is evidenced not by a resurgence of religion where it clearly receded in influence and practice, but in how spiritual and religious tendencies either are resilient and recognizable in secular-named societies or remain lively elsewhere, uninfluenced by secular forces.[90]

Taylor responded to Casanova in *Secularism and Freedom of Conscience* (2011).[91] There, he demonstrates an ability to understand secularism as functioning within "a diversity of beliefs and values" that represents a plurality of citizens within a given society, thereby agreeing with Casanova's challenge to be more nuanced.[92] In representing a dimension of plurality, Taylor appreciates John Rawls's description of an "overlapping consensus."[93] As notable in a lengthy quotation, a wide-angle snapshot of Taylor's thinking along these lines is helpful. He says that

> [a] Christian, for example, will be able to defend fundamental rights and freedoms by invoking the idea that the human being was created in God's image; a Kantian rationalist will say that it is necessary to recognize and protect the equal dignity of rational beings; a utilitarian will maintain that one must seek to maximize the happiness of sentient beings capable both of pleasure and pain; a Buddhist will invoke the core principle of *ahimsa*, nonviolence; and an indigenous person or deep ecologist, referring to a holistic conception of the world, will maintain that living beings and natural forces stand in a relation of complementarity and interdependence and that, consequently, each of them, including human beings, must be granted equal respect. All of them agree on the principle, even though they cannot reach an agreement about the reasons that warrant it.[94]

The postsecular designation, moreover, is not accurate, at least according to Taylor and readers sympathetic to his narrative. Those who jump to Taylor's defense endorse Taylor's distinctions at the onset of *A Secular Age* between three kinds of secularities and the contemporary spiritual and religious searchings—discussed in *A Secular Age* as "the Nova Effect"—that are notable in secular societies.[95]

There are other criticisms. The card-carrying historians Jon Butler and Simon During are concerned about the way Taylor does history in his book.[96] During calls *A Secular Age* philosophical or conjectural history, a genre During feels elides the naming and understanding of specific material causes—"most obviously capitalism and urbanization," which Taylor's historic overview misses—and dwells, instead, in teleological explanations.[97] Furthermore, During is not interested in Taylor's "fullness," "an existentialized/theophanized moral anthropology," which is akin, he explains, to the spiritual impulses articulated and appreciated by Simone Weil.[98] He suggests that Taylor deal with the "mundane," the ordinary experience of common sense and daily routine. Experience of the humdrum daily is more accurate, he insists, in representing an anthropological reality and is not a correlate of the religious-secular and transcendent-imminent terminologies.[99]

Butler, who, unlike others, is discouraged by the three versions of secularity Taylor outlines at the beginning of *A Secular Age*, suggests that Taylor's history is convenient: "It is a history for argument about modernity, the cause of the modern condition, and its possible cure. It is a history of lament and failure intended to propel readers toward a history of meaning and fulfillment."[100]

Aware of the importance of material realities in educational research, I do not take Butler's critique, in particular, lightly. Historical and material realities indeed elicit data and substantiate proposals. Yet I am not sure either of us, Taylor or me, is terribly vulnerable. On Taylor's side, his stated interest in offering an alternative "narrative" for understanding Western secularism canvasses the pages of *A Secular Age*. He is telling a story newly, or differently. Ironically, after nearly nine hundred pages, Taylor feels as if the manuscript we all plodded through is not long enough. As for my appreciation of Butler's critique, I myself am not unaware of the special role of philosophical and theoretical thinking in a philosophy of education. Certain quantifications and evaluations are not always necessary.

Another critic, the social-scientist David Lyon, calls Taylor an antisecularist and wants him to better appreciate certain postsecular dynamics in policymaking, expressions of religiosity that have formulated and gained meaning in response to secularism.[101] Casanova is helpful to Lyon, of course, but Lyon's main concern is to stress the validity of postsecularity in understanding public policy issues and political matters that gain focus and energy in Western societies, such as the wearing of religious garb in public spaces and the persistence and frequency of debates around life issues, such as abortion and euthanasia.[102]

Finally, the multiculturalist Keith Tester suggests that Taylor is not Catholic enough.[103] He wants Taylor to be truer and more genuine about the practices and goals of the Church. Taylor's hero, Tester tells us, is the Renaissance Jesuit missionary Matteo Ricci. Ricci was a scion of cultural adaptation and religious assimilation, notable for his ability to enter into and form relationships with the highest officials of China's reclusive Ming Dynasty. Ricci himself became a ranked official, a mandarin, of the dynasty as one of the Confucian literati. He translated classic works back and forth between Christian and Confucian cultures, constructed a map of the world centralizing China but including Europe and other foreign geographies and cosmologies, and presented to and maintained for the Ming imperial court Europe's latest technological equipment. A recent biographer explains that "by virtue of his intellect, a heroic individual bridges impossible chasms between civilizations, opening up a new world of understanding by the strength of his learning and genius."[104]

Taylor features Ricci in his 1996 address, a "Catholic Modernity," as a seventeenth-century solution for twenty-first-century needs.[105] Tester insists that Ricci was, ultimately, an evangelizing functionary of the Roman

Catholic Church. Tester seems to want to unmask illusory ideas about who Ricci essentially was, and to do the same of the Church itself. His concern with Taylor's version of Catholicism, then, is that it is not a realistic expression of the faith—"Taylor's Catholicism is extraordinarily *un-churched*"—and it is not accountable to its own history.[106]

The theologian John Milbank also takes up the Catholic issue.[107] As he questions—with Butler and During—Taylor's historical method, calling it historicized existentialism, he wants Taylor to better articulate what it means for the Catholic Church to be *incarnational*. In this, Milbank is implicitly inspired by Taylor's concern with modern expressions of excarnation—again, an overt and exclusive rational perspective in the realms of faith and religion—and is explicitly motivated by Taylor's discussion of the role of the "festive" in former hierarchical societies. Readers of *A Secular Age* enjoy Taylor's reminiscing about the ploys and strategies of festive celebrations in cultures—Carnival and Mardi Gras, for instance—which, because of appointed and routine seasons of excessive celebration, maintained dimensions of moral and social equilibrium and a complementarity of social roles in daily life.[108]

As Milbank wants to articulate an anthropology that is more representational of such festive realities—and, thus, incarnational—he wants the same of Roman Catholicism. He points to tendencies of clericalism, a bureaucratic and obsessive morality, and a general denigration of sexuality as anti-incarnational. Titled "A Closer Walk on the Wild Side," his essay calls to mind Lou Reed's 1970s hit song.

Edited by George Levine of Rutgers University with a poignant focus on *A Secular Age*, the eleven essays of *The Joy of Secularism* are almost entirely devoted to a single concept from Taylor's work, fullness.[109] Reminiscent of an ordinary kitchen classic, Irma Rombauer's 1936 *The Joy of Cooking*, the jacket of the book is designed as a traditional red-and-white-checkered tablecloth. The contributions within criticize Taylor's transcendent-dependent version of fullness and suggest alternative naturalistic conceptions of fullness, such as the joy of cooking. Generally, many of the authors seek to preserve the construct, even if they redefine it dramatically. More so, Taylor's assessment of modernity is also generally accepted.

Paolo Costa and Adam Phillips interpret fullness through Freudian perspectives. Costa suggests that Taylor is simply articulating the oceanic sentiment, a sensation better described by Pierre Hadot. For its poignancy and poetry, and for its affinity to Taylor's description of fullness through Bede Griffiths, Hadot's remarks about a certain kind of fullness in his life are worth quoting in entirety:

One happened on rue Ruinart, on the path I took home to my parents' house every day from the petit Séminaire. Night had fallen. The stars were shining in the immense sky. At this time one could still see them. Another took place in a room of our house. In both cases I was filled with an anxiety that was both terrifying and delicious, provoked by the sentiment of the presence of the world, or of the Whole, and of me in that world. In fact, I was incapable of formulating my experience, but after the fact I felt that it might correspond to questions such as *What am I? Why am I here? What is this world I am in?* I experienced a sentiment of strangeness, of astonishment, and of wonder at being there. At the same time I had the sentiment of being immersed in the world, of being a part of it, the world extending from the smallest blade of grass to the stars. This world was present to me, intensely present. Much later I would discover that this awareness of belonging to the Whole was . . . called the "oceanic sentiment." I believe that I have been a philosopher since that time, if by philosophy one means this awareness of existence, of being-in-the-world.[110]

Both Costa and Hadot trace the oceanic sentiment through Sigmund Freud to Romain Rolland. Again, Hadot well represents Costa's point, that "the oceanic sentiment—as I experienced it, . . . is foreign to Christianity because it does not involve either God or Christ."[111] Although Hadot distinguishes it from the "sentiment of nature"—that is, "wonder in the face of nature"—and allows for the possibility of a cosmic sentiment, his oceanic sentiment "is something situated at the level of the pure sentiment of existing."[112] This bridges to Adam Phillips.

Phillips feels that Taylor's yearning for a supernatural being and a Christian anthropological correlate (fullness) for sensing such a being evades the human condition of helplessness. A common repulsion within many of us to a fundamental sense of helplessness cultivates certain dependencies, which Phillips thinks thwart human growth. Looking closely at Taylor, Phillips even ponders the possibility that helplessness and disenchantment are much the same.[113] Phillips bristles at the immaturity that fullness represents, and he explains it as a psychological sentiment indicative of something much different. In this, I am cognizant of a challenge Taylor poses in *A Secular Age*: for religious and Christian practitioners to continually update and expand the dynamics of faith and theology in their lives. He indicates that the theology of a ten-year-old child is not useful for a seasoned adult who has weathered the realities of life. A "childish" (Christian) faith indeed perpetuates an immature perspective.[114]

Beyond two gestures to Freud, many other contributors to *The Joy of Secularism* turn to Charles Darwin, such as Rebecca Stott and David Sloan Wilson. They agree that disenchantment and meaninglessness are contemporary Western problems, but Taylor's interest in reenchantment through an attentiveness or capacity for fullness is not attractive. They remind Taylor that science can enchant us, too, and that discoveries about life and the world yield answers but also expose deeper mysteries. Wilson suggests that the kinds of sensations of enchantment normally cultivated by the arts, such as the effects upon us induced by music or poetry, and religious enchantment in our lives through liturgy or personal prayer, have been superseded: "There is much to look forward to when we appreciate that when it comes to evolution, the future need not resemble the past."[115]

Stott, not unlike Taylor, is concerned about language and recognizes its ability to sensitize us to certain realities. She agrees with Taylor that "secularism is a form of subtraction from religious 'fullness,' . . . that secularism can amount to a 'flattening,' an emptying out of experience, a disenchantment."[116] Rather than forging a religious commitment, however, Stott wants to reclaim notions of the sublime and finds new words and phrases that showcase it. Whereas Taylor deploys the poetry of Gerard Manley Hopkins—its internal method of sprung rhythm, in particular—to nurture an ontic commitment and a correspondent religious sensitivity, Stott turns to Amy Clampitt's poems, describing them as "exquisite expressions of what we might call the Darwinian sublime or the poetics of immersion."[117] Clampitt writes, "But the sun / underfoot is so dazzling / down there among the sundews, / there is so much light / in that cup that, looking, / you start to fall upward."[118]

Akeel Bilgrami, finally, is similar.[119] Like many, he appreciates Taylor's concerns about the dimensions of meaninglessness today in Western culture but is also agreeable with Wilson and Stott. He simply suggests that we should not look to sources beyond us. Our task today is not to flee the world but to be more at home in it, as well as at home in ourselves.

From a different publication, *New Blackfriars*, Kieran Flanagan anticipates an indictment against Taylor's notion of fullness common to many of the contributors to Levine's book. He interprets Taylor's interest in expressions of reenchantment as nostalgic and old fashioned, and he describes Taylor as looking backward to reclaim something long gone.[120]

In *Varieties of Secularism in a Secular Age*, Colin Jaeger claims that Taylor's fullness is nothing other than the Romantic sensibility of William Wordsworth, Friedrich von Schiller, and Percy Bysshe Shelley, poets Taylor himself pointedly and frequently criticizes in *A Secular Age* for the fragile moments of delight they are able to entice. Taylor responds, admitting, "I plead guilty as charged: I'm a hopeless German romantic of the 1790s."[121] Taylor here gestures beyond the poets, however, to Johann Gottfried von Herder's notion of the human community functioning as an orchestra and ongoing dimensions and expressions of reconciliation at play in the wide network of an authentic Christian community and its communion of saints.

Back in the *Joy of Secularism,* the literary critic Bruce Robbins might be the fiercest of Taylor's critics. Michael Warner, Jonathan VanAntwerpen, and Craig Calhoun remain (in their *Varieties of Secularism in a Secular Age*) discouraged and disappointed by Robbins's review of *A Secular Age.* However, George Levine in his *The Joy of Secularism,* and within the same edition, Taylor himself, indicate worthy concerns in Robbins's more recent writing on Taylor. Fundamentally, in his own essay, Robbins has no time for Taylor's fullness. Being secular is about advancing and improving, and not returning to "tiny, isolated medieval parishes that once sustained belief."[122] Robbins, one of the few scholars across a range of publications who wants nothing to do with fullness, also insists that it is only Christian-specific and cannot represent the greater human community. As Christianity fades away from Northern Atlantic societies, so too should preoccupations with experiencing the grace of the Christian God. Finally, a reliance upon the work of imagination in conceiving a notion of Taylor's fullness to begin with is problematic: "Imagination is a sort of magical helper in this story, happened upon when Western man seems most lost in the wasteland of disenchantment, and offering some hope of a happy ending."[123]

Most scholars quite like fullness, however, and labor to preserve it. Peter van de Veer and Jonathan Sheehan want broader, more inclusive interpretations of it, a broadening that Taylor himself also wants.[124] For instance, van der Veer cites spiritual inspirations through Ralph Waldo Emerson, Walt Whitman, Wassily Kandinsky, Tu Wei-Ming, Rabindranath Tagore, and Mohandas Gandhi.[125] More vague and ambiguous than the experience of fullness, van der Veer explains that spirituality in essence—unlike Christian religious or metaphysical commitment—is a bridge that connects "various discursive traditions around the globe."[126] Sheehan, too, wants vastly wide multicultural representation, including agnostic and atheistic expressions of fullness.[127]

The Dewey scholar Philip Kitcher, however, best represents the admirers, and according to Levine, editor of the book, as well as James Wood in his recent discussion of secularism in *The New Yorker,* Kitcher offers the crowning essay.[128] Taylor, Kitcher feels, is onto something fundamentally important with his fullness construct. For Kitcher, the transcendental orientation is wrong, but fullness is indeed an essential aspect of human life, and in a secular age we know it less and less. He espouses impatience with Darwinian atheists who think, too simply, that being religious is about believing doctrines.[129] He celebrates the abilities of religions to create communities, manifest solidarity, inspire charitable and material responses, and enact social justice. He is particularly excited about the personal senses of meaning and purpose found in religion, and he notes the role of Taylor's fullness in facilitating expressions of individual and corporate integrity. Turning to *A Common Faith* (1934), Kitcher cites John Dewey's keen interest in certain episodes in our lives that cultivate a religious attitude or outlook. Kitcher thus explains, "Decades [after the publication of *A Common Faith*], secularism still needs to attend to the cultivation of [a religious] attitude, to elaborate ways in which it can become more widespread and more enduring. . . . I hope to have renewed the quest for what Dewey called a 'common faith,' a complex of psychological states beyond the acceptance of myth, that recognizes secular *human*ism as more than blunt denial."[130]

Today, we need Dewey's religiosity—Deweyian fullness—more than ever, Kitcher claims, and secular humanists must take up the task of generating the existentially transformative experiences that religion has long offered.

## CONCLUSION

Always fearful of relativism in various stripes and sizes and the expressions of individualism so easily recognized in Western culture, Taylor, throughout his career, has maintained a metaphysical conviction that he refers to in *A Secular Age* as an "ontic commitment," an expression I referred to above when discussing both Clarence Joldersma's and Rebecca Stott's research. Such a commitment is at the core of a pedagogy of grace, and stems from the origins of Jesuit higher learning and what I refer to as the Jesuit imaginary.

Taylor's ontic commitment demonstrates a distinction between subjectivity and external realities in natural and supernatural ontologies. As we review the scholarship on Taylor, especially regarding his 2007 magnus opus, as well as the responses Taylor frequently generates for scholarly journals, at conferences, and at Internet sites like "The Immanent Frame," it is clear that Taylor, in a secular age, is willing to be conversant about possibilities and interpretations that challenge or enrich his own.[131] This is also a presupposition of the current context of Jesuit higher education, where students represent all faith traditions, and none.

Regarding fullness, for instance, an essential term in *A Secular Age* and the driving topic of consequent scholarship, Taylor agrees that his philosophical-anthropological expression of human flourishing is not only

Christian.[132] About a reality he assesses to be so fundamentally rooted within the human experience and representative of the human condition, he is open to diverse expressions and articulations. He explains, "I think what we need is a conversation between a host of different positions, religious, nonreligious, antireligious, humanistic, antihumanistic, and so on, in which we eschew mutual caricature and try to understand what 'fullness' means for the other."[133]

Whatever it means, however, for Taylor's fullness, for a pedagogy of fullness, and for a correspondent Jesuit imaginary, the ontic commitment is necessary. Recognizing it and negotiating what such a commitment means is a helpful benchmark for assessing where both Taylor and Jesuit higher learning stand, and the principal criteria each strives to honor. The implications are philosophically broad, informing epistemological assumptions, moral and ethical ideals, political theory, and—the heart of the matter—an existential orientation, to name a few.

## NOTES

1. Charles Taylor, *A Secular Age* (Cambridge, MA: Belknap Press of Harvard University Press, 2007), 737. For an example of Illich's contribution to educational thought, see *Deschooling Society*, by Ivan Illich (London: Calder & Boyars, 1971).
2. Taylor, *Secular Age*.
3. Charles Bingham, "Before Recognition, and After: The Educational Critique," *Educational Theory* 56, no. 3 (2006): 325–44; Charles Taylor, "The Politics of Recognition," in *Multiculturalism: Examining the Politics of Recognition*, ed. Amy Gutmann (Princeton, NJ: Princeton University Press, 1994), 25–73.
4. Bingham, "Before Recognition," 325.
5. Bingham, 327.
6. Bingham.
7. Bingham.
8. Bingham, 328.
9. Bingham, 335–36, 338, 340.
10. Lawrence Blum, "Recognition and Multiculturalism in Education," *Journal of Philosophy of Education* 35, no. 4 (2001): 539–59.
11. Blum, 540.
12. Blum, 541.
13. Blum, 546.
14. Blum, 547.
15. Blum, 555.
16. Julia Resnik, "Contextualizing Recognition, Absence of Recognition, and Misrecognition: The Case of Migrant Workers' Children in Daycares in Israel," *Journal of Curriculum Studies* 41, no. 5 (2009): 625–49.
17. Resnik, 626.

18. Charles Taylor, *Sources of the Self: The Making of the Modern Identity* (Cambridge, MA: Harvard University Press, 1989).

19. Hanan A. Alexander, "Moral Education and Liberal Democracy: Spirituality, Community, and Character in an Open Society," *Educational Theory* 53, no. 4 (2003): 367–87. For another research example of modernity and Taylor, see Stefaan E. Cuypers, "The Ideal of a Catholic Education in a Secularized Society," *Catholic Education: A Journal of Inquiry and Practice* 7, no. 4 (2004): 426–45.

20. Alexander, "Moral Education," 376.

21. Alexander, 367.

22. Alexander.

23. Alexander, 381.

24. René V. Arcilla, *Mediumism: A Philosophical Reconstruction of Modernism for Existential Learning* (Albany: State University of New York Press, 2010), 47.

25. Alexander, "Moral Education," 381.

26. Charles Taylor, *The Ethics of Authenticity* (Cambridge, MA: Harvard University Press, 1991).

27. Charles Taylor, *Philosophy and the Human Sciences: Philosophical Papers, Volume 2* (Cambridge: Cambridge University Press, 1985); Alexander, "Moral Education," 377.

28. Alexander, "Moral Education," 377.

29. Charles Taylor, *Hegel* (Cambridge: Cambridge University Press, 1975).

30. Alexander, "Moral Education," 378.

31. Alexander, 379. Alexander's article represents voices from many camps. Communitarian interests like Taylor's and shared within Alexander's work by thinkers such as Alasdair MacIntyre, Walter Feinberg, Michael Sandel, and Kenneth Strike, are some examples. Among the theorists who are cited for discussions around the topic of moral education and teaching are Nicholas Burbules, David Carr, David T. Hansen, Philip Jackson, Lawrence Kohlberg, Nel Noddings, and Lee Shulman.

32. Karl Hostetler, "The Common Good and Public Education," *Educational Theory* 53, no. 3 (2003): 347–61.

33. Hostetler, 347.

34. Hostetler, 351.

35. Hostetler, 352.

36. Charles Taylor, "Explanation and Practical Reason," in *The Quality of Life*, ed. Martha Nussbaum and Amartya Sen (Oxford: Oxford University Press, 1993), 208–41.

37. Paul Smeyers and Nicholas C. Burbules, "Education as Initiation into Practices," *Educational Theory* 56, no. 4 (2006): 439–49.

38. Smeyers and Burbules, 439.

39. Smeyers and Burbules, 443, 449.

40. Smeyers and Burbules, 444.

41. Charles Taylor, *Human Agency and Language: Philosophical Papers, Volume 1* (Cambridge: Cambridge University Press, 1985).

42. Mark Mason, "The Ethics of Integrity: Educational Values Beyond Postmodern Ethics," *Journal of Philosophy of Education* 35, no. 1 (2001): 47–69.

43. Mason, 48.

44. Mason.

45. Mason, 50.

46. Mason.

47. Mason, 56.

48. Mason, 60.

49. For another research example of Taylor's authenticity, see Mike A. B. Degenhardt, "Should Philosophy Express the Self?" *Journal of Philosophy of Education* 37, no. 1 (2003): 35–51.

50. Clarence W. Joldersma, "How Can Science Help Us Care for Nature? Hermeneutics, Fragility, and Responsibility for the Earth," *Educational Theory* 59, no. 4 (2009): 465–83. For another example of environmental education and Taylor, see Michael Bonnett, "Environmental Concern and the Metaphysics of Education," *Journal of the Philosophy of Education* 34, no. 4 (2000): 591–602.

51. Joldersma, "How Can Science Help Us?" 465.

52. Joldersma, 477; Charles Taylor, *Philosophical Arguments* (Cambridge, MA: Harvard University Press, 1995).

53. Joldersma, "How Can Science Help Us?" 470.

54. Joldersma, 475.

55. Joldersma, 482. For another research example of Taylor's social imaginary in educational thought, see Fazal Rizvi, "Imagination and the Globalization of Educational Policy Research," *Globalisation, Societies and Education* 4, no. 2 (2006): 193–205.

56. Paul Theobald, "A Case for Inserting Community into the Public School Curriculum," *American Journal of Education* 112 (May 2006): 315–34.

57. Theobald, 316.

58. Theobald, 315.

59. Theobald, 318.

60. Theobald, 319.

61. Theobald, 328.

62. Chris Higgins, "Teaching and the Good Life: A Critique of the Ascetic Ideal in Education," *Educational Theory* 53, no. 2 (2003): 131.

63. Higgins, 153.

64. Higgins, 131.

65. Higgins, 137.

66. Higgins.

67. Higgins, 141.

68. Higgins.

69. David Dewhurst, "Education and Passion," *Educational Theory* 47, no. 4 (1997): 477–88.

70. Dewhurst, 482.

71. Robert V. Bullough Jr., Clifford T. Mayes, and Robert S. Patterson, "Wanted: A Prophetic Pedagogy—A Response to Our Critics," *Curriculum Inquiry* 32, no. 3 (2002): 341–47.

72. Robert V. Bullough Jr., Clifford T. Mayes, and Robert S. Patterson, "Teaching as Prophecy," *Curriculum Inquiry* 32, no. 3 (2002): 311–29.

73. Bullough, Mayes, and Patterson, "Wanted," 341.

74. Bullough, Mayes, and Patterson, 342.

75. Bullough, Mayes, and Patterson.

76. Bullough, Mayes, and Patterson. For another research example of the philosophy of teaching and Taylor, see Joseph Buijs, "Teaching: Profession or Vocation?" *Catholic Education: A Journal of Inquiry and Practice* 8, no. 3 (2005): 326–45.

77. Pamela A. Moss, "Understanding the Other / Understanding Ourselves: Toward a Constructive Dialogue about 'Principles' in Educational Research," *Educational Theory* 55, no. 3 (2005): 263–83.

78. Charles Taylor, "Understanding the Other: A Gadamerian View on Conceptual Schemes," in *Gadamer's Century: Essays in Honor of Hans-Georg Gadamer*, ed. Jeff Malpas, Ulrich Arnswald, and Jens Kertscher (Cambridge, MA: MIT Press, 2002), 279–98.

79. Moss, "Understanding," 267.

80. Moss, 270.

81. Johannah Fahey and Jane Kenway, "The Power of Imagining and Imagining Power," *Globalisation, Societies and Education* 4, no. 2 (2006): 161–66.

82. Stephen Denig, "What Would Newman Do? John Cardinal Newman and *Ex Corde Ecclesiae*," *Catholic Education: A Journal of Inquiry and Practice* 8, no. 2 (2004): 162–74.

83. Mike Newby, "Literary Development as Spiritual Development in the Common School," *Journal of Philosophy of Education* 31, no. 2 (1997): 283–94.

84. Neil Burtonwood, "Social Cohesion, Autonomy and the Liberal Defense of Faith Schools," *Journal of the Philosophy of Education* 37, no. 3 (2003): 415–25; Richard Pring, "The Common School," *Journal of Philosophy of Education* 41, no. 4 (2007): 503–22.

85. Marianna Papastephanou, "Arrows Not Yet Fired: Cultivating Cosmopolitanism through Education," *Journal of Philosophy of Education* 36, no. 1 (2002): 69–86.

86. Michael Warner, Jonathan VanAntwerpen, and Craig Calhoun, eds., *Varieties of Secularism in a Secular Age* (Cambridge, MA: Harvard University Press, 2010).

87. John Patrick Diggins, "The Godless Delusion" (review of *A Secular Age*, by Charles Taylor), *New York Times Book Review*, December 16, 2007; Peter E. Gordon, "The Place of the Sacred in the Absence of God" (review of *A Secular Age*, by Charles Taylor), *Journal of the History of Ideas* 69, no. 4 (2008): 647–73; Bruce Robbins, "Disenchanted" (review of *A Secular Age*, by Charles Taylor), *Notre Dame Philosophical Reviews*, 2008, http://ndpr .nd.edu/review.cfm?id=13905.

88. José Casanova, "A Secular Age: Dawn or Twilight?" in *Varieties of Secularism in a Secular Age*, ed. Michael Warner, Jonathan VanAntwerpen, and Craig Calhoun (Cambridge, MA: Harvard University Press, 2010), 256–81; José Casanova, "The Secular and Secularisms," *Social Research: An International Quarterly of the Social Sciences* 76, no. 4 (2009): 1049–66.

89. Michael Warner, Jonathan VanAntwerpen, and Craig Calhoun, "Editor's Introduction," in *Varieties of Secularism*, 22.

90. Robert N. Bellah, "Confronting Modernity: Maruyama Masao, Jürgen Habermas, and Charles Taylor," in *Varieties of Secularism*, 51.

91. Charles Taylor and Jocelyn Maclure, *Secularism and Freedom of Conscience*, trans. Jane Marie Todd (Cambridge, MA: Harvard University Press, 2011).

92. Taylor and Maclure, 4–5.

93. Taylor and Maclure, 11.

94. Taylor and Maclure, 12.

95. Warner, VanAntwerpen, and Calhoun, "Editor's Introduction," 22.

96. Jon Butler, "Disquieted History in *A Secular Age*," in *Varieties of Secularism*, 193–216; Simon During, "Completing Secularism: The Mundane in the Neoliberal Era," in *Varieties of Secularism*, 105–25.

97. During, "Completing Secularism," 108.

98. During, 107.

99. During, 113.

100. Butler, "Disquieted History," 194. For an excellent description of the role and practice of history in Taylor's work, and a Hegelian influence in his thinking, see Terry Pinkard,

"Taylor, 'History,' and the History of Philosophy," in *Charles Taylor*, ed. Ruth Abbey (Cambridge: Cambridge University Press, 2004).

101. David Lyon, "Being Post-Secular in the Social Sciences," *New Blackfriars* 91, no. 1036 (2010): 648–62.

102. Taylor endorses Lyon in a written response. However, I am witness to an exchange between Richard Bernstein of New School and Taylor in New York in 2008. Bernstein, from a conference audience, approached a microphone to query Taylor, protesting something to the effect, "Chuck, you can't not deal with the real issues." Abortion, in fact, was the real issue. Taylor had just been challenged about matters of public and political policy posed by a different interlocutor, and Bernstein was unimpressed. Taylor responded, "Dick, I can. I am a philosopher."

103. Keith Tester, "Multiculturalism, Catholicism and Us," *New Blackfriars* 91, no. 1036 (2010): 665–76.

104. R. Po-Chia Hsia, *A Jesuit in the Forbidden City: Matteo Ricci, 1552–1610* (Oxford: Oxford University Press, 2010), 305.

105. Taylor, "Catholic Modernity," 15–16.

106. Tester, "Multiculturalism," 668.

107. John Milbank, "A Closer Walk on the Wild Side," in *Varieties of Secularism*, 54–82.

108. Taylor, *Secular Age*, 44–47.

109. *The Joy of Secularism: 11 Essays for How We Live Now*, ed. George Levine (Princeton, NJ: Princeton University Press, 2011).

110. Pierre Hadot, *The Present Alone Is Our Happiness: Conversations with Jeannie Carlier and Arnold I. Davidson*, trans. Marc Djaballah (Palo Alto, CA: Stanford University Press, 2009), 5–6.

111. Hadot, 8.

112. Hadot.

113. Adam Phillips, "Freud's Helplessness," in *Joy of Secularism*, 133.

114. Taylor, *Secular Age*, 307.

115. David Sloan Wilson, "The Truth Is Sacred," in *Joy of Secularism*, 184.

116. Rebecca Stott, "The Wetfooted Understory: Darwinian Immersions," in *Joy of Secularism*, 208.

117. Stott, 223.

118. Stott, 224.

119. Akeel Bilgrami, "What Is Enchantment?" in *Varieties of Secularism*, 145–65.

120. Kieran Flanagan, "*A Secular Age*: An Exercise in Breach-Mending," *New Blackfriars* 91, no. 1036 (2010): 699–721.

121. Charles Taylor, "Afterword: *Apologia pro Libro suo*," in *Varieties of Secularism in a Secular Age*, ed. Michael Warner, Jonathan VanAntwerpen, and Craig Calhoun (Cambridge, MA: Harvard University Press, 2010), 320.

122. Bruce Robbins, "Enchantment? No, Thank You!" in *Joy of Secularism*, 90.

123. Robbins, 88.

124. Taylor, "Afterword," 318; Taylor and Maclure, *Freedom and Conscience*, 13, 100.

125. Peter van der Veer, "Spirituality in Modern Society," *Social Research: An International Quarterly of the Social Sciences* 76, no. 4 (2009): 1097–1120.

126. van der Veer, 1097.

127. Jonathan Sheehan, "When Was Disenchantment? History and the Secular Age," in *Varieties of Secularism*, 217–42.

128. Philip Kitcher, "Challenges for Secularism," in *Joy of Secularism*, 24–56; James Wood, "Is That All There Is? Secularism and Its Discontents," *New Yorker*, August 15, 2011, 88.

129. Kitcher, "Challenges," 32.

130. Kitcher, 55–56.

131. "The Immanent Frame," http://blogs.ssrc.org/tif/.

132. Taylor, "Afterword," 316.

133. Taylor, 318.

# CHAPTER FOUR

# RENAISSANCE HUMANISTIC BACKGROUNDS OF JESUIT EDUCATIONAL THOUGHT

The genesis of Renaissance humanism can be appreciated by examining the life and work of the educational theorist and teacher Pier Paolo Vergerio, which in itself represents an originary ancient Greek humanism that so inspired Ignatius of Loyola. Also, evolving conceptions of "arête," notions of human excellence, culminated in ancient Rome as an expression of Ciceronian eloquence. With roots reaching back to ancient Greek sophistry and Isocrates, the rhetoric of Cicero is the foundation of Vergerio's humanism, a paradigm shift in education that represents a fundamental aspect of the tradition of Jesuit education. This tradition commences at the end of the sixteenth century in a pervasive Renaissance humanist milieu and flourishes as a dominant pedagogy in both Western Europe and abroad for over two hundred years.

I begin with Vergerio and his innovative and influential Renaissance humanist educational treatise, a letter penned to Italian royalty. Then I discuss the humanist ethos of ancient Greece and the *septem artes liberales*—the classic seven liberal arts—that chart for Renaissance humanist educators a pathway beyond the existing medieval educational orientation, Scholasticism. When I introduce and define "arête," it will be instructive not only of ancient perspectives but as a benchmark for educational emphases and ideals. Looking at arête—a conception of excellence—in Homeric terms and advancing historically through Isocrates, we can see the emergence of a defining Renaissance humanist educational expression, rhetoric. Given that Ciceronian rhetoric best represents Renaissance humanist education, especially in the Jesuit tradition, I then discuss the meaning and practice of Ciceronian arête. Finally, in the section "Renaissance Remands," I return to Vergerio's life and letter to feature significant elements of Scholastic and Renaissance humanist educations.

## PIER PAOLO VERGERIO AND RENAISSANCE HUMANISM

After moving beyond his hometown of Capodistria—a fourteenth-century city-state allied with the Kingdom of Venice—Pier Paolo Vergerio always remembered the feast day of Saint Jerome. In the Catholic Church's faith and practice, feast days memorialize its more remarkable members, its saints, on their day of dying. The death day is significant because it benchmarks a well-lived life in the individual's preceding years and, after them, an eternal life that is articulated by the precepts of Christian soteriology, that is, the teachings of divine salvation. For Christian believers, the day of dying is not an absolute death but a passing from one kind of life (excellently lived) to another. Jerome, a late-fourth-century scripture scholar and linguist who attained honorable distinction within Roman Catholic rankings as a doctor of the Church, is ultimately celebrated for creating functional Latin translations of the Jewish and Christian scriptures from their original Hebrew and Greek texts. As a compilation, the translation is called the Vulgate.

The boy Vergerio may have been aware of feast days in general and whom they honored, but what seemed so memorable to him were the specific practices enacted in Capodistria on Saint Jerome's Day, September 30, then and now, for Western practitioners of Catholicism. Celebrating the patron saint of the city, this particular feast day was exceptional. Among some of its ritual practices, it offered a banquet—a feast—that was sumptuous and savory in proportions and consumption.

Young Vergerio was definitely aware of this, but it is what *happened* at the banquet that impressed him so much: everyone gathered equitably. Social distinctions of all ranks and classes were set aside, momentarily dismissed, and forgotten. Readers of Charles Taylor's *A Secular Age* will recall his own discussion of religious festivals and their cultural, moral, and social effects. In Vergerio's experience, prince and pauper, master and maid, debonair and debtor all dined together.[1] This was important to young Vergerio for many reasons. For one, an amnesty was achieved: "Vergerio was born into an epoch of violent contrasts and significant struggles."[2] Wars and plagues destabilized and even sundered personal and political relationships, and the brief respite from strife afforded an alternative, more attractive, and impressionable image of relating.

Second, in bringing about the banquet, Vergerio recognized an operative moral expression with flavors both civil and religious. Inequitable class distinctions were leveled by a sense of dignity for persons and an unquestionable inclusion of all in the feast. Moreover, this social inclusion was only possible through the charitable actions of those who had expendable resources to supplement others who had little, or nothing at all, to offer. Each and all donated what they could, but many simply could not contribute. Vergerio noticed that a communal concern was addressed by righteous individuals who themselves knew and demonstrated the virtues of hospitality and generosity. A sense of personal character and a civic correlate are important constructs of Vergerio's mature life.

But Vergerio appreciated the collaborative and inclusive dimensions of the banquet on a level deeply personal. With surrounding political and religious conflict and chaos, the winds of fortune shifted all too easily. Through the course of the boy's formative years, Vergerio's family was both benefactor and beneficiary of the banquet. Third, then, Vergerio intimately experienced these different ways of participating in the feast and their corresponding virtues of giving and being grateful.

Finally, the memories and stories were significant. Well-spoken narratives—the right words and an effective delivery of these words—about Jerome's life, for instance, or about the banquets that commemorated his life, influenced and inspired people. Individuals and audiences were persuaded by the descriptions of the virtues they represented. The feast day banquets were all the better, and so too were those persons and families who participated in them. From the panegyrics and preaching, Vergerio himself formed and nourished vivid images of Jerome and his feast day that sustained and encouraged him well beyond his childhood in Capodistria.[3] Composed, thoughtful, ascetic, scholarly, peaceful: if the world around Vergerio was violent and unattractive, Jerome's life, the banquet that remembered his life, and the kind of world each represented were not. Vergerio appreciated a correlation between an individual sense of self and a communal responsibility. But he also suspected a connection from persuasive speeches about persons and events of moral import to a profoundly personal moral sensibility that was manifested by the speakers and inspired within those who listened.

The expression of social harmony, an individual sense of personal character, a correlation between individual character and one's community, a set of profoundly personal experiences, the impact of morally persuasive words and images: these banquet-related dynamics of Vergerio's young life emerged in his professional life as the ingredients of an innovatory force. In *Orators and Philosophers: A History of the Idea of Liberal Education* (1995), Bruce Kimball explains that Vergerio wrote one of the earliest, if not the first, Renaissance discourses on education.[4] Published in the opening years of the fifteenth century, the treatise, *De Ingenius Moribus et Liberalibus Studiis* [*The Character and Studies Befitting a Free-born Youth*] (c. 1403), represents a paradigm shift—the seeds of a revolutionary change—in Western teaching and learning that continues to inform educational practices.[5] The treatise itself was read and consulted for hundreds of years after its publication, and for at least a century and a half is reported to have been one of the most commonly read manifestos of the Renaissance itself.[6]

Dedicated to Umbertus, the son of Francesco Carrara, the duke of Padua, *De Ingenius Moribus et Liberalibus Studiis* was one of a set of other subsequent educational tracts that "formed the nucleus of Italian humanist pedagogical writings."[7] Leonardo Bruni, Aeneas Silvius Piccolomini, and Battista Guarino are some of the other similarly influential authors. Craig Kallendorf refers collectively to the four as educational reformers of a special brand who "want to leave [educational] institutions mostly intact while improving the quality of the human material that directs those institutions."[8] Vergerio's pedagogical explanation that "the fruits of literature ... are always great, for the whole of life and for every kind of person, but it is ... particularly beneficial to the studious for forming habits of [virtue]" offers a snapshot of the kinds of "human material" that Kallendorf notes.[9]

## HUMANISM AND THE *SEPTEM ARTES LIBERALES*

Generally, humanist educators wanted to implement programs of instruction that formed students more holistically. They tempered the intellectual force of Scholastic education, especially in its dialectic tone, to focus on other aspects of the human condition, such as the power of the will, emotional capacities, aesthetic sensibilities, the work of the imagination, and more; they "sought for something which took in the whole of [one's] life and interests."[10] In doing so, they reevaluated and balanced the classic seven liberal arts.

Such arts—academic disciplines by contemporary standards—were initially regarded as liberal in that free men of ancient citizenries were able to study them. In Greek and Roman antiquity, slaves and others with fewer social and political rights were not afforded such opportunities.[11] Not only were slaves (and women, and foreigners, for instance) not regarded as citizens worthy to participate in the political and social institutions of the given community, such as educational programs; they did not have time. Oppressive political structures aside, slaves and women were simply otherwise occupied. Time was consumed by labor, not afforded leisure. Free men who had the free time to study pursued the arts.

But the arts also freed people. They liberated those who studied them from basic impulses and thoughtless habits into patterns of daily life that were more intentional and intelligent, that is, *deliberate*.[12] Reading, writing, and thinking were naturally empowering as important skills, but education in the liberal arts was particularly celebrated for the way it humanely nourished and nurtured students. That is, the liberal arts cultivated a student's humanity toward an idealized expression of being human.

Werner Jaeger describes this in the ancient Greek context as a special Greek obsession to create "a higher type of man."[13] Jaeger explains that ancient Greece—"a nation of artists and philosophers"—recognized the ability of education to impart knowledge, but also to form personal character, "to shape the living man as the potter moulds clay and the sculptor carves stone."[14] Invented and employed by the Greeks but formally categorized later as the *trivium*—grammar, dialectic, and rhetoric—and the *quadrivium*—music, arithmetic, geometry, and astronomy, the *septem artes liberales* were thought to educate a person for a better, freer, more virtuous life.[15]

Jaeger is worth dwelling on momentarily. He articulates ancient Greek perspective as having an unprecedented sensitivity for human capacity: "From our first glimpse of them we find that the individual person is the center of their thought."[16] Jaeger offers a litany of examples, citing

their anthropomorphic gods, their concentration on the problem depicting the human form in sculpture and even in painting; the logical sequence by which their philosophy moved from the problem of the cosmos to the problem of man, in which it culminated with Socrates, Plato, and Aristotle; their poetry, whose inexhaustible theme from Homer throughout all the succeeding centuries is man, his destiny, and his gods; and finally their state, which cannot be understood unless viewed as the force which shaped man and man's life—all these are separate rays from one great light. They are expressions of an anthropomorphic attitude to life, which cannot be explained by or derived from anything else, and which pervades everything felt, made, or thought by the Greeks. Other nations made gods, kings, spirits: the Greeks alone made men.[17]

But in this Jaeger distinguishes between the subjective dimension of human life and the human condition, explaining that Greek anthropocentrism wrestled with the latter aspect: "The intellectual principle . . . is not individualism but 'humanism,' to use the word in its original and classic sense, . . . from *humanitatis*."[18] Ancient Greeks articulated a universal human nature, and in doing so they pondered how to educate their citizens toward the genuine expression of such a nature. Jaeger stresses that such an ideal was not an abstract, esoteric conception of a specific and fixed image but one grounded in the dynamic realities of daily life in the city-state. The educational programs they pondered and implemented for attaining—or for striving to attain—such an ideal, he instructs, manifest a culture of formation, or of teaching, which offered, ultimately, a "refinement" of the human soul.[19] The culture, the Greek *paideia*—literally, "childrearing"[20]—reveals, further, a purposeful search for an ideal life—again, "a higher type of human being"[21]—that is well understood through the concept of arête.

## ARÊTE FROM THE *ILIAD* TO ISOCRATES

Arête, a kind of excellence that "shows superlative ability and superiority," reveals certain operative virtues that were worth possessing.[22] In the first chapter of his voluminous work *Paideia: The Ideals of Greek Culture* (1939), Jaeger traces the understanding of arête for Greeks themselves. For archaic Greeks, arête represents the physical strength and skill set of a Homeric warrior. Even in Homer, from the *Iliad* to the *Odyssey*, according to Jaeger, the ideal of human excellence evolves into one that is more mindful; that is, the warrior is more intentional in his actions and even descriptive of them. Still later in ancient Greek history, Jaeger notes dimensions of moral comport and virtuosity for arête; and then, with Aristotle (384–22 BCE)—who also ponders the excellence of certain *objects*—the arête of persons assumes patrician overtones. Hesiod, moreover, juxtaposes original Homeric strength and Aristotelian liberality. Hesiod's epic poem *Works and Days* features the ideal of excellence of the common laborer who "wishes to make something of his arête, and he engages, not in the ambitious rivalry for chivalrous prowess and praise which is commended by the code of the aristocrat, but in the quiet strong rivalry of work. In the sweat of his brow shall he eat bread—but that is not a curse, it is a blessing. Only the sweat of his brow can win him arête."[23]

Kimball endorses Jaeger's discussion of arête and articulates three ancient Greek variants of it through, first, Gorgias and the sophists; then, with Plato, Aristotle, and the philosophers; and finally, in a combined version of the two by Isocrates. For the sophists, the philosophers, and the orator, arête represents (1) persuasiveness in the political arena, (2) theoretical knowing and a correspondent personal virtuosity, and (3) a blending of being well spoken and morally upright.[24] In this third variant, Isocrates's blending of rhetorical skill and oratorical integrity revealed a reformed version of sophistry and at the same time evaded Platonic and Aristotelian philosophic esotericism. Through Isocrates, persuasive speech became more accountable and practical. In the domain of education, it also became curricular.

It is this form of intellectually and morally responsible rhetoric, as the Jesuit historian John O'Malley, SJ, describes it, that ultimately schooled the Ancients: "Isocrates and his followers won the battle to educate fourth-century Greece and subsequently the Hellenistic and Roman worlds."[25] Plato's Academy, Isocrates felt, produced—for too long a time span—contemplative individuals disconnected from the daily activities of the community. Aristotle's own school, the Lyceum, would dwell in a natural philosophy that was just as removed from practical concerns.[26] Alternatively, Isocrates's school of rhetoric studied poetry, political discourse, and literature, and offered a curriculum that strove to form politically engaged and morally responsible individuals: "For Isocrates the foundation upon which [rhetoric] was built was ... the study of the poets, not only for the 'grammatical' aspects, ... but also because literature revealed the complexity of the human situation."[27] Isocrates's main educational objective was that individuals would be able to properly navigate the complexities of life, and one way of doing so was through effective civic engagement. This demanded rhetorical skill, the content of which was now deemed credible.

The practice of good speaking is associated with the practices in ancient Greece for living good and intentional lives, practices to which Pierre Hadot refers in his book, *Philosophy as a Way of Life* (1995), as spiritual exercises. Such ancient practices, more commonly associated with the specific exercises of the Epicureans and Stoics, "have as their goal the transformation of our vision of the world, and the metamorphosis of our being."[28] In fact, I turn to Hadot later in the book to further elucidate spiritual exercises in the Jesuit tradition.

Tangentially, education in the Isocratic tradition of rhetoric calls to mind its origins in sophistry, the practice of persuading. Socrates's mission develops out of his impatience with meritless opinions of smoothing-talking, fee-demanding individuals in and around Athens, the sophists. In *American Higher Education: A History* (2006), Christopher Lucas explains that sophistry "evidenced the symptoms of superficiality and the pedantic shallowness for which it [became] notorious."[29] He traces from it expressions of "relativism, skepticism, and radical individualism" and spotlights an oft-referenced dictum of a fifth-century sophist, Protagoras: "Man is the measure of all things."[30] And yet Lucas also cites worthy dimensions of sophist tradition and education in ancient Greece, such as democratic forms of instruction, broad and comprehensive curricular offerings, and iconoclastic speeches that denounced slavery and war.[31] Collectively, the denigrations and accolades of sophistry were a backdrop to Isocrates and his version of arête, oratory.

As Jaeger describes an anthropocentric concern of the Greeks, a corresponding cultural milieu to attend it, and an arête to actualize it, he also stresses the communal reality of ancient Greece: "The man revealed in the work of the great Greeks is a political man. Greek education is not the sum of a number of private parts and skills intended to create a perfect independent personality."[32] Lucas even describes the Greek culture, the *paideia*, as "*common* learning" (emphasis added).[33] In Greece, personal life could not be distinguished from the polis. As the ideal of human excellence in classic Greek regard evolves, the corresponding conceptions of arête will continue to reflect the communal context. The warrior, the worker, and the aristocrat will in Roman sensibility continue to evolve and assume an equally specific and determinately political expression, human arête as "statesman." Humanist regard in its Renaissance rendering will be especially mindful of the statesman and a corresponding verbal and personal eloquence cultivated by Marcus Tullius Cicero.

## CICERONIAN STATESMANSHIP AND THE *STUDIA HUMANITATIS*

Cicero, whom Vergerio designated the "source of all eloquence," had "harnessed," better than other orators both classical and contemporary, "persuasive oratory to the compelling example of an upright life."[34] The morally honorable life implied communal and civic engagement, and this mattered to Vergerio. Francesco Petrarch, who, in 1345 discovered Cicero's personal letters to his fellow citizen and friend Titus Pomponius Atticus, and is commonly regarded as the father of humanism, serves as something of a foil for Vergerio.[35] In Petrarch, Vergerio recognized oratorical prominence and expertise, and he deeply appreciated the Renaissance humanist turn he initiates in his discovery and propagation of Cicero. But in Vergerio's estimate, the life and work of Petrarch portray, and thereby endorse, the life of a solitary poet. Rather than retreating from a troubled world, "Vergerio preferred the political struggles of the orator in the city."[36] Relying heavily on the first-century BCE Ciceronian handbooks *De Inventione* and the *Rhetorica ad Herennium* (which may or may not have been written by Cicero), scholars admit that Vergerio "simply recapitulated" a Ciceronian educational plan decisively invested in political and legislative influence.[37] One stresses that "Vergerio left no ambiguity regarding his position on the social role of a humanist intellectual. In opposition to Petrarch's lifelong ambivalence about political activism,

Vergerio offered an unconditional endorsement. . . . Humanists would assist the proper functioning of government. . . . Public panegyric and written history became the privileged media through which [they] might instill civic values and exemplify their realization in historic deeds."[38]

For Vergerio, as with the ancient Greeks and Romans, the upright life of the individual is that of an individual-in-community. Unlike the Scholastics' interest in esoteric truths, the humanist movement in general demonstrates a practical concern about the daily life of the public. For Vergerio, the practical dimension necessitated an active, responsible execution of one's citizenship.[39]

Through Cicero, rhetorical skill and civic engagement stand out as prescriptions of personal virtuosity more clearly than Isocrates's own reforms. Indeed, Isocrates is the inspiration for and foundation of Cicero, both in comprehensive curricular offerings to students and in an emphasis on oratory.[40] The eloquence of good, effective, persuasive speaking correlates with personal honesty and appropriate causes, but Cicero's eloquence became more personal and fundamentally pedagogical. It extended beyond the mastery of speech, the integrity of its message, and civic effect. It was more profoundly revelatory of the speaker's personal life. It represents the prose *and* the person: "Eloquence was not a technique, but a style of life. The *vir bonus dicendi peritus* ['the better man speaking skillfully'], as Cicero defined the orator, offered the perfect model for the humanism of the Renaissance."[41] In the ancient Roman context, the skilled orator professed a deep sense of personal probity for his own life and those of the community; and, in the Renaissance, women and men yearned for and strove toward an eloquence of personal character. Robert Proctor says that in the tradition of Cicero, "the *studia humanitatis . . .* can perfect one's *ingenium*, or natural talent."[42]

Proctor's study, *Education's Great Amnesia: Reconsidering the Humanities from Petrarch to Freud—With a Curriculum for Today's Students* (1988), also champions Ciceronian rhetoric. Cicero, he insists, "gives poetry, geometry, music, and dialectic as examples of the arts by which young [students] are formed into their humanity."[43] Cicero, Proctor instructs, coined the phrase *studia humanitatis*: "What Cicero calls the *studia humanitatis . . .* are synonymous with the *artes liberales*, that is, with ancient education as a whole, including what would later come to be known as the *trivium* and *quadrivium* of the liberal arts."[44] As a *canonista* taught canon law and a *legista* taught civil law, the *humanista*—in the fifteenth-century Italian original: *umanista*—taught the *studia humanitatis*.[45] These, the *artes liberales* from ancient conception, evolve through Cicero—and the Renaissance humanist return to Cicero, into a more constricted contemporary category, *beaus artes*, or "fine arts." With Cicero and, thus, the Renaissance humanists, the *studia humanitatis* was regarded for its ability to form eloquent persons. Moreover, Ciceronian rhetoric, the capstone expression of the *studia humanitatis*, functioned intimately with and through all the arts. The arts, as I discuss more fully in chapter 5, were not separable disciplines.[46]

The prominence of rhetoric in the Isocratic tradition and a later Ciceronian development of it give insight into the curricular interests of Renaissance humanists like Vergerio. There was an underlying impulse in Vergerio and his colleagues to reevaluate the *septem artes liberales* and to instantiate a renewed and better-integrated expression of them as Ciceronian *studia humanitatis*. Dialectics, the crowning discipline of Scholasticism, was not dismissed, but reoriented, and the role of rhetoric was restored. "The anti-Scholasticism of the humanists was the attempt by practitioners of one discipline to overcome the intellectual domination of another."[47]

## RENAISSANCE REMANDS

Vergerio's humanist letter to the duke's son, Umbertus, frames the humanists' concerns. Kallendorf describes three of its features. In what he refers to as a "moralizing flavor," he suggests that, first, Vergerio's educational plan focuses on the formation of individual character; second, that such formation is to be individually accommodated (i.e., that the process of Vergerio's humanist education manifests a sensitivity to individual students and their own particular talents and limitations); and, third, that the character formation and learning of individual persons and positive civic engagement are interrelated.[48]

The details of *De Ingenius Moribus et Liberalibus Studiis* illuminate its Renaissance distinction in the history of education. In it, Vergerio exudes a special humanist attentiveness to youthfulness and its powers. Espousing the trademark Renaissance investment in Greek and Roman classics, Vergerio turns to Virgil to highlight the Roman poet's own recognition of the plasticity of young persons. Vergerio agrees with this ancient insight, but he places it in educational discourse. He also confesses in his educational plan an urgency— "we must, then, press onwards"—to tap such potential.[49] Moreover, maintaining such youthfulness in the later years of life is necessary and noble: "Even so great a philosopher as Socrates applied himself to the lyre when he was already advanced in years and turned over his fingers to a teacher for guidance."[50] Though Vergerio's interest in youthfulness quickly embraces a moralizing concern for tempering basic impulses and appetites, he manifests, up front and throughout the treatise, an interest in the potency of infancy, certain innate qualities of youthfulness, and the worthiness of nourishing such a dynamism throughout and into the latter years of life. Moreover, the educational interest in youthfulness and powers is, four and a half centuries later, recognized and appreciated by the public intellectual and philosopher John Dewey and his *Democracy and Education* (1916). We will later glance back at Dewey and his conception of growth.

As Vergerio *seizes* youthfulness, his educational ideal does not cultivate or direct it uniformly, but personally. Kallendorf, again, but here more pointedly, explains that Vergerio "goes back to the Greeks ... for an approach to education that is based on a fourfold division amongst letters, gymnastics, music, and drawing, and he develops at unusual length the idea that everyone has different talents and that any general program, must be adapted to the strengths and weaknesses of each student."[51]

Also, well into his treatise, Vergerio explicitly articulates a personally catered—"radically student-centered"—educational approach, and in the same gesture he describes an ideal of ongoing inquiry:[52]

> We have enumerated almost all the chief disciplines, not in order that each person need necessarily understand all of them to the point of being learned, or being considered learned—indeed, each discipline could absorb all a man's efforts, and the capacity to be content with modest wealth. We have done this rather so that everyone might embrace the study most suitable to himself—although all studies are so linked together that no one of them can be well understood if the others are completely unknown.[53]

That is, what students of his program come to know both *is* and *is not* sufficient. A student's knowledge of poetry might assist her desire to write or recite it or speak publicly with its specific images and examples. Another's knowledge of music might let him play it (personally, publicly) well, or compose it, or teach it. Vergerio seems interested in letting students pursue these disciplines with personal investment, and also to be well taught in them by mentors. Teachers were expected to be masterly in their disciplines, but with Vergerio they were also expected to be adaptive to their students' temperaments and interests.[54]

Vergerio's concern for students as individuals, however, does not compromise his desire to offer a balanced, comprehensive curriculum of the liberal arts for all students. Musical instruction will serve the musical boy well, but the boy and his musical capacities will also be well served by poetry and mathematics. Given that holistic pedagogy, moreover, is a characteristic of Renaissance humanism, its replacement by vocationalism in contemporary education and a domineering expression of instrumental rationality—an orientation Taylor laments—in higher education is problematic even today.

As Vergerio's educational program is plentiful and exhaustive in humanist exercises and content, it is also particularly humane. Vergerio explains that "from time to time, . . . one needs to do absolutely nothing and be entirely free from work, so as to meet once again the demands of work and toil."[55] Collecting pebbles and seashells, hunting and fishing, singing and playing the lute—these, too, have educational merit in Vergerio's plan, as does plain and simple rest.[56] Vergerio's fundamental educational interest, however, and one that benchmarks him with curricular distinction, regards an explicit interest in classic rhetoric. The Vergerio scholar and biographer John M. McManamon explains that as a young teacher himself, Vergerio briefly adopted in his own classroom work a commonly used method of teaching and its corresponding curriculum, respectively, Scholastic disputation and dialectical instruction.

Scholastic method and its content generally consisted of a *lectio* (a lesson) by an instructor who explained the meaning and significance of a specific text. The teacher recited scripted sets of questions, referred to as *quaestiones*, to engage the text and its issues rationally and methodically. In turn, students analyzed and debated the questions. Their disputes, or *disputationes*, garnered praise or condemnation in relation to the way they corresponded with veracity—given truths of the matters at hand.[57] Argumentation was the crucial and culminating gesture, and truth was the objective.

O'Malley articulates five educational principles for such a program. The philosophy of Aristotle, particularly regarding his scientific treatises, represented the type of material that was lectured. Second, the main, if not only, objective was to find and name specific truths. Rehearsing and debating options and alternatives, third, argued toward such truths, and options and alternatives were dialectically scrutinized by Aristotelian methods. Fourth, in knowing truths, the educational program hoped to create experts in the fields of law, medicine, and theology, namely, the classic professions. Professionals, finally, would be able to represent the respective comprehensive philosophic truth system of their profession.[58] But students, eventually, "found their writings without heart or warmth, and a reaction was certain to arise."[59]

The philosophers and theologians who perpetuated Scholasticism grew more and more esoteric and meaningless. The concerns they passionately argued had little to do with everyday life. The practitioners "had become lost in contentious details," and, as the historian George Ganss, SJ, further explains, "they had, by distinguishing and subdistinguishing, turned their words so completely into technical terms that no one else felt confident of grasping their meaning."[60]

Desiderius Erasmus, a Renaissance humanist spokesman through his many writings, satirizes Scholasticism most famously in *The Praise of Folly* (1509). His own experience at the Collège de Montaigu of the University of Paris at the end of the fifteenth century and his passionate interest in new expressions of education, politics, and religion stage him as a worthy representative. As Montaigu is an important snapshot in time, Erasmus's own stinging words are an important benchmark. Now consider, "[The] means to happiness is right training or education. Sound education is the condition of real wisdom. And if an education which is soundly planned and carefully carried out is the very fount of all human excellence, so, on the one hand, careless and unworthy training is the true source of folly and vice."[61] These remarks in *De Ratione Studii* [*Upon the Right Method of Instruction*] (1511) map from Vergerio to him a hundred-year push against an educational orientation of inquiry that had evolved into a caricature of itself.

## CONCLUSION

The curricular emphasis on argumentation and Scholasticism's specific goals to be masterly in certain disciplines were not attractive to Vergerio. To him, an educational program of argumentation espoused and even validated the social and religious violence of his era. It reveals yet another one of Vergerio's correlations: the importation of violence into the classroom, which had already conditioned the lives of students. Worse yet, the educational arena perpetuated the cruel demeanor around it. As a student at the University of Padua in particular, the cutthroat verbal debates he endured reminded Vergerio of the brutality of wars and plagues at home in Capodistria.[62]

As a teacher in his own classroom, then, he "found refuge in the Stoicism of Roman rhetoricians."[63] Humanism, inspired by Greek anthropocentrism, disseminated by Isocratic schooling, championed by Ciceronian eloquence, and discovered and reinvigorated by Petrarch, evolved an alternative—a paradigm shift, upon which Jesuit education became globally prolific. Aristotle, who had gained academic prominence in the Middle Ages and became the philosophical face of Scholasticism, was replaced: "a campaign against 'Aristotle' both because of the barbarous style, according to the humanists, in which his works came down to us and because of the even worse style of his followers in the universities. It was a style that did not lead to the philosophical life."[64] In place of a dialectic method and its esoteric objectives, "humanists, [shifted] their interests more to [the individual] and . . . worldly concerns," Ganss continues, explaining that the humanists "revived and substituted ideals drawn from classical literature. One of these was what they named *huma-nitas*. By this term they meant an ensemble of qualities—intellectual force, literary excellence, artistic taste, polished manners, and elegant bearing—all intended to enhance ... a citizen."[65]

Vergerio and his humanist colleagues represented a new educational orientation. First, they intentionally framed portrayals and possibilities of good living. Through the poetic, theatrical, and literary showcasing of exemplary people and the kinds of decisions they represented, literature especially guided students in moral and practical ways. Next, the poetry, theater, and literature came from ancient sources and thereby represented a classicist perspective. The shift supplanted the medieval scholastic practices of dialectical argumentation with ancient Greek and Roman images of conscientious living. Third, the program of education did not hope to create professionals set for life but focused on younger students for a limited number of years. The students could advance to the studies of the professions, but, eventually, they could do so only after completing the humanist program. Finally, such a program purported to be not a system of thought but a moral sensibility. Generally, the humanist agenda hoped to educate students themselves into upright persons.[66]

Vergerio's curricular distinction and educational novelty, however, came through Cicero.[67] Like the other humanists around him, his educational approach looked back to antiquity; but in Roman antiquity, Vergerio was especially convinced by the social and political possibilities of educating in Ciceronian rhetoric. Vergerio "sought to reestablish the orator at the center of public life," and he ushered a willing and waiting Cicero front and center in his educational plan.[68]

Vergerio is not a lone ranger. As we have seen, the authors of other humanist educational treatises subsequent to his also construct and publish influential humanist programs in education; among other humanists in general, he is not alone in turning to Cicero. Recall, however, the Saint Jerome feast day celebrations and the turbulent political and religious milieu of Vergerio's childhood. Moments of personal equity and social harmony, the correlations between individual responsibility and the community, personal experience and virtuous response (e.g., of generosity or gratitude), and the impact of corresponding narratives in the forms of panegyrics and preaching—all hover close to the surfaces of the pages of his treatise. His ability to recognize an affinity between vitriolic dialectics in the Scholastic classroom and the mainstream social and political discord in the world around it is telling. His creation of an educational space more peaceable and diplomatic alone well testifies to the influence of the equitable and cooperative feast day banquet.

But the treatise's staying power in readership, schooling, and educational consciousness attests, again, to its paradigmatic influence.

All this, including Vergerio's particular interest in Ciceronian rhetoric as a manifestation of personal and communitarian enhancement, positions him as a cardinal source and catalyst for yet another paradigm shift in education that occurs through the Society of Jesus. The arc from the Greeks and Romans, to Vergerio, and through the Renaissance humanists, elucidates the tried-and-true lineage of the Jesuit theoretical-educational enterprise, whereby the pedagogies of study, solidarity, and grace are featured in historic and traditional regard, and are appreciated for the Jesuit imaginary they envisage.

## NOTES

1. John M. McManamon, *Pierpaolo Vergerio the Elder: The Humanist as Orator*, Medieval and Renaissance Texts and Studies, vol. 163 (Tempe: Arizona State University Press, 1996), 5.
2. McManamon, 15.
3. McManamon, 7.
4. Bruce A. Kimball, *Orators and Philosophers: A History of the Idea of Liberal Education* (New York: College Entrance Examination Board, 1995), 79.
5. McManamon, *Pierpaolo Vergerio*, 22.
6. George E. Ganss, *Saint Ignatius' Idea of a Jesuit University: A Study in the History of Catholic Higher Education* (Milwaukee: Marquette University Press, 1956), 140.
7. Craig W. Kallendorf, ed. and trans., *Humanist Educational Treatises* (Cambridge, MA: Harvard University Press, 2002), ix.
8. Kallendorf, viii.
9. Pier Paolo Vergerio, *De Ingenius Moribus et Liberalibus Studiis*, in *Humanist Educational Treatises*, ed. Kallendorf, 151.
10. Ganss, *Saint Ignatius' Idea*, 131.
11. Kimball, *Orators*, 13.
12. Martha C. Nussbaum, *Cultivating Humanity: A Classical Defense of Reform in Liberal Education* (Cambridge, MA: Harvard University Press, 1997), 8.
13. Werner Jaeger, *Paideia: The Ideals of Greek Culture, Volume I: Archaic Greece, the Mind of Athens*, trans. Gilbert Highet (Oxford: Oxford University Press, 1945), vxii.
14. Jaeger, xxii.
15. Kimball, *Orators*, 24; and Hastings Rashdall, *Universities of Europe in the Middle Ages, Volume I: Salerno, Bologna, Paris* (Cambridge: Cambridge University Press, 2010), 33.
16. Jaeger, *Paideia*, xxiii.
17. Jaeger.
18. Jaeger.
19. John C. Haughey, *Where Is Knowing Going? The Horizons of the Knowing Society* (Washington, DC: Georgetown University Press, 2009), 16.
20. Jaeger, *Paideia*, 286.
21. Donald N. Levine, *Powers of the Mind: The Reinvention of Liberal Learning in America* (Chicago: University of Chicago Press, 2006), 13.

22. Jaeger, *Paideia*, 5.

23. Jaeger, 71.

24. Kimball, *Orators*, 17–18.

25. John W. O'Malley, "From the 1599 *Ratio Studiorum* to the Present: A Humanist Tradition?" in *The Jesuit Ratio Studiorum: 400th Anniversary Perspectives*, ed. Vincent J. Duminuco (New York: Fordham University Press, 2000), 128.

26. Jaeger, *Paideia*.

27. John W. O'Malley, *Four Cultures of the West* (Cambridge, MA: Belknap Press of Harvard University Press, 2004), 129.

28. Pierre Hadot, *Philosophy as a Way of Life*, ed. Arnold I. Davidson (Oxford: Blackwell, 2008), 127.

29. Christopher J. Lucas, *American Higher Education: A History* (New York: Palgrave Macmillan, 2006), 12.

30. Lucas, 11–12.

31. Lucas, 11.

32. Jaeger, *Paideia*, xxv.

33. Lucas, *American Higher Education*, 135.

34. McManamon, *Pierpaolo Vergerio*, 22.

35. O'Malley, *Four Cultures*, 152; Richard Paul Blum, ed., *Philosophers of the Renaissance*, trans. Brian McNeil (Washington, DC: Catholic University of America Press, 2010), 7; John W. O'Malley, *The First Jesuits* (Cambridge, MA: Harvard University Press, 1993), 208.

36. McManamon, *Pierpaolo Vergerio*, 61.

37. McManamon, 37.

38. McManamon, 58–59.

39. Ganss, *Saint Ignatius' Idea*, 163–64.

40. Levine, *Powers*, 15.

41. Gabriel Codina, "Modus Parisiensis," in *The Jesuit Ratio Studiorum: 400th Anniversary Perspectives*, ed. Vincent J. Duminuco (New York: Fordham University Press, 2000), 40.

42. Robert E. Proctor, *Education's Great Amnesia: Reconsidering the Humanities from Petrarch to Freud—With a Curriculum for Today's Students* (Bloomington: Indiana University Press, 1988), 11.

43. Proctor, 16.

44. Proctor, 16; Ronald Modras, *Ignatian Humanism: A Dynamic Spirituality for the 21st Century* (Chicago: Loyola University Press, 2004), xiii.

45. Proctor, *Education's Great Amnesia*, 7; Modras, *Ignatian Humanism*, xiii.

46. Proctor, *Education's Great Amnesia*, 16.

47. Modras, *Ignatian Humanism*, 57.

48. Kallendorf, *Humanist Educational Treatises*, x.

49. Vergerio, *De Ingenius Moribus*, 31.

50. Vergerio, 33.

51. Kallendorf, *Humanist Educational Treatises*, x.

52. O'Malley, *Four Cultures*, 155.

53. Vergerio, *De Ingenius Moribus*, 57.

54. O'Malley, *Four Cultures*, 155.

55. Vergerio, *De Ingenius Moribus*, 89.

56. Vergerio, 85.

57. Codina, "Modus Parisiensis," 37. See also Philippe Lécrivain, *Paris in the Time of Ignatius of Loyola, 1528–1535*, trans. Ralph C. Renner (Saint Louis: Institute of Jesuit Sources, 2011), 58–59.

58. O'Malley, "From the 1599 *Ratio Studiorum* to the Present," 132.

59. Ganss, *Saint Ignatius' Idea*, 134.

60. Ganss.

61. Desiderius Erasmus, *De Ratione Studii* (*Upon the Right Method of Instruction*), in *Desiderius Erasmus Concerning the Aim and Method of Education*, ed. William Harrison Woodward (New York: Bureau of Publication of Teachers College, Columbia University, 1964).

62. McManamon, *Pierpaolo Vergerio the Elder*, 29.

63. McManamon, 29.

64. O'Malley, *Four Cultures*, 151.

65. Ganss, *Saint Ignatius' Idea*, 137–38.

66. O'Malley, "From the 1599 *Ratio Studiorum* to the Present," 130.

67. McManamon, *Pierpaolo Vergerio*, 81.

68. McManamon.

# CHAPTER FIVE

# THE TRADITION OF JESUIT EDUCATION

The earliest vision of Jesuit higher education augmented a humanistic movement that was in active rebirth when Ignatius of Loyola was completing his studies at the University of Paris, and becomes the heart and the soul of Jesuit education, both in its origins and in its impressive proliferation around the world. Ignatius and his companions did not invent humanism, but they deployed it in a new form through fresh tools and networks. At the University of Paris's Collège de Montaigu and also at its oldest school, the rival Collège Sainte-Barbe, they studied new pedagogies that were in fact old ones, returning to the wisdom of the Greeks, who strove to educate in, through, and of the liberal arts. This combined approach was in contrast to mere Scholasticism, for that had run its course in many ways. Although Scholasticism provided a sharpness of argument and terminology and a precise reading of history, it missed fundamental aspects they considered so important to human formation. They recognized the importance of their holistic approach as a pedagogy and carried it to a new level. That is part of why Jesuit education expanded worldwide.

Just as Saint Ignatius's initial conversion came about by reading of the greatness of saints Benedict, Dominic, and Francis, so the first Jesuits' humanistic approach offered saints and historical figures as mentors. Among other qualities, their pedagogical rationale showcased mentoring's ability to create greatness in our lives, whether via larger aspirations or higher virtues. In many ways, both the Jesuits and a much later figure, the philosopher John Dewey—in a book titled *Democracy and Education*—wanted to develop great civic leaders. Their methods are different, but the civic goal is the same. It is magnanimous, and one to which any of us might aspire in order to become better people.

In 1548, the Jesuit order established a school in Messina, Italy, that was open to students from the general public. Education was not a primary work of the Jesuits, yet it inspired, almost instantly, an international network of schools. The rapid and successful expansion levied a new and principal focus of the order and inaugurated a tradition that survives today. Importantly, the essential components of this tradition reveal important assumptions about human subjectivity and a corresponding worldview, and indeed, how we understand ourselves and the world around us evolved from Renaissance humanist ideals and inspires my three pedagogies of fullness.

## IGNATIUS OF LOYOLA

The opening of their first school for lay students on the island of Sicily in 1548 is an important benchmark for the Jesuits. Only a few years beyond their official 1540 recognition as a religious order in the Roman Catholic Church, their founder, Ignatius of Loyola, would not live another full decade. Yet, at his death in 1556, his leadership and his already globally networked organization had founded 35 schools. Less than fifty years later, at the century's end, the number of schools tallied 245.[1] By 1773, when papal decree suppressed the Society of Jesus worldwide, the organization administered nearly eight hundred schools internationally.[2] The explosion of schools—"[our] world had never seen before nor has it seen since such an immense network of educational institutions operating on an international basis"—and a plan that helped to govern such an institutional expanse, looks to an earlier and actual explosion to explain its origins.[3]

In 1521, Ignatius of Loyola was critically and almost fatally wounded. A cannon ball shattered his right leg while he defended the city of Pamplona from a French invasion.[4] Born Íñigo López de Loyola, he was raised in a noble life of "wealth, prestige, and influence . . . [and] apparently destined to enjoy the extravagant life of a courtier."[5] In Pamplona, where Ignatius was felled, opposing troops reportedly nursed him—though crudely, biographers indicate—and let him be carried by stretcher by his soldier-comrades for a not-insignificant distance to the family castle in Spain's Basque region. At home in Azpeitia in the district of Guipúzcoa, Ignatius convalesced, and in the process—delayed by his own self-conscious demand to rebreak and better set (for appearance) the broken bones in his leg—experienced a conversion.

For those who know about Ignatius and the Jesuits, it is commonplace knowledge that he generally preferred to read romantic and chivalric stories in his youth and that these fantasies informed the dreams he enjoyed of his own future life. Ignatius harbored "ambitions for feats of arms and chivalry, interests in fine clothes and his personal appearance, and romantic episodes.

He manifested certain characteristics: a desire for worldly praise and glory, eagerness to distinguish himself by daring or even reckless deeds against odds, and tenacity in reaching an objective once he had decided upon it."[6]

*Amadis de Gaul* (1508), an immensely popular sixteenth-century Spanish work in the genre of knight-errantry that was later parodied by Miguel de Cervantes in his history-making picaresque proto-novel, *Don Quixote* (1605), had been fuel for Ignatius's imaginative fire. But, at the time of his healing, only spiritual and religious books were available: the four-volume set of Ludolph of Saxony's *Vita Christi* (1374), and one of the volumes of Jacobus de Voragine's *Flos Sanctorum* (c. 1260), offering biographical detail of the lives of Christian saints.[7] Both books would feature prominently in Ignatius's life thereafter. In particular, the latter transformed the vivid ways he imagined the exotic and adventurous life of a knight. Now he was suddenly impressed by the lives of Francis of Assisi and Dominic de Guzmán—heroes of a different kind—and their impact on humanity.

Francis and Dominic, as the founders, respectively, of the Roman Catholic religious orders of the Franciscans and the Dominicans (the Order of Preachers), manifested notable dimensions of basic charity, generosity, determination, and intelligence with tremendous public influence. Francis's dedication to the poor, sick, and destitute and Dominic's smart and persuasive preaching seized Western Christendom with new expressions of Christian living. Their movements animated specific values of Christian scriptural writings, particularly from the four canonical Gospel books. Each individual attracted both women and men into their orders in large numbers. Moreover, each man was sainted, as were particular women and men who joined their organizations and became notable for their lives of service. Already at the time of Ignatius's convalescence, these religious orders, and the memories of the men who founded them, had been operative for over three centuries. At the end of Charles Taylor's *A Secular Age*, when Taylor presses for examples of fullness beyond the phenomenal epiphanies of Bede Griffiths and Václav Havel, he turns to Francis and Francis's ability to participate in and associate (internally and communally, as discussed) through the dynamic of agape.[8]

In Ignatius's autobiography (which he dictated to Juan Alfonso de Polanco at the end of his life and which thus was written in the third person), mending from his cannon ball injury and feeling pensive, he explains that he increasingly realizes that his dreams of romance and chivalry reflect dimensions of immaturity. Excessive personal grooming, a desire for fame, and sexual promiscuity are implicitly recognized in his autobiography as the motivating goals in his life. As he continued to assess goals like these, he felt "dry and dissatisfied."[9] He continued to think of Francis and Dominic, however, and increasingly wanted to emulate their lives and impress others as positively and pervasively.

One biographer challenges his readers to see a profound dynamic at work in the life of Ignatius: "Within his soul there was a force that pressed him to go beyond himself. Of course, a person can be easily deceived by the illusion of wanting to be a saint, because romanticizing about sanctity is a most pleasing experience; however, a conceptual or aesthetic brand of narcissism does not always have the power to change us."[10]

Also, it should be noted that Ignatius's autobiography describes the serious and personal work—in a medieval milieu—of self-reflection taking place: "Interrupting his reading, he sometimes stopped to think about the things he had read. . . . Thus, he pondered over many things that he found good."[11]

Ignatius's personal conversion in 1521, then, well depicts the seeds of what would flourish as the Society of Jesus, the Jesuits. Moreover, events in the years to follow—such as his time spent in the Spanish Benedictine monastery of Our Lady of Montserrat, a longer period living in a cave in nearby Manresa on the Cardoner River, and a pilgrimage to Jerusalem—influence the ways he regards his own sense of self, and how he interacts with others, his writings, his spiritual life, and later decisions about the Jesuit order. Moreover, almost as soon as he left behind his chivalric life, he was genuinely regarded as a pilgrim—not only for walking so much of Europe then and in the years to follow but also for representing, and eventually promulgating in his writings, a modern sensibility of interiority. For instance, he offered tools for naming and evaluating personal desires, discerning life options, and appreciating and renewing sources of joy and excitement. This internal focus helped instantiate habits of reflection and inquiry, which represent the searching dispositions of pilgrim hearts, minds, and souls.[12]

For my theories, however, Jean Lacouture offers an important insight. He does not disregard the convalescence and the consequent change-of-life, nor the travels and encounters that follow, but he indicates that the real conversion in Ignatius's life, the major turning point, took place when, in 1524, he decided to study.[13] The decision to do so seems to have been sparked by a mere inclination, but it also represented a practical assessment by Ignatius to better actualize his own desire to speak and preach publicly, and, generally, to enhance his influence on others with both skills and proper ecclesial credentials.[14] But something else was also at work.

Ignatius's early convalescent-conversion hope of staying in Jerusalem for the rest of his life had deteriorated. Not long after arriving in a city geographically and historically significant to many of the world's major religions, let alone his, he was evicted from the locale by wardens of the Christian sites and monuments. The charge against him was religious zealotry. Disallowed to remain in the Holy Land, Ignatius went back to Europe, returning to the continent at the Italian port of Venice, from which he immediately departed for Spain. In Barcelona, where he was able to receive patronage, he enrolled in a school to study basic grammar. Two years later, he moved to Alcalá, where, at the historic university there, he studied, though reportedly haphazardly, a problem representative not of his habits but of the modus Italicus (an educational model to be discussed shortly). In Alcalá he also lived with and assisted infirmed patients in their daily routines. Scuffles with authorities of the Roman Catholic Church throughout the Spanish Inquisition propelled him on to Salamanca to another prominent educational institution, the University of Salamanca. There, too, coursework was disorganized, and authorities of the Church were even less accommodating. Frustrated with unstructured schooling and, again, the Inquisition, he left Spain and walked toward France.[15]

Lacouture, convinced that Paris was more profound yet for Ignatius and his worldview, explains that Ignatius, still lame from his battle wound at Pamplona, "limped toward what we now know as humanism."[16] A good education—and the credentials that came with it—was still an important objective of Ignatius, and he knew that the University of Paris was then Europe's best institution of higher learning. The biographer Cándido de Dalmases describes Ignatius's hunch that studies in Paris, per reputation, as well as by experience at Alcalá and Salamanca, would demand seriousness of purpose, offer a meaningful curricular structure, and require a focused discipline for navigating degree requirements.[17] In heading there, however, "our gaunt sack-cloth-clad pilgrim was leaving behind the Middle Ages and entering the new world of the Renaissance."[18]

## MODUS PARISIENSIS

Through a course of seven years, Ignatius formally enrolled in three different colleges of the University of Paris and achieved a bachelor of arts degree in the humanities (1532), a licentiate of arts degree in philosophy (1533), a master of arts degree in philosophy (1534), and credentials in theology (1535). Philippe Lécrivain's recent book, *Paris in the Time of Ignatius of Loyola, 1528–1535* (2011), describes the streets, academic buildings, boarding houses, educational programs, and other resources utilized by Ignatius, including the pedagogical, philosophical, and theological atmospheres of the university and of France generally, and this in comparison with European Christendom around them.

Upon arriving in Paris in 1528, Ignatius enrolled at the Collège de Montaigu—"notoriously harsh," and the alma mater of notables John Calvin, Desiderius Erasmus, and François Rabelais. Ignatius, then thirty-seven, studied his course of elementary humanities side by side with schoolchildren.[19] The school was founded in 1314 by Giles Aicelin de Montaigu, the archbishop of Rouen, and originally named the Collège des Aicelin. Pierre Aicelin de Montaigu inherited patronage for the institution in 1388 and changed its name.[20] The college earned distinction much later, however, through Jan Standonck, who was named schoolmaster in 1483.[21] Standonck rebuilt the school from a state of ruin, implemented programmatic reforms—exceptional in comparison not just with other educational programs in Europe but also with neighboring colleges in Paris themselves—and established thereafter its "rigid and ascetic" reputation.[22] His successor in 1504, Noël Béda, endorsed Standonck's reforms and in 1509 issued new statutes, representing and bolstering a long-practiced educational methodology of repetition and recitation but adding to it new humanist elements. Particularly in its Standonck flavor, Erasmus and Rabelais famously satirized the program in their classic works, respectively, In Praise of Folly (1509) and Pantagruel (1532).[23]

While Ronald Modras refers to the Collège de Montaigu as a "bastion of scholastic intransigence," Lécrivain focuses upon an educational program that was pioneering.[24] For the first time in any college of its kind, students—in accord with Béda's 1509 statutes—were grouped together with others of similar educational experience and knowledge; hence Ignatius's placement with young beginners. Students only advanced to more difficult levels after completing tests and demonstrating mastery of subject matters at hand, a succession at Montaigu that began with Latin grammar and ended in the study and practice of rhetoric.

Moreover, student groupings by ability and experience were further divided into smaller sections of ten. As Montaigu arranged students into appropriate levels of instruction and offered an ascending pattern of advancement, it also introduced a subdividing system of decuriae (ten), whereby students studied and interacted with one another more intentionally. Through the special appointment of one of them as a decurio, some students exercised leadership roles that helped guide their classmates.[25] Besides introducing a system of graduation through examinations, a strategic division of classes, and a student prefect, Montaigu also instituted a note-taking program for personally registering newly learned vocabulary, in particular.[26]

Gabriel Codina looks closely at the Collège de Montaigu in its Standonck-Béda years and notes a decisive influence upon it by the Brethren of the Common Life. A popular fourteenth-century lay Christian spiritual movement of individuals, the members of the Brethren lived commonly and simply in communal settings and devoted their lives to pious practices. Through Standonck, Montaigu offered students a form of religious instruction enjoyed by the Brethren, Devotio Moderna.[27] A trademark feature of the group, Devotio Moderna—or New Devotion—was developed and propagated by the group's founder, Gerard Groote, a graduate of the University of Paris who was a critic of Scholasticism.[28] Groote's method facilitated imaginative practices of scenes from the Christian scriptures. Practitioners were encouraged to vividly imagine scenes in Gospel passages and to engage the teachings, healings, meetings, and such through their own conceptions and sense perceptions. Devotio Moderna offered an imaginative practice that allowed for deeply personal investment but also cultivated a possibility for best imitating Christian living in its original expressions.[29] As Codina notes, affinities between the Brethren and Montaigu through the system of *decuriae*—for instance, the deployment of Devotio Moderna at Montaigu, a practice that originated with the Brethren—was adapted and implemented in a pedagogical context. Students, through an exposure to *pietas litterata*, were encouraged to practice aspects of the Devotio in order to vividly and personally imagine persons and expressions of Christian living, to be inspired by them, and to emulate such examples in their own lives.[30]

Nonetheless, the Scholastic flavor was prominent. In 1509, when Erasmus publishes *The Praise of Folly*, he suspects—like Pier Paolo Vergerio a century and a half before him—that something has gone terribly awry in education. He likewise indicts Scholastic methods and content as the main culprit. He wonders, for instance, what happened with a cultivation of practical knowledge that would help individuals better navigate the tasks and toils of daily life. One scholar suggests that his criticism of Scholasticism can be summarized in three problems: a method of ceaseless questioning, an eventual obsession with esoteric theological analysis, and a lack of correspondence between theological issues and the lives of the theologians asking the questions.[31] Erasmus looks back to Montaigu, to Standonck's Scholastic rigidities of recitation and repetition of questions, and he thinks not of classrooms but of "sweatshops" and "torture chambers" where boys, herded through lessons of Latin diction, cowered under the blows of "rods, switches, and straps" at every slight mispronunciation or grammatical mistake.[32] Criticizing Scholastic grammarians, Erasmus describes that "what makes them [happy] is a certain strange conviction they harbor about their learning. Though in fact most of them pound nothing but sheer nonsense into the boys' heads, still, by all the gods! how they look down their noses even at Palaemon and Donatus," mythical and real classic experts in elocution.[33]

And yet, at the time of Erasmus's writing, the ill-remembered Scholastic intransigence (as characterized by Modras above) was receding. Montaigu, already introducing new educational elements to its program, did indeed maintain an older methodology, but also implemented new elements that structured classrooms accordingly and endeavored to meet the educational needs of students; and offered content that would come to be recognized as distinctly humanist. One source stresses at least one strident humanist dimension. It agrees that Montaigu perpetuated Scholastic problems deplored by Erasmus and Rabelais, but it also explains that, eventually, in their programs of student progression and evaluation, Montaigu and other colleges were exceptionally personal: "The student's progress from one intellectual plateau to the next depended more on the individual's own capacity to learn than on systematic lockstep movement from a lower grade to the higher."[34] An older method and its ability to accommodate new organizational features—including new content, through literature, for instance—impressed Ignatius, as did the significant personal gestures of such a pedagogy.[35]

It is in the next year, however, in a different school, the Collège de Sainte-Barbe, where humanism would impress Ignatius more profoundly. "To get from Montaigu to Sainte-Barbe," Lécrivain explains, "there was just one street to cross, the Rue Saint-Symphorien. But, in reality as in spirit, choosing to study at the latter college was to accept entering, if not into a new world, . . . at least into a universe where there was [even] more openness to innovation."[36] Five of Ignatius's first colleague-friends, who would eventually form the Jesuit order, studied at Sainte-Barbe with him. Likewise, it was at such a school—in "the Barbiste tradition"—at the Collège de Guyenne—where an important Renaissance humanist, Michel de Montaigne, studied.[37]

Historians note that, by 1517, the humanist educational movement that began in Italy through the likes of Vergerio over a hundred years earlier had finally penetrated the Parisian programs, and that the Collège de Sainte-Barbe—where, by Ignatius's time, "a great wind of freedom prevailed"—most readily and fully embraced new curricular perspectives.[38] Allan Farrell explains that "what actually took place at [Sainte-Barbe] was a remodeling of the curriculum in order to make the classics in very fact the foundation of the higher studies."[39] Again, as with Vergerio, Sainte-Barbe refashioned the content of its studies to lessen its concentration upon the study of logic and skillfulness in dialectics and to offer, alternatively, greater contact with ancient Greek and Roman literature and rhetorical expression. Student discourse focused less on argument and more on eloquence. A Vergerian correlation is indeed recognizable. Argument and eloquence were regarded not just for their tenors of speaking but also for the kinds of issues they dwelled upon and the personal and relational perspectives they represented.

The adaptation of humanist perspectives at the University of Paris portrays, on one hand, an older and in many ways resistive medieval mind-set that gave the university its original institutional impetus and, on the other hand, a Renaissance humanist outlook that hoped to both restore ancient sentiments and implement new educational practices. The Jesuit historian John O'Malley, SJ, explains that two institutions, one represented by the medieval university and the other by humanist education instituted per Vergerio's influence at primary and secondary schools, "were confronting and trying to accommodate each other."[40] But another distinction that is more geographical in nature is also telling.

Two educational systems—one in Paris, and the other at work throughout Italy and Spain—imply incentives and intentions of their own. Oppositional in many ways to one another, they are known as the Modus Parisiensis and the Modus Italicus. Respectively, each model points to an originating institutional archetype represented by the University of Paris and the University of Bologna. The respective expectations and authoritative influences of professors and students manifest important distinctions. Paris generally represented a professor-centered educational model, whereas Bologna generally represented a student-centered educational model. For instance, in Italian schools, students invited willing and waiting professors to offer their teachings, and they paid them—if at all—in accord with the services rendered. Students lived and studied without their oversight, and they maintained significant dimensions of power in negotiating their educational needs, which, in the Italian context, prioritized professional training.[41] Hastings Rashdall's monumental work, *The Universities of Europe in the Middle Ages* (1895), cites Bologna and Salerno for preeminence, respectively, in law and medicine.

Paris, conversely, was recognized for theological expertise. In Paris, unlike in the Italian schools, students sought after and paid professors for the learning they offered, and professors themselves, who were much more in control, determined the time, place, and content of their courses. Students would go to their professors for classes, and eventually lived in nearby boarding houses or even on the same premises. A unified expression of this educational style was implemented in 1452, when a more centralized system of authority placed a governing matrix over all the Parisian colleges. Codina explains that "in a sense the whole city functioned as a great school, moving together from the sound of the Angelus in the morning, through to the evening, following the same rhythm of hours, calendar, rules, practices, customs, religious and student celebrations, and general style of life."[42]

The general differences between the Modus Parisiensis and the Modus Italicus are telling. Per the strategies newly implemented by Montaigu and experienced by Ignatius, the Modus Parisiensis offered order, regularity, and discipline, dynamics already quite different than those Ignatius struggled with in the Italian-influenced universities at Alcalá and Salamanca. The Modus Italicus that he knew offered exceptional flexibility for students, regardless of preparedness and experience, to take courses and pursue subjects as desired:[43] "Each [college] set up its own requirements, and the methods of teaching varied in large measure according to the taste and capabilities of individual schoolmasters. What system of teaching there was, consisted of an adaptation of the prevailing . . . practice of holding public lectures open to" any student of any age.[44]

Although programming at the Collège de Montaigu and the Collège de Sainte-Barbe, as well as the lectures on the theology of Thomas Aquinas at the Dominican convent on rue Saint-Jacques, facilitated a decisive Scholastic atmosphere, the humanist hue was bright. More emphatically, Lacouture says that in Ignatius's educational years, "the world grew fast, and humanity stepped to center stage."[45] Ignatius had personally witnessed, explains another, "the final phase of the change from the old to the new education, which was in a sense the translation from Medievalism to the Renaissance."[46] In Ignatius's educational experience at Paris—one that was for him so much better than the initial educational forays at Barcelona, Alcalá, and Salamanca—the Modus Parisiensis was both Scholastic and Renaissance humanist: it was old methods of repetition and recitation; new methods of imagination; fixed and exhaustive schedules; specific placement and gradual ascent; examinations and individualized assessment; the subjects of the *trivium* and *quadrivium* in Ciceronian *studia humanitatis*; and first-century classics and thirteenth-century Aquinas.

The practices of the two prototypes merged to form a new one. Ignatius and those individuals around him who formed the Jesuit order were educated by the best of what Europe then offered. In the generations to follow, they would build an educational enterprise of their own. In doing so they would endorse, imitate, and globally disseminate the Scholastic-Renaissance humanist essence of the Modus Parisiensis.

## DOCUMENTATION AND DISSEMINATION OF JESUIT EDUCATION

Although the opening of the Collegio di San Niccoló in Messina in 1548 is a defining moment for Jesuit education, it is not without precedent. After the official approval of the Society of Jesus in 1540 by Pope Paul III, the Jesuits, one of the first nonmonastic religious orders in the history of the Church, began attracting members in large numbers.[47] Fifteen hundred had joined by the time of Ignatius's death.

From the personal experience of the founders, the Jesuits knew the importance of good education and they looked for ways to similarly educate their own new recruits. Moreover, almost as instantly as the group was formally established, it began its intercontinental mission. Francis Xavier, a roommate of Ignatius at the Collège de Sainte-Barbe beginning in 1529, departed Rome and the European continent less than a year after the order was instituted. His travels to India and Japan and his death on the shores of China (on the island of Sancian) memorialized his name to present-day recognition.

Education was not to be a primary focus of the order, let alone one of its ministries, so Ignatius and his advisers first looked for established programs to use in educating their new members. Sending recruits to Paris was the preferred option, so in 1541 the Jesuits established there, briefly, a residence of Jesuit students (referred to as "Scholastics"). Instability in the city, religious inhospitality at the University of Paris, a lack of funding, and renewed political conflict made the early Jesuits' alma mater unfeasible as a place for establishing a Scholastic residential program. Instead, the Jesuit Scholastics were sent on to Louvain.[48]

Per memories of Ignatius's own experience in Alcalá and Salamanca, the exceptional education of the first Jesuits at Paris—and, after 1540, from experiences with other options—the Jesuits were highly discouraged. In the Modus Italicus, the pedagogy at the University at Padua, where even other Scholastics were sent to study, was particularly disappointing, so Jesuit superiors there and elsewhere began being more selective about existing programs or established ones of their own. In *The First Jesuits* (1993), O'Malley explains that in the early years there were seven institutions for Scholastics, Jesuit college-residences at Alcalá, Coimbra, Cologne, Louvain, Paris (as mentioned), Padua, and Valencia: residences of the order where the Scholastics could study in existing university programs as well as ones within their own quarters.[49] The efforts at Padua led to a description of ideals, rules, and practices in the *Constituciones Collegii Patavini* [*Constitutions of the College of Padua*] (1545) by Juan Alfonso de Polanco. It was one of the first of the Jesuits' own educational treatises and a document that formally endorsed the Modus Parisiensis enjoyed by Ignatius and his colleagues at Montaigu and Sainte-Barbe. It was preceded only by *Fundacion de Colegio* [*Foundations of a College*] (1541), a Spanish-written document instructing the process of establishing the ill-fated program for the new Jesuits who had been sent to Paris.[50]

As the Jesuits became educationally involved with their own new members in programs throughout Europe, they also found themselves at about the same time becoming publicly engaged in schools in Spain, at Gandía, and in India, at Goa. Because of their own educational pedigree, their great appreciation for education, and an interest in educating their new members and others, the early Jesuits began teaching in established schools and offering structure and substance to deficient programs. In Gandía, through the influence and patronage of its duke, Francis Borgia—a close descendent of the infamous Borgia pope, Alexander VI, and soon to be a Jesuit himself—the Jesuits were particularly successful. Progress by the Jesuits there gained the recognition of Paul III, who in 1546 designated the institution at Gandía a *studium generale*, a term authorizing university status. The next year, Paul III issued an exceptional permission to the Jesuit order. His decree, the papal bull *Licet Debitum* (1547), allowed an unparalleled privilege throughout Christendom: any Jesuit, anywhere, was authorized to teach any subject.[51]

The assistance Jesuits offered at Gandía, as well as their educational endeavors in Italy and India, manifested educational agility and interest and propelled the Jesuits, through the invitation of Paul III, to establish the Collegio di San Niccoló. The leader of the small and reportedly talented delegation to Sicily, Jerónimo Nadal, in the same year founded another school in nearby Palermo. In that year and the next one, the Jesuits, moreover, assumed full responsibility for the school they had been assisting in Goa, Saint Paul's College, and started new institutions in Naples and Venice. However, almost as soon as Nadal, also an alumnus of the University of Paris, disembarked in Sicily and took steps to establish San Niccoló at Messina, he composed a new educational document for the order, *Constitutiones Collegii Messanensis [Constitutions of the College of Messina]* (1548). This document is significant because it specifically and officially endorsed the Modus Parisiensis for the Jesuits. This document—"one of the seminal documents in Jesuit education"—also demonstrates direct lineage leading to the development and publication of the definitive 1599 *Ratio Studiorum*.[52]

Nadal wrote the *Constitutiones Collegii Messanensis* in two parts, the first dealing explicitly with the character formation of students, and the second pertaining to academics, such as courses and the like. In the spirit of the Modus Parisiensis, the curriculum offered courses of the *trivium* for younger and beginning students and, for students able and prepared for higher studies, courses of the *quadrivium*.[53] Nadal was already reflecting what would emerge as a system of education in primary, secondary, and tertiary levels. Also, Nadal's ability as a pedagogue and an educational administrator was noted by Ignatius, who requested of Nadal a more comprehensive and detailed educational document—explaining, for instance, the scheduling of classes, effective teaching methods, educational exercises, and useful course materials. Nadal delegated the task of writing the new, more specified treatise to his Jesuit colleague at Messina, Annibal Coudret, who penned *De Ratione Studiorum Collegii Messanensis* [*Plan of Studies for the College at Messina*] (1551). Beyond the administrative details of establishing and running a school, Coudret's document, the first by the Jesuits to be titled a "ratio," perpetuated the Jesuits' interest in a structured and purposeful program concerned with both the individual needs of students and coursework in the humanities.

Knowing the accomplishments of Nadal, Coudret, and their colleagues at Messina, Ignatius—seriously invested in the success of the recently founded Roman College near him, "the darling of his enterprise in education"—used the *De Ratione Studiorum Collegii Messanensis* as an early template in Jesuit education for teachers working in the Roman College (1551) as well as in new Jesuit schools being founded in Germany, France, Portugal, Spain, the Netherlands, Austria, Bohemia, and Poland.[54]

## THE *RATIO STUDIORUM* AND THE ROLE OF "STUDY"

The *Ratio atque Institutio Studiorum Societatis Iesu* [*The Official Plan for Jesuit Education*] (1599) reflects, then, a fifty-year process. As the earlier documents generated by Coudret, Nadal, and Polanco led to its genesis, the publication of *De Ratio et Ordine Studiorum Collegii Romani* [*The Plan and Order of Study of the Roman College*] (1579), commissioned by then–superior general of the order (and former duke of Gandía) Borgia and written by Jesuit Diego de Ledesma, reveals the clearest resemblance of the later definitive *Ratio*. Also referred to as the *Ratio Borgiana*, the nascent 1579 edition, as well as the final 1599 version, hoped to offer a useful and informative pedagogical and administrative matrix for Jesuit education in international dispersion that could at the same time be identifiable with the flagship Jesuit institution in Rome.

O'Malley explains that, at the end of the sixteenth century, "the Jesuits had had enough experience in education to try to codify their methods and ideals, and they did so by producing the famous *Ratio Studiorum*, or plan of studies," a document that offered guidance in establishing and running schools around the world for four hundred years.[55] He refers to it as "a codification of curricular, administrative, and pedagogical principles," which had the ability to assure and sustain proper educational quality in disparate geographical and cultural contexts.[56] Another scholar describes it as a set of job descriptions mirroring the Modus Parisiensis. The core of the document is "none other than a collection of thirty series of rules corresponding to distinct offices, counting no less than 467 articles."[57] Another yet explains that the *Ratio*, "to put it in its simplest term, was a handbook on how to teach . . . first and foremost, the *Ratio* is a manual of practice on how to conduct a class."[58] Finally, and more succinctly, the historian Philip Gleason calls the *Ratio* a document of "exotic nomenclature."[59]

However it is described, George Ganss, SJ, insists that the *Ratio* must be understood from its sixteenth-century context: "In nation upon nation there was a widespread lack of order and plan in education. City upon city had no secondary or higher schools of importance; and in those which existed in other cities, the organization was generally poor."[60] Ganss cites a widespread historical need for educational improvement and, at least on some level, a degree of systematization, so the qualitative aspect of what was being offered cannot be overlooked: "The *Ratio* contains a comprehensive design intended to ensure an immersion into classical culture, mastery of material, quickness of mind, sensitivity to individual ability, and personal discipline."[61]

The educational theorist Robert McClintock, however, offers a substantive insight about the *Ratio*. McClintock agrees with the administrative description of the *Ratio* in establishing schools and in endorsing a method of teaching. He recognizes, however, a recurring educational practice in the *Ratio* that, in his estimation, is not characterized by instruction per se, or specific learning objectives, a pedagogical technique often wrongly associated with the *Ratio*. More personally, the *Ratio* offers a program of "study." McClintock references "study," "a word that recurs over and over" in the *Ratio*, as the treatise's ethos.[62] As the *Ratio* constantly encourages study, it also describes a helpful demeanor for engaging it, its virtuous benefits, its relationship to the common good, and the need, even, to take breaks from it.[63]

As McClintock discusses the personal and communal merits of study, so too he considers the kind of teaching that occurs in such a program; in part, the *Ratio* dictates what seems to be a pedagogy of inspiration.[64] He describes the general style of a Jesuit teacher as "hortatory and heuristic, rather than didactic."[65] Jesuit teachers, O'Malley similarly says, "tried to influence their students more by their example than by their words."[66] In doing so, McClintock explains that the Jesuits, per their *Ratio*—that is, through the kind of studying and teaching it facilitated—encouraged in their students a personally integrating, self-reflective dynamic.

In its humanist regard for character development and virtuous living, and its modern philosophical ability to reflect personally and existentially, study offers a tool for self-formation that can be employed throughout the course of one's life.[67] McClintock explains that "study itself is neither a single path nor the final goal; it is the motivating power by which men form and impose their character upon their role in life. Through study each man reaches out to the resources of nature, faith, and reason, to select from them as best seems to suit his situation and to develop powers by which he can turn the accidents of time, place, and station into a work of achieved intention."[68]

As Erasmus represents McClintock's description of study, McClintock's real hero is Michel de Montaigne, a Renaissance humanist philosopher who, in writing numerous freethinking and self-reflective compositions across a limitless range of topics in his *Essays*, first published in 1580, introduced a decisively modernist philosophical method. We looked at them earlier through Stephen Toulmin's *Cosmopolis* (1990). Recall, Montaigne was a student of the humanist "Barbiste tradition." Here, in regard to McClintock's discussion, Descartes's era-altering focus upon the individual self, and, slightly before him, Montaigne's reflecting and writing, display a philosophically game-changing subjective turn. Montaigne's method—"to assay," as in "to try," demonstrated through the essays—is an exemplary expression of McClintock's study. Montaigne's is a self-exploring, self-empowering, self-determining philosophical activity akin to the ideals of study preserved and promulgated in the Jesuit *Ratio*: "It is a marvel how much of a place this College holds in Christendom; and I believe there never was a brotherhood and body among us that held such a rank, or to sum up, that produced such results as these [Jesuits] will, if their plans continue. . . . [The Jesuits are] a nursery of great men in every sort of greatness."[69]

Aldo Scaglione, author of *The Liberal Arts and the Jesuit College System* (1986), voices a similar comparison. Endorsing McClintock and citing Montaigne, but specifically about the rhetorical dimension of Jesuit humanist pedagogy, Scaglione says that Jesuit education functioned "for the purpose of *Bildung* rather than sheer instruction, formation of the mind and personal character rather than erudition, following what could be referred to as Montaigne's . . . idea of education."[70]

## PART IV OF THE JESUIT *CONSTITUTIONS* AND THE MANDATE TO ADAPT

As Ganss suggests the importance for knowing the historical context of the *Ratio*, one that reveals a generally haphazard and anemic pan-European educational milieu, McClintock points to humanist and modernist philosophic outlooks. But Ganss offers a further encouragement, one that is also reflected in the Erasmus-McClintock conception of study. Ganss reports that the *Ratio* is ancillary to an earlier educational document of the Jesuits, part IV of the *Constitutions of the Society of Jesus*.[71]

In 1547, Ignatius, assisted by his secretary and "autobiographer," Polanco, the author of the treatise for the scholastics' educational program at Padua, commenced an organized formulation of the *Constitutions* (ratified in 1558). Resembling the codes and strictures of the Collège de Montaigu at the University of Paris, it articulates the ideals, structures of governance, and basic rules of the Society of Jesus.[72] Part IV, the educational content of the *Constitutions*, was inspired by Nadal, also an author of earlier educational treatises for the Jesuits. As Nadal had delegated Coudret in 1551 to write the fuller *ratio* of his *constituciones* of the inaugural Messina program, Nadal simultaneously composed *De Studii Generalis Dispositione et Ordine* [*A University or a Studium Generale*], much of which influenced and shaped the composition of part IV.[73] The value of study in forming persons and influencing the common good is discussed, as are encouragements to safeguard study and learning from distractions, such as through spiritual "mortifications," lengthy prayers, time-consuming meditations, and even obligations and activities that entice students away from the work of study.[74] However, Ganss's encouragement to regard the *Constitutions*—"it deserves to rank as a classic of . . . educational philosophy"—as a precursor and foundation of the *Ratio* focuses on a crucial dynamic in part IV, a mandate of *adaptability*.[75] Educational programs and personnel involved in such programs were to be astute about both the particular sociocultural contexts wherein they worked and the students with whom they were working.

Jesuit education, then, established and administered on a global scale by the guidance of the *Ratio Studiorum*, was, per the *Constitutions*, to be mindful and respectful of differing cultures and conditions. Ignatius "was strongly insistent on the adaptability of his regulations to times, places, and persons. Expressions such as 'especially in these times' and 'consideration should be given . . . to persons, times, and places' occur with great frequency" in part IV.[76] Some examples of what this adaptation pertains to include the general implementation of a curriculum, the assessment of individual students, whether Latin should be spoken, the appropriateness of lecturing, and even how and when to do personal study.[77]

However, as the stamp of adaptability demarcates the educational work of the Jesuits, it went further. Howard Gray, SJ, explains that, beyond "part IV," the *Constitutions* as a whole facilitates an "education in attention, reverence, and devotion" for all aspects of life and work.[78] As educational programs were to be culturally and socially pliable, so were the Jesuits themselves. Ignatius, Gray says, "envisioned a group able to work on the frontiers of the Church and even in lands and enterprises that were not part of Christendom. In other words, the work of the Jesuits demanded capability and flexibility, . . . [and specific elements of their training offered] ways to test the ability . . . to live this kind of life."[79]

Not unlike Montaigne's own style of assaying, training and formation for a life as a Jesuit offered (and still does) "experiments," in Jesuit parlance, which assessed and stretched the emotional, intellectual, and spiritual plasticity of its members. An experience generally through the course of a month (mostly in silence) of the *Spiritual Exercises*, a residential assignment to a care facility to physically help patients or residents with daily needs, and an intentional period of traveling or journeying represent, respectively, the "long retreat," the "hospital experiment," and the "pilgrimage," each assayed Jesuits in special ways.

In many ways, Terence voices an apropos humanist sentiment: "Nothing human is foreign to me."[80] The *Constitutions* instruct that "a deep and authentic involvement with . . . local culture should be fostered, according to regional differences, by sharing the life and experiences . . . and by trying to understand . . . cultures from within."[81] Contemporary translations of Terence reference the inappropriateness of harboring the prejudices of "nationalisms" or "particularisms" that mitigate an "openness toward different forms of cultures, diverse citizens, and differing mentalities."[82] The historian Kathleen Mahoney, author of *Catholic Higher Education in Protestant America: The Jesuits and Harvard in the Age of the University* (2003), remarks that the "balance struck between the structure of the *Ratio Studiorum* and the flexibility encouraged by the *Constitutions* served the peripatetic Jesuits immensely well, whether in the courts of China, the jungles of Latin America, or frontier outposts along the Mississippi."[83] But another nod toward Montaigne is necessary, especially per the ancient adage of Terence.

As McClintock explains an important affinity between Montaigne and Jesuit education through the dynamic of study, its inward focus attests to an outward variant. As practices of introspection, reflection, and discernment explore and befriend dimensions of subjectivity, students are more genuinely curious and interested in the world around them. This is partly what Bernard Lonergan tries to convey about the connection between the self and the social. Montaigne's *Travel Journal* (1581) shows him tasting foods and enjoying and questioning the conventions and customs of foreign contexts, and his essay "Of Cannibals" (1580) unmasks a commonplace attitude toward difference and his own alternative disposition: "Each man calls barbarism whatever is not his own practice; for indeed it seems we have no other test of truth and reason than the example and pattern of the opinions and customs of the country we live in."[84]

Cognizant of the need to be malleable and accommodating in foreign contexts, Gray dwells upon the dimension of personal experience in Jesuit education. To make his case, he cites not only the *Constitutions* and other writings, such as Ignatius's *Spiritual Exercises* (1548), but also Ignatius's actual life—the accident in Pamplona, his convalescence, his failure in Jerusalem, his studies in Paris—to amplify an astute regard in all things Jesuit for what it means to adjust and acclimatize oneself geographically, culturally, intellectually, and spiritually. Farrell is even more emphatic, citing the "exigencies of circumstance" and Ignatius's ability to respond in effective and productive ways as a notable personal skill.[85]

In the realm of education, Joseph Daoust says, "Experience, both personal and of one's society and culture, is to be taken seriously as the starting point of [Jesuit] education."[86] But Ganss's point—recognized at least implicitly by McClintock's description of study in the *Ratio*—is the profoundly personal, cultural, and historical adaptability of Jesuit education itself, an adaptability that precedes and informs the understanding and implementation of the infamously codified *Ratio Studiorum*. In curricular terms, the humanist coursework prescribed by the *Ratio* for Jesuit schools cannot be "a static block of contents, but rather . . . a structured, engaged, dynamic, content-rich process involving the personalities of the teachers and the students."[87] Claude Pavur argues that the *Ratio*—a four-hundred-year-old document generally considered long outdated and, at times in the history of Jesuit education, restrictive and even arresting of the tradition itself—is in fact timely. Educators today, he laments, "have lost the skill of constructing a humanist curriculum architectonically."[88]

## THE IGNATIAN *SPIRITUAL EXERCISES*

Pavur is particularly helpful in comparing the *Ratio* with Ignatius's *Spiritual Exercises*. Written in the aftermath of his conversion and partly inspired by the reading of Ludolph of Saxony's *Vita Christi* at the time of his convalescence, the *Exercises* was generally a work in progress during the Paris years and a bit after, but was not published until 1548. Even in its earliest form, however, the insights of the *Exercises* were preached and taught publicly and privately by Ignatius and his increasing numbers of companions during his time in Paris (1528–35). It is the *Exercises* that often attracted individuals—such as the colleagues at Paris—to join Ignatius and the emerging organization. It is also the contents of the *Exercises* that drew the ire of the Spanish Inquisition during Ignatius's brief stays in Alcalá and Salamanca, and kept eyebrows raised even in Paris.

The Jesuit John O'Malley calls the *Spiritual Exercises* "one of the world's most famous books . . . in that category one of the least read and least well understood."[89] The psychoanalyst Carl Jung compares it with yoga and alchemy as one of three benchmark advances in the history of individuation and imagination.[90] Albert Hyma describes it is the culminating gesture of the Christian Renaissance, a humanist movement whose origins Hyma locates in Groote and his Brethren of the Common Life and that later flourishes through institutions like the Collège de Montaigu.[91] Pierre Hadot describes its essence as resembling the spiritual exercises practiced in ancient Greece by the early schools of philosophy.[92]

One clear example of Hadot's association to antiquity is through an imaginative exercise in Ignatius's work that cultivates a cosmic vision of reality, what Hadot refers to as "a view from above." Such a perspective, he explains, "leads us to consider the whole of human reality, in all its social, geographical, and emotional aspects, as an anonymous, swarming mass, and it teaches us to relocate human existence within the immeasurable dimensions of the cosmos."[93] Hadot further argues that the epic poetry of Homer offers views of the world through the eyes of the gods "who look down upon mankind's battles and passions from the heights of the heavens of the mountaintops, without, however, being able to resist the temptation of intervening from time to time on behalf of one or the other."[94] Plato, as well as Cicero, Lucretius, Seneca, Marcus Aurelius, and Lucian—men known as Cynics, Epicureans, or Stoics—have their own versions of the view from above, and they also deal with impulses to intervene in positive and constructive ways for societies and persons.[95] Ignatius provides his through the Trinitarian gaze upon the world, an especially imaginative meditation that lets the practitioner of Ignatius's *Exercises* see the world and, more pointedly, its inhabitants—"the old and the young, the rich and the poor, the happy and the sad, some being born and some being laid to rest"—from the cosmic vantage of the divine life (a trinity) of the Christian God.[96] And as with the Homeric epics, as well as with the ancient philosophical ways, one is impelled to intervene in a certain manner.[97]

Ignatius's *Spiritual Exercises*, more basically, is a manual of meditations offered in the forms of prayers, instructions, rules, scripture, and specific scenes from the life of Jesus that invite a deeply personal assessment of one's own life, a process of discernment regarding options and possibilities, an opportunity for making a choice of existential import, and the cultivation of a graced worldview. Philip Endean describes the work as decisively modern. Let alone the sixteenth-century ability to write, print, and disseminate treatises, the dimensions of interiority and autonomy in Ignatius's work (recall

Jung's historic designation of the *Exercises* as well as Ignatius's own abilities to reflect deeply about his own life during his convalescence) exude both a modern philosophical milieu ready to explore aspects of subjectivity and a Renaissance humanist regard for personal growth.[98]

The humanist aspect, furthermore—an essential ingredient of curricula in Jesuit education—is salient in the *Exercises* in its existential thrust. As Renaissance humanist educators focused more on the realities and complexities of daily life by turning educational efforts away from speculative truths to the real concerns of life, fifteenth-century humanists were cultivating the dynamism of the *Spiritual Exercises* crafted by Ignatius. Like humanists, the *Exercises* essentially ask, "How ought I live my life?"[99] But the introspection and consequent decisions that may occur propel the practitioner beyond the specific concerns of her or his individual life to the conditions of the lives of others. As personal and existential as the meditations of the *Exercises* are, Gray laments how they have been disregarded as individualistic and isolating, and challenges scholars to recognize that the overall experience is "relentlessly oriented to the life one lives outside of solitude—in the arena of public life, to the future."[100] The authors of *The Jesuit Mystique* (1995) agree: "That spirit of discernment, which in effect means the capacity to see with lucid self-knowledge what is necessary to be done, is not a rarefied spiritual skill. It is not cultivated in isolation from human commerce; it is refined with involvement in the all-too-human world of muck, muddle, and misery. It is a practical skill, a way of being in the world."[101]

Such engagement of the world is what Daoust refers to as the "Ignatian Educational Paradigm," a dynamic in the humanist tradition that hopes for a strong connection between a sense of personal eloquence and one's surroundings.[102] Dimensions of subjectivity and social engagement echo the Ciceronian ideal of individual virtuosity and communal investment, but the Jesuit expressions testify to more intimacy and intensity. Spiritual discernment and the Montaigne-McClintock dynamic of study burrow further into a self who cannot *not* be willing and able to positively engage the surrounding world.

Pavur's comparison of the *Ratio* and the *Exercises* cites six points of congruence, intersections that not only teach us more about the two documents themselves but also reinforce a humanist ethos of the Jesuit order. First, each treatise is noticeably pedagogical. For example, specific activities are prescribed. The *Ratio* stipulates of students a repetition of prose in a classroom context. The *Exercises* specifies for practitioners an imagination of a Gospel scene. Repetition was regarded by Ignatius as a strategy not for memorizing content and mechanically repeating it but for interiorizing it and being informed by it. Second, in the spirit of the Modus Parisiensis, both offer a program of advancement, that is, moving through culminating stages to a better, more informed, and enlightened place. Third, each document provides structures that are user friendly, ones that can be adapted personally. Educational practices in the *Ratio* and prayers in the *Exercises* can and even should be self-stylized. Fourth, both documents are highly detailed, offering lengthy descriptions for preparing for an examination or for doing a meditation. Fifth, in the spirit of Renaissance humanism, each facilitates a genuinely personal experience that necessitates an appropriation of insights and a corresponding response. Again, the *Ratio* and the *Exercises* lead toward existential realities that encourage practitioners to make important decisions about their lives. Finally, both are intentional of a "radically open disposition to God."[103] This sixth aspect is significant in that it cultivates a certain worldview. It is also an essential orientation of Taylor's fullness, and an expression of its ontic commitment.

About this religious dimension, Paul Crowley explains, "Ignatian spirituality, classically rooted in the *Spiritual Exercises* of St. Ignatius of Loyola, is an approach to transcendence rooted in a staunch incarnationalism . . . shot through with a certain hopefulness about the human project."[104] Such hope for persons—manifested educationally and spiritually in the Jesuit perspective—deeply troubles philosophers and theologians of a different ilk, and represents a fundamental anthropological difference. At this juncture, however, the Jesuit hope for persons and their potentials partly represents the impulsion in Jesuit education for Ciceronian eloquence, an ideal the Jesuits refer to in the *Ratio* as *eloquentia perfecta*.[105]

## *ELOQUENTIA PERFECTA*

Per Cicero, *eloquentia* was represented by the combined realities of rhetorical ability and moral character. Again, it was reflected in Cicero's definition of the orator, "*vir bonus dicendi peritus*," that is, "the better man speaking skillfully."[106] An individual's life was indistinguishable from tangible communal concerns. The Renaissance humanists' return to the ancient sources in general reflects the operative humanist sentiment that "good literature produces good citizens."[107] Cicero's own deployment of the *septem artes liberales*, his *studia humanitatis*, however, manifested a synthetic and unified educational approach that had been unbalanced and fragmented by medieval-era professionalism. The scholastic disconnect between theologians and their lives was evidence of this, but so too was the obsessive focus upon singular expressions of the arts, an exploitation of any of them—dialectics, namely, for theologians—into disciplines.

The culture of eloquence in the Jesuit system reflected Cicero's own three principles of rhetoric: teaching, delighting, and moving. These—respectively, *docere, delectare,* and *movere*—were deployed in the Jesuit system through, again, the methods of the Modus Parisiensis, and manifested a unique educational atmosphere.[108] Inspired by Ciceronian virtuosity and the Ciceronian curriculum—and further motivated by Renaissance humanists such as Vergerio, who shifted his educational efforts to Ciceronian ideals—the Jesuits desired to educate the whole person. *Eloquentia perfecta* is thereby a holistic educational ideal about bodily health, the intellect, self-expression, aesthetic and emotional faculties, and the spiritual yearnings of individuals who are socially concerned.[109] Ciceronian rhetoric helped frame this inasmuch as it maintained the Ciceronian ideal of an integrated *studia humanitatis*. As Gerald McKevitt notes, "Mastery of *eloquentia perfecta,* or articulate wisdom, meant not merely the ability to communicate with ease and elegance, but 'the capacity to reason, to feel, to express oneself and to act, harmonizing virtue with learning.'"[110] Mahoney reinforces this ideal in curricular discourse, explaining that the subject matters of the *studia humanitatis* "were brought together at a given point . . . under a particularly disciplinary umbrella, such that they reinforced and complemented one another; for example, in the development of 'perfect eloquence.'"[111]

A renaissance of an integrated *studia humanitatis* as well as an interest in cultivating the humanity of their students necessitated active and personally engaging educational exercises: "Orations had to be delivered, not just studied; poetry had to be recited, not just read; plays had to be staged, [and] . . . with plays came music and dance."[112] Modras reports that Jesuit education originated and institutionalized the student pageant.[113] In studying, memorizing, reciting, imagining, acting, singing, dancing, and praying, students were striving toward an *eloquentia perfecta.* But their educational activities reflect the efforts of their Jesuit teachers, who were writing scores, scripts, and lyrics, staging and directing productions—which necessitated even more artful efforts of students and teachers, such as set designers, makeup artists, and costume tailors—which took place both in the schools and in public squares.[114]

The expression of Ciceronian rhetoric was systematic in the Jesuit order as a whole. In *Jesuit Political Thought: The Society of Jesus and the State, c. 1540–1630* (2004), Harro Höpfl says that in all their efforts, Jesuits were widely eloquent: "Colleges, churches, and residences were built to impress. A concern with persuasiveness and presentability is evident throughout [their] organization."[115] An ethos of *eloquentia perfecta* as such, Jodi Loach insists, "brought about a cultural revolution."[116] Ganss indicates the hospitality in the schools for students from across a wide spectrum of socioeconomic classes, and he emphasizes that they benefited by possibilities for upward mobility.[117] Loach, however, is interested in a force of personal and social striving toward greatness—"*magis*" in the Jesuit lexicon, and a Latin root of greatness—which, according to her, was an ideal of the Jesuits that was prevalent in the schools in particular and resulted in an undermining of social hierarchies around Europe: "A spirit of emulation favoured the emergence of an elite at once studious and pious."[118]

From the seventh chapter of the first book of Cicero's *De Officiis* (44 BCE), Jesuit educators over the centuries loved to quote Cicero's Platonic inspired insight, "*Non nobis solum nati sumus*," that is, "We are not born for ourselves alone."[119] It represented for them their educational superlative of *eloquentia perfecta*. Two important characteristics, *pietas* and *Christianitas*, framed and bolstered the ideal.

Being pious was not only and specifically a religious expression but also a personal virtue of originary Greek and Roman humanism, as classic (and Latinized) *pietas*.[120] That is, it was not what is today regarded as piety, the act of being obsequious, or exceptionally reverent, or prayerful. Daoust points to Virgil's pious Aeneas in the *Aeneid* (c. 19 BCE) as a worthy example, a piety that Nicholas Mosley discusses in Homeric terms, a state of character, a virtue, or a person imbued with the ancient Greek conceptions of arête discussed above.[121]

*Pietas* in ancient antiquity, and later with the Jesuits, is to be recognized not in its limited contemporary conceptions of ritualism and demeanor but for its character-in-community formation, the cultivation of an upright individual who is socially concerned. Nadal, the founder of San Niccoló at Messina and in many ways the first pedagogue of the Jesuit order, prioritized *pietas* in his educational tracts as the highest objective of Jesuit education.[122] For the Jesuits, it offered an ideal that was comprehensive of the humanist elements in their educational programming and was also reflective of the order's religious sensibility. Integrated with upright character and social concern were aspects of Christian faith and a corresponding worldview. The instillation in one's life of *pietas*—a mature, virtuous, socially concerned, and religious self—manifested as *Christianitas*, that is, a way of being Christian.

Being Christian was an essential ingredient of Renaissance humanism. For Erasmus, Christ was *eloquentia perfecta*.[123] And even before Erasmus, Vergerio and the other early Renaissance humanist pedagogues were themselves Christian. It was their Christian humanism that sparked the Renaissance, and inspired the Jesuits. The use of literature in their schools showcased *pietas*

*litterata,* ancient Greek and Roman and early Christian writings that featured moral comport and social impact. From Ignatius's own experience of
Groote's *Devotio Moderna* at Montaigu, his Saxony-inspired *Exercises,* and a
modern regard for personal discernment, the Jesuits activated and enhanced
their students' imaginations of *pietas-in-Christianitas,* a Jesuit variant of the
individual-in-community. In Renaissance humanist sensitivity, Mahoney
explains that the "Jesuits expended their energies molding students into virtuous, lettered, Christian gentlemen who would contribute to the good of
society as leading citizens; . . . [the Jesuit's] endeavors were rendered *ad civi-
tatis utilitatem*—for the sake of the city."[124]

Students were encouraged to be imaginative, with high ideals, but they
could actually practice *Christianitas* in their schooling. Organizational units
known as "confraternities"—almost a fifteenth-century version of current
community engagement programs—facilitated reflection upon charitable
virtues and actual social engagement. It was a form of praxis. In essence,
students were able to join extracurricular activities that participated in particular social service projects in the local community. It was these "Marian
sodalities"—Jesuit-sponsored groupings not just of students but also of members of the greater community in groups of their own, such as associations of
artisans, merchants, and professionals—that helped exact the seventeenth-
century social revolution Loach recognizes.[125]

The Jesuits themselves were encouraged to reveal *Christianitas* in their
teaching, offering special care and concern for students. As O'Malley ob-
serves, "They repeatedly inculcated in one another the importance of loving
their students, of knowing them as individuals, of enjoying a respectful *familiaritas* with them."[126] This *familiaritas* in the educational context echoed an
instruction in the Jesuits' *Constitutions* to practice *cura personalis* within their
own context, that is, within the governing structures of the order. The expression of personal care that was to be afforded each member of the expanded
international organization influenced the works and projects of the organization, particularly in its educational endeavors.

According to their own educational documents, for instance, through
the personal elements of "study" and adaptability, the methods of the Modus
Parisiensis and the contents of the liberal artisan social action groups, and in
a style of teaching, the Jesuits—using *pietas* and *Christianitas* as archetypes—
framed the prospects of a good life. A gesture to one of Vergerio's Renaissance
humanist colleagues is helpful in recognizing anthropological assumptions
and the context of *eloquentia perfecta.* Giovanni Pico della Mirandola exudes
an existential flair—"thou mayest fashion thyself in whatever shape thou shalt
prefer"—in his *Oration on the Dignity of Man* (1486).[127] Bidding his audience

to recall "Delphic precepts" of self-knowing as well as the classical education of the seven liberal arts—that is, the philosophical and humanist traditions—Pico encourages individuals beyond limited socioreligious expectations of human life to a greatness—again, from Jesuit diction, a *magis*—of which each and all are worthy: "Let a certain . . . ambition invade your souls, so that, not content with the mediocre, we shall pant after the highest and (since we may wish) toil with all our strength to obtain it."[128]

One scholar interprets Pico as having a regard for "an especial and unprecedented potency in human life toward self and social transformation."[129] It was a hopefulness not unlike Vergerio's, who, in his letter, reminds us that "every period of life has the capacity to yield something splendid."[130] Evidenced in the *Constitutions*, Ignatius himself knew and embraced such hopefulness, echoing Pico's *Oration* in particular.[131] Jesuit education, in turn, was in many of its aspects reflective of a dignified, hope-filled Christian anthropology.[132] Again, the Jesuits expressed an excitement for what and who their students were and could be. About humanity, Jesuits were hopeful.

## SANGUINITY AND SUPPRESSION

Because of such hopefulness, Blaise Pascal hated the Jesuits. There were other reasons, too. Polymathic and notable for accomplishments in philosophy, mathematics, physics, and theology, Pascal was also a Jansenist, a member of a morally rigorous sect of Roman Catholicism. Popular in France in his day, Jansenism—named in reference to the early-seventeenth-century Dutch theologian, Cornelius Jansen—preached and taught that humans are morally weak and depraved. The pessimistic regard for the human condition was fueled by the Christian doctrine of original sin, especially through the influence and, within Roman Catholic thinking, the high stature, of Augustine of Hippo. Jansenist teaching, which was condemned at the time of Pascal, insisted that human nature was fundamentally corrupt and in constant need of divine intervention. The convent of Port-Royal in Paris served as the headquarters of Jansenist thought, and the movement's suspicious sentiments about human nature were propagated throughout France in a network of Port-Royal schools, the Petites Écoles de Port-Royal, of which Jean Racine—who eventually severed any association with the schools—is a notable alumnus.[133]

Pascal's contentions with the Jesuits—famously voiced in his *Lettres Provinciales* (1657), an apologetic for Jansenism—is recognizable through both the basic anthropological and theological principles of the Jansenists and their schools. In many ways the Petites Écoles de Port-Royal in France were alternatives to the Jesuit system. Although both established curricula in the classics of Renaissance humanism, the Port-Royal schools focused less upon the strictures, guidelines, and scholastic overtones of the Modus Parisiensis. They also offered instruction not in Latin, but in the vernacular, French.[134] The schools tried to cultivate a different atmosphere. They were not necessarily more leisurely, but they afforded students both more independence and more personalized attention. Also, as the Jesuit schools were writing dramas and staging productions, the Port-Royal educators condemned theater.[135]

It would be unfair to caricature the Jesuit *Ratio* and the global network of Jesuit schools as an impersonal educational bureaucracy and the Port-Royal schools as quaint countryside seminars in humanism, but the images lend themselves to ideological descriptions perpetuated by the different traditions. Pascal's posthumously published *Pensées* (1669) may indeed reflect the genuine humanist sentiments of such schools. The success of the Port-Royal schools, however, was impeded by the Roman Catholic Church's 1653 condemnation of Jansen's teaching and, not long thereafter, was extinguished by a consequent breakup of the Port-Royal network.

Pascal found the Jesuits to be morally lax and charged that they offered Roman Catholic penitents easy absolution from their sins.[136] If the Port-Royal schools were less regimented and freer, ironically, their general code of conduct, penances, asceticisms, and the religious rituals of their daily life were not. Pascal, whose sister professed her life as a nun in a Port-Royal convent, indicted the Jesuits for practicing casuistry, which, according to the Jansenist critique, was an analytical tool for reasoning away personal culpability and corresponding consequences. As much as the Jesuits truly adapted and appropriated their teaching—"to persons, times, and places"—in accord with the ideals of their *Constitutions* and *Spiritual Exercises*, this may well have been one of its expressions. Recognizing the complexities of life and the unique contexts of individual persons in distinctive situations, the Jesuits did indeed seem reluctant to condemn people for their struggles. Instead, they counseled people to engage personal problems constructively and urged individuals to keep living. It was another expression of the pilgrim orientation of the Jesuits: "The consequences for Jesuit moral advice were enormous. Because no one was irrevocably lost, because free will had a role in leading people toward or away from [the bad], there was ... room to be charitable and consolatory during an individual's moral off seasons—not in the absurd ways mentioned by Pascal, but in such a way as to sustain a person's sense of dignity and hope."[137] Such esteem and hope for the people they encountered represented a dignified anthropocentrism, and it infiltrated the Jesuit order. Their educational enterprise was not excepted.

I mentioned above that Ignatius was regarded as a pilgrim. It was an image and an ethos he himself cultivated in the order.[138] Terence's mantra, "Nothing human is foreign to me"—cited above in the context of adapting to "persons, times, and places" in part IV of the Jesuit's *Constitutions*—helps in characterizing a corresponding individual and institutional orientation. Nadal had claimed that a highway rather than a house was a worthy symbol of the Jesuits.[139] In his writings, he reminded his Jesuit colleagues that they were not monks who lived quiet lives removed from the world, but that the world itself was their house.[140] This was a scandalous reality in Christendom, one that liberated the members of a Catholic religious order from a traditional model of consecrated religious life, one that had never *not* been regimented by the common prayer of the divine office, as mentioned above. As Jonathan Wright notes, Catholics and non-Catholics alike did not know how to categorize this nonmonastic entity: "[Ignatius's] scoundrels . . . 'left the shade of ancient sloth and inactivity, in which the other monks grow gray,' and '[came] forth to engage in toils.' It seemed to some as if Jesuits were not quite regular clergy—like those monks who lived in cloistered communities and chanted matins, lauds, and vespers together—and not quite members of the secular clergy, such as parish priests."[141]

Kathleen Mahoney appreciates Nadal's metaphor of the world as a place of home and reinforces it with the "pilgrim" distinction that was associated with Ignatius and, consequently, the Jesuit organization itself: "The Jesuits . . . caught up in the Age of Discovery, radically reconceptualized the spatial dimensions of religious life, claiming the entire world as their 'house' and the journey itself as a constitutive element of their mission and communal life."[142]

Wright explains that the order "was known for its willingness to adapt to certain aspects of foreign cultures. . . . Measured cultural assimilation . . . was to be found in virtually every Jesuit mission field."[143] Again, recognizing Montaigne's own inquisitive and interested travels, though limited, and his assessment of foreign cultures in, respectively, *Travel Journal* and "Of Cannibals," are helpful. With the Jesuits, however, Wright describes an interest and ability in learning the customs of other peoples and explains that the Jesuits demonstrated efforts for learning and for preserving foreign languages. Mahoney claims that an "openness to the world and cultures . . . was recognized by contemporaries and historians as quintessentially Jesuit and essential to their resounding success as a religious order."[144] Their own *Constitutions* instruct that they are to learn "local" languages.[145] The Jesuits thus wrote dictionaries of the French-Huron and Latin-Persian-Annamese languages; they constructed grammars in Latin American Tupi and Guarani; and they conducted scholarship in Indian Sanskrit, Tamil, and Telugu.[146]

The Italian *paisano* Jesuits Matteo Ricci and Roberto de Nobili are paradigmatic characters of such inculturation. They gained honorable and unprecedented statuses in highly protected and revered political and religious
regimes. Ricci, who was for Taylor an important prototype, was allowed to
become a Confucian literato of the Ming Dynasty; and de Nobili, in Madurai, was permitted to live the life of a Hindu sannyasi of the Brahmin caste.[147]
Mahoney's characterization of such an outlook is long but helpful. She offers
a description of a Jesuit ideal and includes within it the dimension of adaptability that is espoused in treatises of the society:

> What the Jesuits of the sixteenth and seventeenth centuries under-
> stood more thoroughly than other religious orders was the impor-
> tance of adapting their ways to the specific places in which they were
> working. Other religious orders sometimes limited their efficacy as
> missionaries by insisting that non-Europeans adopt European ways,
> without themselves adapting to local cultural norms. In contrast, the
> Jesuits learned native languages, read indigenous literature, donned
> native dress, and adopted local customs, sometimes struggling against
> the temptation of going, "too native."[148]

Like other Jesuits throughout Europe and around the world in general,
respectively, Ricci and de Nobili wrote detailed letters about the people,
customs, and geographies from their headquarters in Bejing and Madurai.
Letter writing, in fact, was a Jesuit requisite. In the lifetime of Ignatius alone,
nearly seven thousand letters came and went from his administration in
Rome, most of which have been collated in a twelve-volume set, the *Mon-
umenta Historica Societatis Iesu* (1894), and long enjoyed as an important
window for historically appreciating the Renaissance.[149] Even at the time
they were written, the Jesuits' correspondences were highly instructive, as
were their travels: "Europe learned about the world and the world learned
about Europe."[150]

That the Jesuits harnessed political powers on the European continent
and abroad, that they religiously colonized foreign cultures, that their own
*Ratio Studiorum* bureaucratized and even dehumanized education, and that
they themselves failed their own ideals individually and corporately are
significant parts of the story and subjects for a future publication. Wright's
book, *God's Soldiers: Adventure, Politics, Intrigue, and Power—A History of the
Jesuits* (2004), is not unbalanced. It cites criticisms about the Jesuit order,
showcasing, for instance, openly professed enemies and their concerns—John
Donne, Voltaire, Pascal, Thomas Jefferson, and Napoleon—as well as the

Jesuits' institutional missteps. It is also hagiographic, and thus champions the achievements and distinctions of Ignatius and his organization.

At the end of the book, however, Wright offers a compelling argument. He ponders the 1773 worldwide suppression of the order by Pope Clement XIV, a complicated international process not disconnected from the Jansenist controversy a hundred years earlier or the Jesuits' widespread efforts to adapt to foreign culture and assimilate religious symbols and gestures.[151] Given that there is truth to allegations of Jesuit collusion in power and prestige in many places, Wright challenges readers to see the 1773 (temporary) demise of the order, and the consequent eradication of its hundreds of schools and libraries—"a quarter of a million students forced to make other arrangements"—as symptomatic of a dynamic far bigger than the Jesuits.[152] Their suppression is not, for Wright, simply a decisive, isolated moment reflective of the Jesuit order itself, but also revealing of a long, complex development that benchmarks, with the 1773 suppression, a significant moment in the history of Western secularism.[153] This major blow to a global Christian superpower would emerge in other expressions of conflict and the struggle for influence and power between secular and religious entities over the next couple hundred years.

## CONCLUSION

I have discussed the tradition of Jesuit education from the perspective of its myriad origins, such as the life of the founder and, more particularly, his educational experiences. These experiences attest to specific Scholastic structures of schooling and Renaissance humanist curricular developments at the University of Paris. They demonstrate a waning medieval mind-set and a burgeoning modernity.

The *Ratio Studiorum* is important for obvious reasons, but especially so in its Montaigne-like assaying dynamic of study; its capacity to adapt to times, places, and persons; and its affinities to the *Spiritual Exercises*. Though the *Exercises* manifests a modern sensitivity of subjectivity and interiority, the work also offers exercises in social assessment and engagement akin to ancient Greek spiritual exercises.

Further, the culmination of Ciceronian eloquence as Jesuit *eloquentia perfecta*—an ideal understood through the humanist conceptions of *pietas*, *Christianitas*, and *familiaritas*—reinforces the pedagogical context of the Jesuit educators. Recognizing an imprint of Pico's *Oration on the Dignity of Man*, these reveal a hopeful existential orientation in Jesuit education for humanity, an orientation with philosophical-anthropological assumptions and a corresponding social regard. Finally, by contextualizing both a sense of Jesuit educational hopefulness—sanguinity—and the suppression of the Jesuits, we find a clearer sense of their goals and the theological and geopolitical realities of the day. This sanguinity is countered by Pascal's Augustinian-influenced sense of human depravity, and the suppression is recognized as an expression of Western secularism.

At the end of this lengthy chapter, allow me, however, to also offer a recapitulation of the specific pedagogical practices of the Jesuit tradition. Of the nearly seven thousand letters that passed in and out of Rome during the course of Ignatius's life, one letter, commissioned by Ignatius to the Spanish Jesuit Antonio Araoz, discussed the fundamentals of Jesuit education.[154] Written by his secretary Polanco at the end 1551—when the flagship educational institution, the Roman College, had been established that year, and when Nadal and Coudret had in the same year written important educational documents, as discussed above—this letter demonstrates that the order itself was becoming increasingly involved in the work of education, that such work would become a priority of the group, and that the results, so far, were not only outstanding but also multifariously excellent, as revealed through the students, the order, and the local communities around the schools. The letter offers a good summary statement of Jesuit educational ideals.

The letter endorses a Renaissance humanist curriculum of a Ciceronian *studia humanitatis* in the methodology of the Modus Parisiensis. It is emphatic in stressing the necessity to provide a humanist foundation for students before offering more specific courses in the professions, and it suggests multiple kinds of activities that can personally engage and educationally activate individual students.

However, because students need to be participatory in a variety of ways, especially through rhetorical demonstrations, they also need to study, an important pedagogical expression highlighted by McClintock. Study is not merely a strategy for advancement within the school—through, for instance, the graduating structures of the Modus Parisiensis—but is also regarded as a life practice, a process of self-development that is ongoing. In fact, the educational experience as a whole virtuously shapes and guides the student for life. In its global scale and outreach, the Jesuit tradition is known for its immediate educational objectives and for how it informs the continual process of life. And this education itself is a continual process.

Through his secretary, Polanco, Ignatius explicitly mentions that the order itself will also be significantly influenced. The teaching profession will continue to enhance the learning and growing of the teaching Jesuits themselves, as well as those involved in the work of Jesuit education.

And this, Ignatius dictates, though expensive to offer, is to be freely available. Benefactions can certainly be accepted and even requested, but tuition is not to be an obstacle to anyone. Students of all socioeconomic classes are to be welcomed, but the social concern is broader yet. Ignatius is excited about the way teachers and students alike will immediately engage and influence the surrounding community. The school milieu as a whole is to be socially concerned, and the school is to be seen as a vehicle of social outreach to assist hospitals, shelters, and other venues.

In many ways, Vergerio's feast days continued. Hospitable to all, equitable, morally inspiring, virtuous, personal, and rhetorical, the ingredients of the Saint Jerome's Day banquet were present in his own educational treatise, and through the Jesuit tradition, they gained methodology and global momentum. Institutionalized and systematized by pedagogies at the University of Paris, the early Italian Renaissance evolved from Ciceronian eloquence into an *eloquentia perfecta*. Qualified by the ideals of *familiaritas*, study, *pietas*, and *Christianitas*—that is, a personally invested educational program, possibilities for holistic self-development, a kind of virtuosity, and a social expression—Jesuit *eloquentia perfecta*, in turn, represents a conception of human subjectivity and a corresponding worldview. These components of the self and the social represent the fundamental ethos of the pedagogies of fullness.

## NOTES

1. Bruce A. Kimball, *Orators and Philosophers: A History of the Idea of Liberal Education* (New York: College Entrance Examination Board, 1995), 95.
2. John W. O'Malley, *The First Jesuits* (Cambridge, MA: Harvard University Press, 1993), 16.
3. O'Malley.
4. Cándido de Dalmases, *Ignatius of Loyola: Founder of the Jesuits*, trans. Jerome Aixalá (Saint Louis: Institute of Jesuit Sources, 1985), 39–40.
5. Douglas Letson and Michael Higgins, *The Jesuit Mystique* (Chicago: Jesuit Way, 1995), 3.
6. George E. Ganss, ed., *Ignatius of Loyola: Spiritual Exercises and Selected Works* (New York: Paulist Press, 1991), 14.
7. Dalmases, *Ignatius*, 43.
8. Charles Taylor, *A Secular Age* (Cambridge, MA: Belknap Press of Harvard University Press, 2007), 729.
9. Ignatius of Loyola, *The Autobiography*, in *Ignatius of Loyola: Spiritual Exercises and Selected Works*, trans. Parmananda R. Divarkar and ed. George E. Ganss (New York: Paulist Press, 1991), 71.
10. José Ignacio Tellechea Idígoras, *Ignatius of Loyola: The Pilgrim Saint*, trans. and ed. Cornelius Michael Buckley (Chicago: Loyola University Press, 1994), 123–24.
11. Ignatius, *Autobiography*, 70.

12. The educational philosopher David Hansen explains an educational sensibility of "intellectual, ethical, and aesthetic journeying" right, where one is an ability or orientation that informs my pedagogies of fullness. See David T. Hansen, *The Teacher and the World: A Study of Cosmopolitanism as Education* (New York: Routledge, 2011), 2.

13. Jean Lacouture, *Jesuits: A Multibiography*, trans. Jeremy Leggatt (Washington, DC: Counterpoint, 1995), 5.

14. Idígoras, *Ignatius*, 227.

15. Gabriel Codina, "Modus Parisiensis," in *The Jesuit Ratio Studiorum: 400th Anniversary Perspectives*, ed. Vincent J. Duminuco (New York: Fordham University Press, 2000), 29.

16. Lacouture, *Jesuits*, 4.

17. Dalmases, *Ignatius*, 106.

18. Lacouture, *Jesuits*, 4.

19. Letson and Higgins, *Jesuit Mystique*, 9–10.

20. Hastings Rashdall, *Universities of Europe in the Middle Ages, Vol. I: Salerno, Bologna, Paris* (Cambridge: Cambridge University Press, 2010), 515.

21. Dalmases, *Ignatius*, 108; Albert Hyma, *The Christian Renaissance: A History of the "Devotio Moderna"* (Hamden, CT: Archon Books, 1965), 245.

22. Rashdall, *Universities, Vol. I*, 512; *Vol. II, Pt. I*, 261; *Vol. II, Pt. II*, 663.

23. Dalmases, *Ignatius*, 108.

24. Ronald Modras, *Ignatian Humanism: A Dynamic Spirituality for the 21st Century* (Chicago: Loyola University Press, 2004), 65; Philippe Lécrivain, *Paris in the Time of Ignatius of Loyola, 1528–1535*, trans. Ralph C. Renner (Saint Louis: Institute of Jesuit Sources, 2011), 57–58.

25. Codina, "Modus Parisiensis," 36.

26. Codina, 43.

27. Codina.

28. Hyma, *Christian Renaissance*, 23, 35–40.

29. Hyma, 164.

30. Codina, "Modus Parisiensis," 42–44.

31. John W. O'Malley, *Four Cultures of the West* (Cambridge, MA: Belknap Press of Harvard University Press: 2004), 105.

32. Desiderius Erasmus, *The Praise of Folly*, trans. Clarence H. Miller (New Haven, CT: Yale University Press, 2003), 79.

33. Erasmus.

34. Letson and Higgins, *Jesuit Mystique*, 137.

35. Hansen describes a rich dynamic of loyalty to traditions and a simultaneous reflective openness to new possibilities that is insightful. See Hansen, *Teacher and the World*, 11, 40, 70.

36. Lécrivain, *Paris*, 59.

37. Codina, "Modus Parisiensis," 45.

38. Lécrivain, *Paris*, 92. Allan P. Farrell, *The Jesuit Code of Liberal Education: Development and Scope of the Ratio Studiorum* (Milwaukee: Bruce, 1939), 31; George E. Ganss, *Saint Ignatius' Idea of a Jesuit University: A Study in the History of Catholic Higher Education* (Milwaukee: Marquette University Press, 1956), 30.

39. Farrell, *Jesuit Code*, 31.

40. John W. O'Malley, "How the First Jesuit Became Involved in Education," in *The Jesuit Ratio Studiorum: 400th Anniversary Perspectives*, ed. Vincent J. Duminuco (New York: Fordham University Press, 2000), 58.

41. Codina, "Modus Parisiensis," 31–32.

42. Codina, 33.

43. John W. Padberg, "Development of the *Ratio Studiorum*," in *The Jesuit Ratio Studiorum: 400th Anniversary Perspectives,* ed. Vincent J. Duminuco (New York: Fordham University Press, 2000), 82.

44. Farrell, *Jesuit Code,* 93.

45. Lacouture, *Jesuits,* 4.

46. Farrell, *Jesuit Code,* 31.

47. As nonmonastics, the Jesuits—formally, the Society of Jesus—became an officially chartered religious organization of Roman Catholicism that is not obligated to traditional communal patterns of life and long-practiced routines of the Divine Office (or Psalter), nor are their members geographically or physically bound to cloistered residences.

48. O'Malley, *First Jesuits,* 202.

49. O'Malley.

50. Padberg, "Development," 81.

51. O'Malley, *First Jesuits,* 202.

52. William V. Bangert and Thomas M. McCoog, *Jerome Nadal, SJ, 1507–1580: Tracking the First Generation of Jesuits* (Chicago: Loyola University Press, 1992), 69.

53. Bangert and McCoog, 68.

54. Bangert and McCoog, 69.

55. O'Malley, "How the First Jesuits Became Involved," 70.

56. O'Malley.

57. Codina, "Modus Parisiensis," 34.

58. Letson and Higgins, *Jesuit Mystique,* 141.

59. Philip Gleason, *Contending with Modernity: Catholic Higher Education in the Twentieth Century* (Oxford: Oxford University Press, 1995), 6.

60. Ganss, *Saint Ignatius' Idea,* 213.

61. Letson and Higgins, *Jesuit Mystique,* 143.

62. Robert McClintock, "Toward a Place for Study in a World of Instruction," *Teachers College Record* 73, no. 2 (1971): 176.

63. Claude Pavur, trans., *The Ratio Studiorum: The Official Plan for Jesuit Education* (Saint Louis: Institute of Jesuit Sources, 2005), 189 [§434], 190 [§435], 192 [§443, 444], 200 [§475].

64. Pavur, 48 [§129].

65. McClintock, "Toward a Place for Study," 176.

66. O'Malley, *First Jesuits,* 227.

67. McClintock, "Toward a Place for Study," 161.

68. McClintock, 165.

69. Donald M. Frame, trans., *Michel de Montaigne: The Complete Works—Essay, Travel Journal, Letters* (New York: Everyman's Library, 2003), 1167.

70. Aldo Scaglione, *The Liberal Arts and the Jesuit College System* (Philadelphia: John Benjamins, 1986), 57.

71. Ganss, *Saint Ignatius' Idea,* 211.

72. Codina, "Modus Parisiensis," 44.

73. Bangert and McCoog, *Jerome Nadal,* 86–87.

74. Ignatius of Loyola, *The Constitutions of the Society of Jesus and Their Complementary Norms: A Complete Translation of the Official Latin Texts* (Saint Louis: Institute of Jesuit Sources, 1996), 136–37 [§324.4, 325.B], 142 [§340.2], 150 [§356.D], 160 [§384.14].

75. Ganss, *Saint Ignatius' Idea*, 207.

76. Ganss, 79.

77. Ignatius, *Constitutions*, 144 [§343.B], 150 [§351.1], 160 [§382.K], 180 [§455.A], 182 [§462.5].

78. Howard Gray, SJ, "The Experience of Ignatius Loyola: Background to Jesuit Education," in *The Jesuit Ratio Studiorum: 400th Anniversary Perspectives*, ed. Vincent J. Duminuco, SJ (New York: Fordham University Press, 2000), 11.

79. Gray, 12.

80. Modras, *Ignatian Humanism*, 83, 289.

81. Ignatius, *Constitutions*, 171 [§100].

82. Ignatius, 171–72 [§111].

83. Kathleen A. Mahoney, *Catholic Higher Education in Protestant America: The Jesuits and Harvard in the Age of the University* (Baltimore: Johns Hopkins University Press, 2003), 11.

84. M. A. Screech, trans., "Of Cannibals," in *Michel de Montaigne: The Complete Essays* (London: Penguin Classics, 1991), 152. It might be worth recalling Taylor's critical assessment of Montaigne and the difference manifested in this characterization.

85. Farrell, *Jesuit Code*, 135.

86. Joseph Daoust, "Of Kingfishers and Dragonflies: Faith and Justice at the Core of Jesuit Education," *Conversations on Jesuit Higher Education* 19 (2001): 15.

87. Claude Pavur, "The Curriculum Carries the Mission: The *Ratio Studiorum*, the Making of Jesuit Education, and the Making of the Society of Jesus," *New Jesuit Review* 2, no. 5 (2010). www.newjesuitreview.org/newjesuitreview/Home.html.

88. Pavur.

89. O'Malley, *First Jesuits*, 37.

90. Kenneth L. Becker, *Unlikely Companions: C. G. Jung on the Spiritual Exercises of Ignatius of Loyola—An Exposition and Critique Based on Jung's Lectures and Writings* (Leominster, UK: Gracewing, 2001), 47–55.

91. Hyma, *Christian Renaissance*, 270.

92. Pierre Hadot, *Philosophy as a Way of Life*, ed. Arnold I. Davidson (Oxford: Blackwell, 2008), 127.

93. Hadot, 245.

94. Hadot, 239.

95. Hadot, 238–50; Sarah Bakewell, *How to Live, Or, A Life of Montaigne: In One Question and Twenty Attempts at an Answer* (New York: Other Press, 2010), 112.

96. Ignatius of Loyola, *The Spiritual Exercises of Saint Ignatius: A Literal Translation and a Contemporary Reading*, ed. David L. Fleming (Saint Louis: Institute of Jesuit Sources, 1991), 71–73.

97. As Dean Brackley argues in *The Call to Discernment in Troubled Times: New Perspectives on the Transformative Wisdom of Ignatius of Loyola* (New York: Crossroad, 2004), the Trinitarian gaze is an essential and defining mediation on Ignatius's *Spiritual Exercises*.

98. Philip Endean, "The Spiritual Exercises," in *The Cambridge Companion to the Jesuits*, ed. Thomas Worcester (Cambridge: Cambridge University Press, 2008), 52.

99. William C. Spohn, "Developing a Moral Conscience in Jesuit Higher Education," in *Jesuit Education 21: Conference Proceedings on the Future of Jesuit Higher Education*, ed. Martin R. Tripole (Philadelphia: St. Joseph's University Press, 2000), 395.

100. Gray, "Experience," 8.

101. Letson and Higgins, *Jesuit Mystique*, 110.

102. Daoust, "Of Kingfishers and Dragonflies: Faith and Justice at the Core of Jesuit Education," 14–15.

103. Pavur, "Curriculum."

104. Paul Crowley, "The Jesuit University and the Search for Transcendence," *Conversations on Jesuit Higher Education* 22 (2002): 10.

105. *Ratio Studiorum*, 155 [§375].

106. Codina, "Modus Parisiensis," 40; O'Malley, "From the 1599 *Ratio Studiorum* to the Present," 129.

107. Modras, *Ignatian Humanism*, 79.

108. C. Jane Gosine, and Erik Oland, "*Docere, Delectare, Movere*: Marc-Antoine Charpentier and Jesuit Spirituality," *Early Music* 11 (2004): 520.

109. Ganss, *Saint Ignatius' Idea*, 176.

110. Gerald McKevitt, "Jesuit Schools in the USA, 1814–c. 1970," in *The Cambridge Companion to the Jesuits*, ed. Thomas Worcester (Cambridge: Cambridge University Press, 2008), 280.

111. Mahoney, *Catholic Higher Education*, 43.

112. O'Malley, *Four Cultures*, 168.

113. Modras, *Ignatian Humanism*, 81.

114. Modras.

115. Harro Höpfl, *Jesuit Political Thought: The Society of Jesus and the State, c. 1540–1640: Ideas in Context* (New York: Cambridge University Press, 2004), 20.

116. Jodi Loach, "Revolutionary Pedagogues? How Jesuits Used Education to Change Society," in *The Jesuits II: Cultures, Sciences, and the Arts 1540–1773*, ed. John W. O'Malley, Gauvin Alexander Bailey, Steven J. Harris, and T. Frank Kennedy (Toronto: University of Toronto Press, 2002), 71.

117. Ganss, *Saint Ignatius' Idea*, 167.

118. Loach, "Revolutionary Pedagogues?" 66–67.

119. John W. O'Malley, "How Humanist Is the Jesuit Tradition? From the 1599 *Ratio Studiorum* to Now," in *Jesuit Education 21: Conference Proceedings on the Future of Jesuit Higher Education*, ed. Martin R. Tripole (Philadelphia: St. Joseph's University Press, 2000), 190.

120. The Greek linguistic expressions of piety are beyond the scope of this book. However, given the charge of impiety against Socrates and his discussion of it in the *Apology*—as well as the four versions of piety that are considered in *Euthyphro* and the numerous references to piety in the *Republic*—the *Platonic Dialogues* would provide a useful starting point.

121. Daoust, "Of Kingfishers and Dragonflies," 15; Nicholas Moseley, "Pius Aeneas," *Classical Journal* 20, no. 7 (1925) 387–400. Moreover, see *The Oxford Classical Dictionary, Second Edition*, ed. N. G. L. Hammond and H. H. Scullard (Oxford: Clarendon Press, 1970), 833: "Virgil's 'pius Aeneas' significantly expresses the Roman ideal in his religious attitude, in his patriotic mission, and in his relations with father, sons, and comrades."

122. O'Malley, "How Humanist Is the Jesuit Tradition?" 135.

123. Codina, "Modus Parisiensis," 40.

124. Mahoney, *Catholic Higher Education*, 41.

125. Loach, "Revolutionary Pedagogues?" 66.

126. O'Malley, *First Jesuits*, 226–27.

127. Giovanni Pico della Mirandola, *Oration on the Dignity of Man*, trans. Elizabeth Livermoore Forbes, in *The Renaissance Philosophy of Man: Petrarca, Valla, Ficino, Pico,*

*Pomponazzi, Vives,* ed. Ernst Cassirer, Paul Oskar Kristeller, and John Herman Randall Jr. (Chicago: University of Chicago Press, 1948), 225.

128. Pico della Mirandola, 227.
129. Christopher J. Lucas, *American Higher Education: A History* (New York: Palgrave Macmillan, 2006), 72–73.
130. Craig W. Kallendorf, ed. and trans., "Pier Paolo Vergerio, De Ingenius Moribus et Liberalibus Studiis [The Character and Studies Befitting a Free-Born Youth]," in *Humanist Educational Treatises* (Cambridge, MA: Harvard University Press, 2002), 73.
131. Ignatius, *Constitutions,* 220 [§547].
132. O'Malley, "How Humanist Is the Jesuit Tradition?" 191.
133. Félix Cadet, ed., *Port-Royal Education: A Sketch of Its History with Extracts from Its Leading Authors* (Syracuse: C. W. Bardeen, 1899), 111.
134. Cadet, 38.
135. Cadet, 321.
136. Jonathan Wright, "The Suppression and Restoration," in *The Cambridge Companion to the Jesuits,* ed. Thomas Worcester (Cambridge: Cambridge University Press, 2008), 267.
137. Jonathan Wright, *God's Soldiers: Adventure, Politics, Intrigue, and Power—A History of the Jesuits* (New York: Doubleday, 2004), 167.
138. Modras, *Ignatian Humanism,* 79; O'Malley, *First Jesuits,* 15.
139. Bangert and McCoog, *Jerome Nadal,* 40.
140. O'Malley, *First Jesuits,* 67–68.
141. Wright, *God's Soldiers,* 50.
142. Mahoney, *Catholic Higher Education,* 152. Also, Hansen's recent book articulates conceptions of "home" in pedagogical light—a "cosmopolitan orientation"—that demonstrates affinities to the Jesuit sensibility: "From a cosmopolitan perspective, persons are always leaving *and* remaining at home" (p. 57). For a fuller discussion, see Hansen, *Teacher and the World,* 56–59.
143. Wright, *God's Soldiers,* 117.
144. Mahoney, *Catholic Higher Education,* 11.
145. Ignatius, *Constitutions,* 179 [§449.B].
146. Wright, *God's Soldiers,* 121.
147. R. Po-Chia Hsia, *A Jesuit in the Forbidden City: Matteo Ricci, 1552–1610* (Oxford: Oxford University Press, 2010); Vincent Cronin, *A Pearl to India: The Life of Roberto de Nobili* (New York: E. P. Dutton, 1959).
148. Mahoney, *Catholic Higher Education,* 153.
149. John Padberg, ed. *Ignatius of Loyola: Letters and Instructions* (Saint Louis: Institute of Jesuit Sources, 2006), ix.
150. Wright, *God's Soldiers,* 132.
151. Stanisław Obirek, "Jesuits in Poland and Eastern Europe," in *The Cambridge Companion to the Jesuits,* ed. Thomas Worcester (Cambridge: Cambridge University Press, 2008), 143–44.
152. Wright, *God's Soldiers,* 216.
153. Wright, "Suppression and Restoration," 263; Wright, *God's Soldiers,* 215.
154. Padberg, *Ignatius of Loyola,* 360–63.

# CHAPTER SIX

# HIGHER EDUCATION
# IN A SECULAR AGE

Let me now turn to the realities of contemporary higher education, discussing them in three broad strokes: institutional fragmentation, superficial subjectivity, and instrumental epistemics. As Charles Taylor speaks in *A Secular Age* and elsewhere about the "malaises of modernity"—the ways cultural and social disquietudes compromise possibilities for fullness in our lives—maladies of the contemporary era also exist that are particular to the context of higher education. Likewise, they jeopardize possibilities of relating, growing, and flourishing. The contemporary university is less collaborative, less personal, and less educative than it should be. Problems related to the holistic dimensions of higher education in institutional, subjective, and epistemological realities are not disassociated from the impersonal or noxious dimensions of modernity when they represent the ways Taylor's work is used and appreciated in educational theory.[1] My broad stroke issues are not always easily distinguishable from one another and even gain momentum from the effects of each other, but they are nonetheless three distinct illnesses notable for higher education in a secular age.

In defining and explaining these three contemporary problems, it is not difficult to substantiate descriptions of them from a host of different thinkers and writers. Some, traditional philosophers, such as Karl Jaspers and Alfred North Whitehead, write their own "idea" about the university, and historians and current commentators also think and write helpfully about influences, movements, and trends in higher education. These many voices work together to manifest the concerns of fragmentation, superficiality, and instrumentality. Furthermore, the various contributions from different scholarly perspectives resonate with many of Taylor's concerns, and assist in exposing how higher education in a secular age reflects the crisis of fullness that propels this book.

As many kinds of experts corroborate in their critiques, they demonstrate a relationship between a general cultural milieu and higher education itself that we see in this quotation from Robert Maynard Hutchins, an important figure in the history of higher education in the United States:[2] "Things are no better outside the university than within. . . . In a world gone mad over technology, science, [and] the production of material goods, . . . it is natural that the world has steadily become more and more unphilosophical or antiphilosophical. Why worry about something as vague, useless, confusing, contradictory, and menacing as philosophy seems to be?"[3]

Hutchins's ability to describe a correlation between the depersonalizing and mechanistic forces of modernity and the life of universities is essential in guiding us to maintain Taylor's own cultural critique. It also allows us to recognize the corresponding existential costs of relationship and perspective he describes. Though it is worth asking whether universities spur cultural problems or exacerbate existing ones, or whether higher education can or should alleviate such problems, answers to these questions are contingent upon considerations that I will take up in my next book. My own hope is that the university does not muster or mimic social ills but mitigates and even ameliorates both within and around it those that compromise human flourishing. However that can be achieved, Hutchins's insight at least reminds us that the illnesses of higher education discussed in this chapter are principally recognized in how they impede Taylor's dimensions of relating, or, said otherwise, lead to profligating the buffers of modernity.

Before continuing this discussion, however, it is worth recognizing a tension inherent within my three basic assumptions. It concerns the role of the humanities in higher education's many instantiations, such as liberal arts institutions, places of highly specialized and sophisticated research, campuses with undergraduate or graduate student populations, and combinations of any of these points of focus. It is fair to ponder when, where, and why the humanities can or should be studied, and to what ends. It is also reasonable to wonder which kinds of institutions I have in mind. Again, possible responses are so numerous that I have necessarily limited the scope of conversation about the humanities as well as institutions of higher education to general terms.

My basic supposition, however, is that the three maladies are directly related to the humanities—both in how they have been affected and in the solutions they represent. My second assumption is that most American universities are generally susceptible to or participatory in these three problematic dynamics. Third, I presume that good undergraduate education—whether in small liberal arts colleges or large research universities—should facilitate a meaningful engagement of topics in the humanities, offering an expansive educative exposure that can inform students who either advance through the academy to different levels or leave it for other life options.

## INSTITUTIONAL FRAGMENTATION

I regard institutional fragmentation as the parsing of the university into disciplinary pursuits, a slicing or fracturing of what generally has been considered an integrating or synthesizing venue of intellective activity. Official designations of early institutions of higher learning in the twelfth and thirteenth centuries as *studia generale* reflected a place of higher learning "where students from all parts are received."[4] *Studia generale* became more sophisticated and institutional, however, and were recognized as universities in how they represented various branches of learning that were ultimately connected and supportive of each other in a unified way. The seven aspects of the *trivium* and *quadrivium*—that is, the *septem artes liberales* and the subsequent *studia humanitatis*—are dimensions of learning that Pier Paolo Vergerio and other Renaissance humanists attempted to restore in the fifteenth and sixteenth centuries, were not celebrated for how they competed against one another but for how they represented a mutually supportive curriculum of learning.[5] In the university they also represented a conception of knowledge, albeit vast, as a unity itself. As we will see throughout this chapter, many thinkers recognize the university as a locus that should in essence function as a cohesive institution whereby different academic perspectives merge to inform and enhance one another.

Jonathan Cole's book *The Great American University* (2009) portrays the fragmented reality of current universities astutely. Just as he is able to name aspects of higher education that were lost as the university diversified and specialized through the scientific advancements of the nineteenth century, he is also able to show us what has been gained.[6]

Cole's long book is structured in three parts. First, he describes how small, "sleepy" colleges in the United States morphed into powerful national forces of scientific and economic transformation. Then he explains how university-based research has improved the quality of living for people around the world. Finally, he highlights specific threats upon and within research universities in recent years—such as governmental censoring, international competition, dogmatic attitudes, commercialization, and inequalities of resources—which compromise senses of academic integrity and mission.

Seeing the university today as particularly fractured, Cole readily admits that the patterns and practices of higher education divide the university into overly autonomous entities that are less collaborative, communicative, and cooperative. He laments "program creep," which can burden and distort basic objectives of a given institution.[7] He depicts university campuses as filled with pockets of isolation, and then details, first, the difficulty—if not impossibility—of insights and discoveries being shared and discussed; second, a diced and inflexible budget system that hampers the possibilities of growth in many areas; and, third, a generally stymied intellectual advancement for dealing with some of the most pressing issues of the day.[8] Because of the buffers that impede dialogue, growth, and inquiry, he indicates that we desperately need the "breadth of knowledge produced by . . . sharing of ideas and expertise. This is especially true when it comes to tackling problems such as global climate change, economic development, and finding the causes of disease or poverty and eradicating them.[9]

And yet, some of the basic essentials of our daily lives—things we could not imagine living without—resulted specifically from isolated, highly specialized, disciplinary university research in its fragmented modus operandi. Electric toothbrushes, refrigeration, Doppler weather predictions, Gatorade, automated teller machines, barcodes for scanning purchasable goods, and the internet are some of the objects he celebrates while negotiating just of few hours of a day of his own.[10] American research universities, he explains, are, in global comparison, simply the best, a credential achieved through the production of an incredibly "high proportion of the most important fundamental knowledge and practical research discoveries in the world."[11]

Describing an institution that is essentially fractured, Cole points to Clark Kerr's designation of the modern American research university as the "multiversity," "a somewhat chaotic and constantly changing place."[12] Cole explains how the multiversity functions as an institution of higher education "with many parts and missions that, taken together, comprised a multidimensional 'city' where parts were loosely integrated, rather than a small village or town that was truly coherent."[13] As president of the University of California from 1958 to 1967 and author of the widely read *Uses of the University* (1963), Kerr explains that the "modern American university is not Oxford, nor is it Berlin; it is a new type of institution in the world."[14]

Kerr's European references point to John Henry Newman and Wilhelm von Humboldt. Newman's classic *The Idea of the University* (1873), based on his own experience at Oxford and his founding of the Catholic University of Ireland in 1851, and Humboldt's establishment of the University of Berlin in 1810, manifest two considerably different models. The one that had evolved into Kerr's multiversity became a unique entity influenced by these forms and others, the origin of which is benchmarked by the opening of Johns Hopkins

University in 1876 under Daniel Coit Gilman's presidency: "The first American university to emphasize research rather than undergraduate teaching," Johns Hopkins—inspired by the scholarly impetus of Humboldt's Berlin model—pioneered what eventually became a wholly new model.[15]

In *Multiversities, Ideas, and Democracy*, George Fallis discusses four distinct archetypes of the university, all of which inform the emergence of the American multiversity. There is, of course, Newman's university, an institution that offers curricular programs in the liberal arts that function to form the intellectual, moral, and social sensibilities of undergraduate students, and there is Humboldt's university, an institution that focuses upon research pursuits for graduate students and scholarly advancement.

Along with these two conceptions of the university, there are two others. The first is the medieval university, as "Paris and Bologna are the two archetypal—it might almost be said the only *original* universities."[16] Along with Salerno, these institutions' unequivocal objectives are to train individuals in the three traditional professions: theology, law, and medicine. The fourth and final conception is what Fallis describes as an underappreciated model, the Scottish prototype, the idea of the university enlivened by the institutions at Edinburgh, Aberdeen, Glasgow, and St Andrews that allowed for an egalitarian access of students into their programs and pioneered applied sciences—economics, political science, and psychology, to name a few—that have long been commonplace.[17]

As influences of the four ideals of the university collectively represent the reality of many American universities today, Newman's archetype best frames for our purposes a counterdynamic of university fragmentation. In *The Idea of the University: A Reexamination* (1992), Jaroslav Pelikan quotes Newman as saying, "If we would rightly deem of it, a University is the home, it is *the mansion-house, of the goodly family of the Sciences*, sisters all, and sisterly in their mutual dispositions" (emphasis added).[18] The role of theology as an integrating, synthesizing, and culminating expression of university pursuits represents for him specific—and unambiguously religious—epistemological and cosmological orientations that tend toward a holistic conception of reality. He explains in "discourse III" of *The Idea of a University*, "I lay it down that all knowledge forms one whole, because its subject matter is one; for the universe in its length and breadth is so intimately knit together."[19] This represents a metaphysical commitment that is also reflected by the philosophers Karl Jaspers and Jacques Maritain in their statements about universities in, respectively, *The Idea of the University* (1946) and *Education at the Crossroads* (1943). Each describes a unity of knowledge that should somehow be represented or replicated by the functioning of the university.[20]

In *God, Philosophy, Universities* (2009), Alasdair MacIntyre points to the overarching philosophical system of Thomas Aquinas—and before him, Aristotle—as inspirational with ideas of a purposive and cohesive universe, and explains how academic pursuits within universities work together in forming understandings of such an expansive realm.[21] He also recalls how theology was an essential ingredient of this synthesizing orientation long before Newman's description of the university in the middle of the nineteenth century for its capacity to gather, or at least capstone, myriad academic perspectives.

Furthermore, in *Knowledge Matters* (2011), Craig Calhoun, an expert on Charles Taylor, recently discusses commonplace assumptions of the university that continue to persist, one of which endorses this Aristotelian–Thomistic–Newman–MacIntyre line of thought. These assumptions attempt, he explains, "to integrate the whole universe of knowledge, approaching and ideally connecting all or at least many subjects. That is, they are not narrowly specialized technical institutes."[22] If scholars and practitioners of higher education are reluctant to endorse conceptions of reality and knowledge in unified and holistic dimensions, and, moreover, are not interested in drawing a correlation between them and universities' efforts, Calhoun's caveat here encourages any of us to be cognizant of what constitutes the differences between university study and vocational training.

As academic programs fractured and dispersed into disciplinary interests—scientific ones, namely—of their own, they lost an essential component of university functioning. MacIntyre asks, "What disappeared? Enquiry in relationship to other disciplines and [the possibility] that the various disciplines contribute to a single shared enterprise."[23] Jaspers stands right behind him and suggests that the real issue about disciplinarity is a communicative one. Inquiry can be fueled and furthered to greater accomplishments through an interactive and conversant academic community. For Jaspers, a dialogic orientation is a university fundamental: "Communication of all with all is necessary. . . . Here is the living core of university life."[24] The contemporary German philosopher Jürgen Habermas is also interested in an essential dialogical commitment. In "The Idea of the University: Learning Processes" (1987), he seems uncomfortable with religious and metaphysical conceptions of reality and knowledge, yet looks for a constitutive element of the university, asking, "Does anything remain upon which an integrating self-understanding of universities could be founded?"[25] He lands where Jaspers staked a claim: in communication.[26]

Like MacIntyre—and Jaspers and Habermas, for that matter—Anthony Kronman argues for an explicit "reconnection" to such modes of communicative inquiry in *Education's End* (2007).[27] Moreover, in moving from Newman's ideal of a curricular hegemony to the dialogic hopes of MacIntyre, Jaspers, and Habermas—and, as we will see, to Kronman's interest in what the humanities in the university can achieve existentially—we can better appreciate the pervasiveness of fragmentation, and thus the mending powers of dialogue.

Passionately interested in classics of the Western canon of literature and philosophy, Kronman argues that university disciplinarity devalues the humanities. When we lose the humanities, we lose an ability to ask questions about the meaning of life, a fundamental dimension of humanity that Taylor's fullness represents. Queries about the meanings and purposes of life are not being entertained and explored in universities: "We need the humanities to meet the deepest spiritual longing of our age, whose roots lie in the hegemony of science itself. At the very heart of our civilization, with its vast powers of control, there is an emptiness that science has created and cannot fill."[28] In fragmented university environments, students are either conditioned into indifference or—as more explicitly related to Kronman's driving concern—they look beyond the university for answers to their basic existential needs. The solutions some of them reach are misguiding or simplistic. Kronman is greatly disturbed by the prevalence of prospering evangelical organizations in the United States today—"the surge of fundamentalist belief"—that attend to important existential impulses of searching individuals in naive and artless ways.[29]

Kronman's particular value, however, is in his ability to share MacIntyre's concern that the multiversity becomes so pointed and narrow in endless directions that other points of focus are dismissed or discounted: "Certain questions go unasked or, rather, if they are asked, it is only by individuals and in settings such that as few as possible hear them being asked."[30] Characterized by the sociologist Robert Bellah as a "cafeteria," or by other scholars as the "full-service university," or a "giant bazaar" where students shop for the specifics goods that will meet their particular utilitarian needs, the multiversity is widely recognized for its existential deficiencies.[31]

In his 1867 *Inaugural Address: Delivered to the University Students of St. Andrews*, John Stuart Mill warns an academic community to avoid pursuits and perspectives whereby one confines him or herself "to a smaller and smaller portion of the whole extent" of knowledge.[32] Writing in his autobiography the year he died, Mill himself movingly describes a conversion in his life that brought him—the son of the intellectually prominent James Mill and an exceptionally studied individual himself—face-to-face with the existential wisdom of the humanities, and, eventually, his own heart. In the long, heartheavy, and personally despondent winter of 1826, William Wordsworth was his medicine.[33] "Poetry and art . . . [were the] instruments of human culture" that offered a brilliant man a new sense of meaning and purpose.[34] He confesses, "I found the fabric of my old and taught opinions giving way in many fresh places."[35]

In front of the students and faculty of St Andrews four decades later, he compared the knowledge of a specialized, constricted pursuit to a pinhead that merely punctuates the ambit of human industry.[36] Mill was not arguing against the serious efforts of research and a striving for expertise, nor exceptionally focused interests that are personally empowered by curiosity and discipline. He was attempting to contextualize the time and place for highly specialized efforts, and in turn espouse the benefits of well-rounded, unified, and holistic educational influences. Though long, this quotation from MacIntyre describes myopic quests of a number of disciplinary contexts on the topic of the human person, and then he asks a telling question:

> From the standpoint of physics human beings are composed of fundamental particles interacting in accordance with the probabilistic generalizations of quantum mechanics. From that of chemistry we are the sites of chemical interactions, assemblages of elements and compounds. From that of biology we are multicellular organisms belonging to species each of which has its own evolutionary past. From that of historians we are intelligible only as emerging from the long histories of social and economic transformations. From that of economists we are rational profit-maximizing makers of decisions. From that of psychology and sociology we shape and are shaped by our perceptions, our emotions, and our social roles and institutions. And from that of students of literature and the arts it is in the exercise of our various imaginative powers that we exhibit much that is distinctive about human beings. But how do all these relate to each other?[37]

The issue of institutional fragmentation in modern research universities is yet another expression of a secular age and, in the interests of this book, can be evaluated as to how it participates in the crisis of fullness.

## SUPERFICIAL SUBJECTIVITY

In *Education at the Crossroads*, Maritain exclaims that the "cult of specialization" demonstrated by the fragmentation of the university into its instrumental scientific pursuits "dehumanizes" students.[38] This section of the chapter and the next one, "Instrumental Epistemics," build on the insights and expressions of the fractured nature of the multiversity described above. Both thus burrow more deeply into the personal, *dehumanizing* concerns of higher education in a secular age.

The dynamic of personal superficiality references numerous common practices in higher education today and is specifically named by the current leader of the Jesuit organization as a contemporary problem that higher education should allay.[39] The breakdown of curricular programs in the humanities at the end of the nineteenth century and the beginning of the twentieth century dramatically decreased undergraduate students' exposure to the thinking, imagining, inquiring, and intuiting activities commonly associated with studies in the humanities. In accord with the images of the fragmented university given above that compare the multiversity to a cafeteria or a bazaar, students were able to begin choosing their way toward useful undergraduate degrees. This also meant that students could avoid certain courses. In doing so, students became more career oriented, and universities let students negotiate practical programs for specific professions. One particular problem of superficiality, then, regards vocationalism, the training of students for certain jobs that supplants the educating of students as certain kinds of persons.

The main concern about superficiality, then, pertains to the *unformed* realities and *unexercised* capacities of well-trained students. As students of higher education dwell less, if at all, in the images of literature, the plights of history, the questions of philosophy, the possibilities of theology, and even just the basic data of joy, gratitude, and grief, to name only a few, so much less of their personal capacities is enacted and exercised. They are less personally invested in the fact that so many of their intellective capacities are simply not engaged. In a recent book, a social critic characterizes current undergraduate students as slumped, chatting, snacking, bored, and undisciplined.[40] As expressions of superficiality are recognized through the problem of vocationalism in higher education, they are also noted through the lacks of interest and disengagements of students.

As with institutional fragmentation, I would like to contextualize superficiality with Newman's classic prototype. The "gentleman" he famously describes as a formative outcome of higher education in "discourse V" of the *Idea of the University* might be unattractive to scholars of the idea of the university for different reasons. Newman explains that higher education should cultivate within its students not a Christian, nor a Catholic, but gentlemanly demeanor that is characterized by "a cultivated intellect, a delicate taste, a candid, equitable, dispassionate mind, a noble and courteous bearing in the conduct of life."[41] These are the objectives of his ideal university. Readers today would generally not be convinced that Newman was not in fact interested in the Christian and Catholic outcomes, though in fairness to Newman he is quite clear in the *Idea of the University* that he is speaking about liberal education qua liberal education. Regardless, the middle-nineteenth-century context within which he was writing also manifests sexist and bourgeois regard. I am not invested in either preserving or dismantling Newman's gentleman, but I do want to honor a motivating sensibility behind it, which is the cultivation of a virtuous person.[42]

Whether intentionally or not, an apposite correlate is wonderfully reflected in the Spanish philosopher José Ortega y Gasset's writings on higher education, *Mission of the University*, a set of lectures about the university composed and delivered in 1930 and then reevaluated and formally published in 1944. Kerr offers a description in the introduction to a more recent edition as a work reflecting its own especial contexts, such as Ortega y Gasset's early Jesuit education in Spain; his later studies at German research universities; the Spanish dictatorships, beginning in 1923, of Miguel Primo de Rivera y Orbenaja and, in the years after 1936, Franciso Franco y Bahamonde; and his own existential interest as a philosopher. Ortega y Gasset offers an ideal of the university as contextually influenced as any of them, if not more explicitly so.[43] These are reflected in the *Mission of the University* through his interest in a unified schema of knowledge that corresponds with an ordered, albeit vast, universe; a desire to cultivate democratic sensibilities in students; and an insistence that issues of daily life will be directly and meaningfully engaged.

As Newman envisages the gentleman in his university, Ortega y Gasset grieves the presence of the "new barbarian" in universities around him. Such an individual is a "laggard behind the contemporary civilization, archaic and primitive in contrast with his problems, which are grimly, relentlessly modern."[44] More squarely within the realm and responsibly of the university, "this new barbarian is above all the professional man, more learned than ever before, but at the same time more uncultured—the engineer, the physician, the lawyer, the scientist."[45] Ortega y Gasset is particularly concerned about a tendency toward professionalism, or vocationalism.

In *Mission of the University*, Ortega y Gasset focuses intensely upon the ways university students can assess current events critically and evaluatively. He yearns for a higher educative pedagogy that dwells in the "vital ideas" of the day, the broader realities of culture, and the connections that can be drawn between the two.[46] For him, the training of professionals misses this and represents an educational failure that is reflected in the "dehumanizing" characteristic of which Jaspers speaks. For undergraduates, vocational training, scholar per scholar, is the great sin of the university. The superficial training it offers represents an insufficient and incomplete education of individual persons. If Newman's gentleman seems to be a bit aristocratic, the assumption is that he is not shallow.

Fallis reminds us of Newman's interest in this educational kind of fullness when he writes in "discourse V" about acquiring knowledge for its own sake: "A liberal education . . . should not be preparation for a job, not to gain mastery of one discipline. Rather, it should be a broad education."[47] MacIntyre agrees, but in referencing Newman he gets more to the point of character formation:

> The aim of a university education is not to fit students for this or that particular profession or career, to equip them with theory that will later on find useful applications to this or that form of practice. It is to transform their minds, so that the student becomes a different kind of individual, one able to engage fruitfully in conversation and debate, one who has a capacity for exercising judgment, for bringing insights and arguments from a variety of disciplines to bear on particular complex issues.[48]

MacIntyre emphasizes the role of philosophy alone in expanding and enriching our lives, but he also specifically discusses the activities of dialogue and debate that deepen and personalize the dynamic of inquiry within students. Kronman also explains how the humanities, especially through literature, stir emotions and stimulate imaginative thinking.[49] Kronman, of course, espouses an antivocationalist regard and, like others, indicts the university as guilty in how it fails to educate students. Although Fallis, MacIntyre, and Kronman have specific agendas of their own, they share with each other a passionate regard for substantiating and developing subjectivity. Through different intellective emphases, they want to educate people for the complexities of life. In their works we can appreciate the rational, emotional, and imaginative enhancements of subjectivity in the context of higher education.

Like Jaspers, Maritain, Newman, and Ortega y Gasset above, Alfred North Whitehead is yet another philosopher who discusses university education. As scholars and thinkers bemoan specialization, he beckons to "generalization," whose spirit, in his assessment, should govern universities.[50] He exudes an interesting Renaissance humanist sensitivity through an interest in the growth and development of students, and he recognizes the ability of education to cultivate the innate human capacity—"the principle of progress is from within"—for the improvement and enrichment of one's life.[51]

I considered Vergerio's ability at the beginning of the fifteenth century to name and discuss the dynamic of youthfulness in education as well as in life.

Likewise, we were able to appreciate John Dewey's similar concept of growth. Whitehead himself speaks of the "rhythmic character of growth," and he discusses the responsibility of teachers at all levels of education—higher education included—to appreciate such a capacity in the lives of their students and for establishing the kind of environment that fosters it.[52] He criticizes specializing trends that narrow the interests of students and thereby stunt the growth they can enjoy.

Ironically, in Whitehead's collection of essays *The Aims of Education* (1929), a set of addresses for conferences and academic communities ranging from 1912 to 1928, the last address to be composed, "Universities and Their Functions"—the one dealing specifically with higher education and the need for generalization—was delivered at the Harvard Business School. In this address, Whitehead expresses an interest in maximizing a deeply personal educational impact and thereby emphasizes a challenge for higher education to offer students a wide exposure of courses. He also repeats his insights about the Renaissance humanist and Deweyan power of youthfulness, encouraging universities to tap into and nourish all of an individual's intellective capacities. In this, he is especially pointed about the role of imagination. Its abilities to enable a person to assess current realities about one's life and the world and ponder alternatives not only testify to profound personal investments of analysis, evaluation, and hope but also help catalyze transformations of the self and the social. In fact, imaginative capacity is a nonnegotiable educative expression for Whitehead: "A university is imaginative or it is nothing."[53]

Similar to the growth construct, Whitehead explains that young people are easily imaginative and that higher education should offer methods that exercise the imagination within the university and beyond, preserving it as a way of life.[54] Part of Whitehead's goal is to home in upon a sense of individual investment and the dimensions of excitement, curiosity, confidence, and possibility that are associated with imaginative capacity.[55] In this, he reveals affinities with Dewey in other ways. Not only does Dewey speak to the problems of vocational education in *Democracy and Education*—"No one is just an artist and nothing else, and in so far as one approximates that condition, he is so much the less developed human being; he is a kind of monstrosity"—but he also amplifies the dimension of self-investment through his description of personal interests:[56] "To be interested is to be absorbed in, wrapped up in, carried away by, some object. To take an interest is to be on the alert, to care about, to be attentive. We say of an interested person both that he has lost himself in some affair and that he has found himself in it. Both terms express the engrossment of the self."[57]

The concept of interest in Dewey's rendition represents and substantiates the depth and breadth of personal imagination that Whitehead wants, and both philosophers also speak to an inherent connection to discipline. Dewey couples interest and discipline as "correlative aspects," and Whitehead speaks of the need for imaginative education—again, a self-invested learning process—to be persistent throughout life.[58] In this, and furthermore, both Whitehead and Dewey speak, then, of an educational way of life. Relating an imaginative orientation toward life more specifically to the university, Whitehead says, enticingly, that "education is discipline for the adventure of life; research is intellectual adventure; and the universities should be homes of adventure."[59]

Martha Nussbaum agrees. In *Not For Profit: Why Democracy Needs the Humanities* (2010)—a concise follow-up to her earlier book, *Cultivating Humanity: A Classical Defense of Reform in Liberal Education* (1997)—she echoes Whitehead in an important way.[60] In *Not For Profit*, she wants higher education to provoke in the life of a student a "daring imagination," and with it, sharp and searching critical and analytical thinking and acute empathetic abilities that engage the predicaments and complexities of others and the world—educational outcomes that are, for her, unqualifiedly cultivated by the humanities.[61]

Her book frames the devaluation, if not demise, of the humanities by economic and instrumental drives both within and around the university. Science and technology can indeed enhance the quality of life, and the kinds of financial investments and payouts they proffer are not negligible. But the "profit motive" that compels so much of higher education cannot be the only motive, let alone a primary one.[62] As her book begins, she turns to the Indian and American intellectuals Rabindranath Tagore and Bronson Alcott and proclaims that, in being so driven by cost/benefit pedagogies and programs, "we seem to be forgetting about the soul"—that is, the deeply personal and profoundly substantial abilities to think, imagine, and relate.[63]

In his 1826–27 winter of depression, Mill's soul was touched. A new perspective filled his life, and a correlation can be made between Nussbaum's appreciations of the humanities and their role in higher education and Mill's. Defining the university as a place that should not train men professionally but nourish and cultivate human beings, expressing a concern about vocationalism that has been noted throughout this section, Mill wants universities to offer intellectually rounded, personally invested, character forming, and socially engaged higher education.[64] Furthermore, his sentiments are represented in the insights and challenges of Dewey, Fallis, Kronman, MacIntyre, Newman, Ortega y Gasset, and Whitehead, especially with regard to the substantial and existential dimensions of the human experience. When Mill emerges from his melancholy—an awakening to joy energized by artistic thoughts, images, and feelings—he admits that he, "for the first time [in his life], gave its proper place, among the prime necessities of human well-being, to the internal culture of the individual."[65]

## INSTRUMENTAL EPISTEMICS

When Mill nears the end of his address at the University of St Andrews—a thoughtful and hopeful assessment of the idea of the university in line with those of Habermas, Jaspers, Maritain, Newman, Ortega y Gasset, and Whitehead—Mill also dwells in the campus-wide possibilities of open and communicative inquiry, personally dedicated and disciplined scholarship, collaborative and kindred academic entities, effective and inspiring teaching, and the cultivation of young adults who will live graced by broad intellectual, moral, and social regard. As these thinkers collectively reference interests, imaginations, analyses, evaluations, insights, feelings, and communications as necessary higher educative abilities, it is Mill who is most eloquent in assessing the aesthetic sensitivities of our lives, powers that bring "home to us all those aspects of life which take hold of our nature on its unselfish side, and lead us to identify our joy and grief... with good or ill... and... to take life seriously."[66]

Such sensitivities, George Fallis explains, cannot be cultivated when all educative efforts focus solely on the betterment of technical rationality: "The experience of joy and love, of sadness and grief, of honour and dignity, are part of being human, and cannot be approached through reason alone."[67] When we engage the work of higher education and educate young adults, then, we should begin in a perspective of the human condition that "recognizes that an autonomous individual possessed of instrumental reason cannot be complete."[68] Like many others, Fallis finds tremendous value in offering courses in the humanities in higher education, especially literature courses— he discusses the contributions of Lionel Trilling's life and scholarship, and in particular his *The Liberal Imagination* (1950) with great respect—in provoking and apprising myriad personal sensibilities. But it is Mill, again, who describes the effects of such an educational exposure so alluringly: "He who has learned what beauty is will desire to realize it in his own life."[69]

As we have pondered the fractured intuitional realities of the modern university and its tendencies to educate persons *insubstantially*, this malaise of higher education focuses on the problem of instrumentality. Together, fragmentation and superficiality represent individualizing efforts (of departments, disciplines, careers, concerns). Likewise, instrumentality also reveals an isolating dynamic. It represents a way of knowing that is decisively rational, and it is evaluated for its practical utility. Knowledge as such can be qualified as advantageous, economical, efficient, factual, and so on. Because it is too often regarded as wholly representative of human intellect, it overshadows or suppresses other intellective powers.

As practitioners and philosophers of the university recognize the value of a cohesive, communicative campus and the need for, broadly, *generally* educated individuals, they also see the importance of personal discovering and knowing that emerge in multiple ways. Christopher Lucas, author of *American Higher Education* (2006), explains that "the clear tendency in American higher education throughout the last quarter of the nineteenth century, more than anything else, was one of concessions to the demand for more utilitarian learning."[70] We can thereby appreciate the possibilities of "integrated learning," a conception of Parker Palmer and Arthur Zajonc's that is worth considering.

The tendency toward scientific knowing is an expression of institutional fragmentation and personal vocationalism, and it is the same with instrumental rationality. Julie Reuben's book and Lucas's, both astute and authoritative in discussing higher education in the United States, focus precisely on an epistemic shift in American university life. In *The Making of the Modern University* (1996), Reuben "examines the transition from the nineteenth-century broad conception of truth to the twentieth-century division between facts and values."[71] The personal sources of curiosity and inquiry, she explains, became forces for forming fast and hard solutions, and the success of rational expression "was judged by practical results."[72] She persists, instructing that "in the nomenclature of the twentieth century, only 'science' constituted true knowledge."[73] She spends much of her book showing how, through the industrial and scientific advances of society and the university, moral and spiritual insights lost validity and significance.

As many of the critics of modernity turn more than three centuries back to René Descartes, so does Lucas. Cartesian epistemology represents a paradigmatic shift that constricted human knowing. In his historical overview he explains how, through Descartes, the idea of science alone narrowed in meaning and became meticulous and scrupulous in how it was conducted, what it observed, and the claims it could make.[74] Lucas cites the stalwart minds and methods of Descartes, Isaac Newton, and Galileo Galilei to articulate a refined scientific orientation that became commonplace and, in turn, is representative of contemporary knowing: "Exact and certain knowledge apprehended by the mind (Descartes), measured mathematically (Newton), and demonstrated by experimentation (Galileo)" characterize a singularly valid epistemic option today.[75] He continues, reinforcing the fact that, as the understanding of science transformed and tapered, "scientific distrust of unproven hypotheses had the further effect of emphasizing the importance of the *utility* of knowledge."[76]

As Lucas explores history to assess the life of American higher education, he explains that such a trend toward the utility of knowledge was ostensible and patent at its most in the land grant universities of the United States. Such institutions of higher education—the A&M universities for "agriculture" and "mechanics," and in general what are now regarded as state universities— flourished significantly by either expanding existing programs or originating new ones through federal land grants for universities that would devote pro- gramming to pointed national production interests.[77] Cole explains that the Morrill Act of 1862, signed into law by President Abraham Lincoln, "the first newly created land-grant school under the Morrill Act was Kansas State Uni- versity," was an investment in individuals and a society, both of which could be measured in "payoffs."[78]

In *The Heart of Higher Education: A Call to Renewal* (2010), Parker Palmer and Arthur Zajonc—authors who also have very recently expressed regret about contemporary trends in American higher education: "something essential has gone missing"—offer a rich description of knowing, to which they refer as "integrative learning," that is not assessed and evaluated for its payoffs.[79] The kind of epistemology they endorse is recognizably broader than one rooted in Cartesian rationality and thereby more inclusive of the many aspects of human knowing. They explain that epistemic power in our lives, "rightly understood, has paradoxical roots—mind and heart, hard data and soft intuition, individual insight and common sifting."[80] In *The Heart of Higher Education*, they thus propose various aspects of a kind of pedagogy that "support a way of knowing that involves much if not all of the whole self" in learning about one's life and the world.[81] As Mill speaks of the need to feel and assess the fundamental joys and grievings of our lives, Palmer and Zajonc speak of the human experiences of awe, wonder, and humility as capacities that augment and enlarge knowing.[82]

More holistic than instrumental, the integrative approach makes con- nections between students' lives and their courses. It also connects courses with other courses, students with their own experiences, students with the greater environment around them, courses with personal experience and the environment, and so on. "A truly integrative education engages students in the systematic exploration of the relationship between their studies of the 'objective' world and the purpose, meaning, limits, and aspirations of their lives."[83] As we have been recognizing the educative importance of uniquely personal interests, imaginations, analyses, evaluations, insights, feelings, and communications, Parker and Zajonc look for ways to evaluate and appreciate all these relationships with the external world.

Earlier in the book, I discussed an inner/outer distinction of knowing that is criticized by Taylor. In supporting John McDowell's epistemic perspective, Taylor criticized conceptions of human knowing that establish an "inside/outside distinction" between individuals and the external world, instructing that the personal, interior construals of a subject's knowing capacities are not mere representations of an exterior world brought into the mind in some way and that, furthermore, inner construals (thoughts, feelings, insights, imaginations) are not disconnected from the influences of an outside world. Taylor realizes that we can certainly buffer ourselves from certain influences, and are conditioned in a secular age to buffer many realities, but he wants us—as do so many thinkers—to better appreciate an epistemology that is always in some way relational. Palmer and Zajonc are looking for ways to better welcome and integrate these various connections within the self and between the self and the social. As Taylor speaks against the inner/outer qualification, he also speaks throughout all of *A Secular Age* about the porous subject who—pervious to and permeable by the external conditions one engages *as well as* by the internal construals one exchanges—the mind is not Descartes's lonely *res cogito*—is able to better know fullness.

Just as significantly, the kind of education that Palmer and Zajonc want represents Taylor's relational interests. As discussed by Taylor as a philosophical-anthropological construct, fullness, a dimension of subjectivity that is waning in a secular age, corresponds to experiences of realities qualified by Taylor as natural and supernatural. Knowing such realities forges an ontic commitment, an epistemic connection to which Palmer and Zajonc are open. For them it is an indispensable expression of human spirituality that, when lacking, lessens something about our own experiences and our own lives. We and our world are somehow reduced, less *fulfilled*: "[A] diminished anthropology is a natural corollary to our diminished ontology."[84]

In proposing integrative learning, Palmer and Zajonc not only let us imagine a holistic epistemic perspective that is inclusive of the many capacities of our own lives, but they also remind us that our ways of knowing do not have to be as fractured, and thus limited, as the institutions of higher education that are persistently criticized today. Moreover, the broad spectrum of capacities for gaining knowledge—represented by thinking, feeling, intuiting, and more, some of the same realities of which Taylor speaks with regard to the participatory and associative dimensions of agape—also represents not a superficial but a personal and genuine investment by and engagement of students. Perhaps Jaspers, in *The Idea of the University*—where he speaks of the incongruity between narrow scientific pursuit and total personal commitment[85]—sums this all up in explaining that the mission of the real university "demands the serious commitment of the whole [person]; . . . it must aim for formation of the whole [person], for education in the broadest sense of the term."[86]

## CONCLUSION

Vitiating the problems not only of instrumentality but also of fragmentation and superficiality, Palmer and Zajonc offer a worthy critique of contemporary higher education. But not unlike so many of the thinkers discussed here, they also look beyond the university to embrace the complications and convolutions, both prosaic and profound, of the world we inhabit. In many ways, daily life is really what the focus is, and as philosophers, historians, and commentators of higher education keep human existence in purview, they also represent general existential concerns about the meanings and purposes of our lives. Palmer and Zajonc wonder at the end of their book that if universities cannot prepare people for the "messiness of real life," including "the complexities and cruelties" of the world, what is the purpose of higher education.[87]

At the University of Chicago, Hutchins pondered the same reality in his generation. Similarly concerned about the problems of higher education that we have considered, he says that a modern mania for the facts of science, mechanics of technology, and possessions of capitalism dull so many aspects of our lives—such as thinking, feeling, imagining, intuiting, and communicating; that is, skills and capacities I have recognized in each component of this chapter as suppressed or disregarded. Moreover, these human abilities are generally engaged and developed by studies in the humanities in the context of higher education.

Like Palmer and Zajonc, Hutchins is also concerned about the messiness of life. In *The University of Utopia* (1953) he explains that, as higher education obsesses only upon evidences and verifications, we ourselves are less able to negotiate the uncertain, complex realities inside us and around us, a capacity made possible, he explains, through the "useless, confusing, contradictory, and menacing" practice of philosophy.[88]

The contemporary university can indeed be evaluated as less collaborative, less personal, and less educative than it should be. Parsed, isolated, individualistic, vocational, professional, economical, and "barbaric" are just some of the qualifications used to describe its current predicament. The problems of higher education in institutional, subjective, and epistemological realities—specifically discussed as institutional fragmentation, superficial subjectivity, and instrumental epistemics—are like the impersonal and noxious dimensions of modernity considered through Taylor's concern for fullness. As an entity that is ever more fractured, pragmatic, and rational in its institutional, personal, and epistemic pursuits, it also manifests a buffered orientation that impedes dimensions of fullness.

Fullness as a phenomenal experience, recognized as being yearned for in the works of recent scholars, and further discussed in epistemic expression and moral-ethical relating, is an existential construct—a philosophical-anthropological reality—about which one can be educated. For a higher educative context specifically invested in its holistic possibilities, this is why I articulate the pedagogies of fullness.

## NOTES

1. The four themes in the second chapter, described as "snapshots" and "parlors of discourse," are "recognition," "the good life," "instrumental rationality," and "hypergoods." In representing aspects of personal identity, holistic expressions of knowing and relating, and essential life values, I draw our attention to their easily noticeable affinities for institutional, subjective, and epistemic concerns.

2. Hutchins, along with Alexander Meiklejohn and Michael Oakeshott, represents a uniquely American reform movement in higher education that was eventually referred to as the General Education movement. In Hutchins's *The Higher Learning in America* (1936) and *Education for Freedom* (1943), Meiklejohn's *The Liberal College* (1920) or *The Experimental College* (1932), and Oakeshott's *The Voice of Liberal Learning* (1989), and other writings, they each wrestle intelligently and passionately with the transformation of American higher education from collegiate programs structured by fine arts curricula to university disciplines dominated by scientific research. Early in the twentieth century, Hutchins, Meiklejohn, and Oakeshott grieved a dismantling of humanities curricula and the loss of existential and moral foci they offered. Their discussions of liberal learning in its ability to free contemporary women and men into dimensions of personal flourishing and communal responsibility still enlighten educational scholars.

3. Robert Maynard Hutchins, *The University of Utopia* (Chicago: University of Chicago Press, 1953), 50–52.

4. Hastings Rashdall, *The Universities of Europe in the Middle Ages, Volume I*, ed. F. M. Powicke and A. B. Emden (Oxford: Clarendon Press, 1987), 5.

5. Stephen Ferrulo, *The Origins of the University: The Schools of Paris and Their Critics, 1100–1215* (Palo Alto, CA: Stanford University Press, 1985), 33–36.

6. Cole's ability to critique and appreciate the contemporary university is not insignificant to this project. You might recall from the first chapter Stephen Toulmin's discouragement,

articulated in his *Cosmopolis* (1990), about the current state of philosophy—we should "return to its pre-17th-century traditions, and try to recover the lost ('*pre*-modern') topics" (p. 11)—and an initial proposal in the book to discount Modernity almost entirely. Taylor passionately values specific elements of Modernity, punctuating his writings with an admiration for the human rights and dignities—let alone scientific and political evolvements in technologies and democracies—that Enlightenment thinking motivated and insisted. In *The Ethics of Authenticity,* Taylor sides with neither the all-out "knockers" of Modernity or its full-blown "boosters," and encourages us to be just as discerning (p. 11). Cole is able to do likewise. So is Toulmin, too, in fact. He knows that we cannot start over in philosophy with a "clean slate" (p. 175). Interestingly, and not unrelated to my discussion in this chapter, Toulmin ponders how Modernity might be humanized and considers the role of higher education in helping him explore possibilities (pp. 184–86).

7. Jonathan R. Cole, *The Great American University: Its Rise to Preeminence, Its Indispensable National Role, Why It Must Be Protected* (New York: PublicAffairs, 2009), 35.

8. Cole, 489.

9. Cole, 490.

10. Cole, 194–95.

11. Cole, 5. Also discussed in the book are the discoveries in universities of momentous achievements, such as DNA, and more adverse realities, such as the atomic bomb.

12. Cole, 140.

13. Cole, *Great American University,* 140; Clark Kerr, *The Uses of the University* (Cambridge, MA: Harvard University Press, 2001), 18.

14. Kerr, *Uses of the University,* 1.

15. Cole, *Great American University,* 19.

16. Hastings Rashdall, *The Universities of Europe in the Middle Ages, Volume I: Salerno, Bologna, Paris* (Cambridge: Cambridge University Press, 2010), 17. See also George Fallis, *Multiversities, Ideas, and Democracy* (Toronto: University of Toronto Press, 2007), 27: "Hastings Rashdall challenged and overturned this long-standing conclusion regarding the origins of the university. He argued—and his viewpoint has prevailed—that professional education had always been the distinguishing characteristic of the university."

17. Fallis, *Multiversities,* 18–33.

18. Jaroslav Pelikan, *The Idea of the University: A Reexamination* (New Haven, CT: Yale University Press, 1992), 57.

19. John Henry Newman, *The Idea of a University,* ed. Frank Turner (New Haven, CT: Yale University Press, 1996), 45.

20. Karl Jaspers, *The Idea of the University,* ed. Karl W. Deutsch (Boston: Beacon Press, 1959), 2, 38; Jacques Maritain, *Education at the Crossroads* (New Haven, CT: Yale University Press, 1943), 76.

21. Alasdair MacIntyre, *God, Philosophy, Universities: A Selective History of the Catholic Philosophical Tradition* (New York: Rowman & Littlefield, 2009), 73–86.

22. Craig Calhoun, "Introduction," in *Knowledge Matters: The Public Mission of the Research University,* ed. Diana Rhoten and Craig Calhoun (New York: Columbia University Press, 2011), 2.

23. MacIntyre, *God, Philosophy, Universities,* 174.

24. Jaspers, *Idea of the University,* 37.

25. Jürgen Habermas and John R. Blazek, "The Idea of the University: Learning Processes," *New German Critique* 41 (1987): 3–22, at 18.

26. Habermas and Blazek, 20.

27. Anthony Kronman, *Education's End: Why Our Colleges and Universities Have Given Up on the Meaning of Life* (New Haven, CT: Yale University Press, 2007), 241.

28. Kronman, 229.

29. Kronman.

30. MacIntyre, *God, Philosophy, Universities*, 174.

31. Christopher J. Lucas, *American Higher Education: A History* (New York: Palgrave Macmillan, 2006), 303–4. According to Pelikan, Newman also named images for what were then emerging as multiversities as a bazaar or "pantechnicon." See Pelikan, *Idea of the University*, 57.

32. John Stuart Mill, *Inaugural Address: Delivered to the University Students of St. Andrews* (Memphis: General Book, 2010), 6.

33. John Stuart Mill, *Autobiography* (New York: Penguin Classics, 1989), 121.

34. Mill, 119.

35. Mill, 127.

36. Mill, *Inaugural Address*, 6.

37. MacIntyre, *God, Philosophy, Universities*, 175.

38. Maritain, *Education*, 11.

39. Adolfo Nicolás, superior general of the Society of Jesus, in his April 2010 address, "Depth, Universality, and Learned Ministry: Challenges to Jesuit Higher Education Today," speaks about the "globalization of superficiality" (Conference Address, Universidad Iberoamricana, Mexico City), 2, www.loyola.edu/Justice/commitment/NicolasSJ.JHE.April23.2010[1].pdf.

40. Mark Fisher, *Capitalist Realism: Is There No Alternative?* (Winchester, UK: Zero Books, 2009), 23.

41. Newman, *Idea of a University*, 89.

42. Newman, 91.

43. Clark Kerr, "Introduction," in *Mission of the University*, by José Ortega y Gasset, ed. and trans. Howard Lee Nostrand (New Brunswick, NJ: Transaction, 1991), xi–xiii.

44. Ortega y Gasset, *Mission*, 28.

45. Ortega y Gasset, 28–29.

46. Ortega y Gasset, 30.

47. Fallis, *Multiversities*, 20.

48. MacIntyre, *God, Philosophy, Universities*, 147–48.

49. Kronman, *Education's End*, 72.

50. Alfred North Whitehead, *The Aims of Education and Other Essays* (New York: Free Press, 1967), 25.

51. Whitehead, 39.

52. Whitehead, 39–40. Whitehead's rhythmic character of growth is articulated in a cyclic pattern of human freedom that passes through the phases or stages of "romance," "precision," and "generalisation" (p. 31).

53. Whitehead, 96.

54. Whitehead, 93.

55. Whitehead, 97.

56. John Dewey, *Democracy and Education: An Introduction to the Philosophy of Education* (New York: Free Press, 1944), 307.

57. Dewey, 126. Here, I think it is also worth naming a tension between an ability for educational topics across a wide range of options to initiate and cull personal interests in students (Whitehead's "generalization," humanist curricula, etc.) and the role of academic disciplines and specialization, per se, in honoring and liberating interest into a path of its own.

58. Dewey, *Democracy and Education*; Whitehead, *Aims of Education*, 97.

59. Whitehead, *The Aims of Education*, 98.

60. Martha C. Nussbaum, *Cultivating Humanity: A Classical Defense of Reform in Liberal Education* (Cambridge, MA: Harvard University Press, 1997); Martha C. Nussbaum, *Not for Profit: Why Democracy Needs the Humanities* (Princeton, NJ: Princeton University Press, 2010).

61. Nussbaum, *Not for Profit*, 7.

62. Nussbaum.

63. Nussbaum, 6.

64. Mill, *Inaugural Address*, 2–3.

65. Mill, *Autobiography*, 118.

66. Mill, *Inaugural Address*, 33.

67. Fallis, *Multiversities, Ideas, and Democracy*, 399.

68. Fallis, 399.

69. Mill, *Inaugural Address*, 34.

70. Lucas, *American Higher Education*, 151–52.

71. Julie A. Reuben, *The Making of the Modern University: An Intellectual Transformation and the Marginalization of Morality* (Chicago: University of Chicago Press, 1996), 2.

72. Reuben, 47.

73. Reuben, 2.

74. Lucas, *American Higher Education*, 93.

75. Lucas.

76. Lucas.

77. Lucas, 152–59.

78. Lucas, 199.

79. Parker J. Palmer and Arthur Zajonc, *The Heart of Higher Education: A Call to Renewal* (San Francisco: Jossey-Bass, 2010), 3.

80. Palmer and Zajonc, 22.

81. Palmer and Zajonc, 32.

82. Palmer and Zajonc, 22.

83. Palmer and Zajonc, 10.

84. Palmer and Zajonc, 101.

85. Jaspers, *Idea of the University*, 12.

86. Jaspers, 3.

87. Parker and Zajonc, *Heart of Higher Education*, 38.

88. Hutchins, *University of Utopia*, 50–52.

# CONCLUSION

# FORMING A LEARNED IMAGINATION

We have seen how imagining a way of living and relating is an essential dimension of Charles Taylor's *A Secular Age*. The "social imaginary" he discusses at length there and elsewhere represents, quite literally, the way people envision a social existence with one another.[1] It includes ways by which people envision or imagine the combined reality of a sense of self and ways of engaging the world, both of which speak to the relational prospects of fullness in one's life. It is Bernard Lonergan who so effectively highlights the intimate connection he represents of subjective and social realities. In his work, the correlation between the two suggests that genuine intellectual, moral, and religious transformations of an individual's life make the world a better place.

Forming a learned imagination for students of Jesuit education—that is, a Jesuit imaginary—is my purpose with the pedagogies of study, solidarity, and grace. A Jesuit imaginary is fueled by the distinctive tradition and pedagogy of the Society of Jesus, the Jesuits, and regards the self, society, and our world hopefully. In how the self is studied, how solidarity with alterity is ever possible, and how the world and we are graced, hope is prevalent in the pedagogies of fullness. Recall my discussion of the positive regard just for individuals noted of the Jesuit order. The organization exuded a robust hope for human potential that was countered by an alternative philosophical anthropology of Jansenism, as personified in the writings of Blaise Pascal.

I name the elements of this anthropological hopefulness in educational terms as essential ingredients of the pedagogies of fullness. The strategies of "study" and "solidarity" rely upon aspects of *assaying* and *adapting*, both of which are represented in Giovanni Pico della Mirandola's *Oration on the Dignity of Man* (1486), an exhortation of existential regard that celebrated the awesome possibilities for better selves and societies. These personal and social transformations are not dissociated from Taylor's existential conception of fullness, and, through Pico, they emerge from the tenets of Renaissance humanism.

The components of Renaissance humanism are educational aspects inspired by an originary Greek humanism. They were promulgated through *paideia*, enacted in ideals of arête, and specified by conceptions of *eloquentia*. After waning in the Middle Ages, they reemerged at the cusp of the fifteenth century through Pier Paolo Vergerio's passionate, and hopeful, educational interest in the virtuous character of individuals and corresponding civic engagement. The feast day of Saint Jerome (c. 340–420), in its dimensions of social equity and civic morality, and the personal virtues of giving and gratitude, fueled for Vergerio a peaceably educative, personally transformative, and socially cooperative imaginary that he attempted to actualize.

I also offered the crystallization and international dissemination of Renaissance humanist education through the Jesuits. Emulating the Modus Parisiensis that Ignatius of Loyola and the first Jesuits encountered at the University of Paris through the Collège de Montaigu and Collège de Sainte-Barbe, supplementing deficient academic programs throughout Europe and elsewhere, and eventually building schools of their own, Jesuit education was pervasive for well over two hundred years until its hiatus beginning in 1773. By generating principal educational documents in part IV of the *Constitutions* (1558) and as the *Ratio Studiorum* (1599) and, respectively, emphasizing the possibilities of "study" and "adaptation," the Jesuits were able to establish a humanist educational network featuring the Ciceronian *studia humanitatis*, structured programs of personal advancement, individual attentiveness to students through *cura personalis* and *familiaritas*, the combined ideals of *eloquentia perfecta* and *pietas*, and a social-civic expression of *Christianitas* that survives today.

Although current expressions of Jesuit higher education in the United States are vulnerable to the contemporary problems of fragmentation, superficiality, and instrumentality around and within them, recent gestures through the highest superiors of the Jesuit organization suggest a steadfast relationship with the humanist origins of Jesuit education and investments in addressing specific social ills regarding the rights and dignities of the underprivileged, the forces of socioeconomic poverty, and environmental and ecological devastation. Kolvenbach's "learned solidarity" epitomizes the three international addresses offered by his predecessor, successor, and himself.

The pedagogies of fullness help to equip students of Jesuit higher learning with a common imaginary. Deeply and personally inquisitive, easily adaptive and widely relational, and open to the inexplicable is one way to frame the Jesuit imaginary. Holistic of self, justly related, and receptive of beauty is another way to regard it. So, too, are conceptions of being at home with oneself and with others, and of being hospitable to an Other. The Jesuit imaginary, a real possibility for students of Jesuit higher education, envisions and hopes for the dimensions of relating what Taylor yearns for in a secular age. By embracing Taylor's existential concern in our own secular age—and thereby rejuvenating his sense of fullness through our studious, adaptive, and graced students—the Jesuit higher educational pedagogies of fullness allow us to gain an abundant "moving toward." In doing so, they reenchant the world, and us.

## NOTE

1. Citing Benedict Anderson's book *Imagined Communities: Reflections on the Origin and Spread of Nationalism* (New York: Verso, 2006), as inspirational of the social imaginary construct, a specific interest of Taylor's is to demonstrate an ancillary role of specific ideas and philosophical conceptions involved in how communities and societies are formed. Michéle Le Dœuff's book *The Philosophical Imaginary*, trans. Colin Gordon (Palo Alto, CA: Stanford University Press, 1989); and Cornelius Castoriadas's 1975 book *The Imaginary Institution of Society*, trans. Kathleen Blamey (Cambridge, MA: MIT Press, 1987) both frame Anderson in helpful ways. Le Dœuff's feminist perspective and Castoriadas's analysis of Marxism show both the force and the frailty of overarching social theories.

# BIBLIOGRAPHY

Abbey, Ruth, ed. *Charles Taylor*. Cambridge: Cambridge University Press, 2004.

Adler, Mortimer J. *The Paideia Proposal: An Educational Manifesto*. New York: Simon & Schuster, 1998.

———. *Reforming Education: The Opening of the American Mind*, edited by Geraldine Van Doran. New York: Macmillan, 1990.

Albert, Lillie. "The Call to Teach: Spirituality and Intellectual Life." *Conversations on Jesuit Higher Education* 18 (2002): 38–42.

Alexander, Hanan A. "Aesthetic Inquiry in Education: Community, Transcendence, and the Meaning of Pedagogy." *Journal of Aesthetic Education* 37, no. 1 (2003): 1–18.

———. "Moral Education and Liberal Democracy: Spirituality, Community, and Character in an Open Society." *Educational Theory* 53, no. 4 (2003): 367–87.

———. *Reclaiming Goodness: Education and the Spiritual Quest*. Notre Dame, IN: University of Notre Dame Press, 2001.

———, ed. *Spirituality and Ethics in Education*. Brighton: Sussex Academic Press, 2004.

———. "What Is Common about Common Schooling? Rational Autonomy and Moral Agency in Liberal Democratic Education." *Journal of Philosophy of Education* 41, no. 4 (2007): 609–24.

Ancelovici, Marcos, and Francis Dupuis-Déri. "Interview with Professor Charles Taylor." *Citizenship Studies* 2, no. 2 (1998): 247–56.

Anderson, Benedict. *Imagined Communities: Reflections on the Origin and Spread of Nationalism*. New York: Verso, 2006.

Appiah, Kwame Anthony. *Cosmopolitanism: Ethics in a World of Strangers*. New York: W. W. Norton, 2006.

———. *The Ethics of Identity*. Princeton, NJ: Princeton University Press, 2005.

Appleyard, Joseph, SJ, and Howard Gray, SJ. "Tracking the Mission and Identity Question." *Conversations on Jesuit Higher Education* 18 (2000): 4–15.

Araujo, Robert J. "What Is Jesuit Higher Education: The Service of Faith and the Promotion of Justice?" In *Jesuit Education 21: Conference Proceedings on the Future of Jesuit Higher Education*, edited by Martin R. Tripole, 25–36. Philadelphia: St. Joseph's University Press, 2000.

Arcila, René V. *For the Love of Perfection: Richard Rorty and Liberal Education*. New York: Routledge, 1995.

———. *Mediumism: A Philosophical Reconstruction of Modernism for Existential Learning*. Albany: State University of New York Press, 2010.

Aristotle. *Nicomachean Ethics*, in *The Basic Works of Aristotle*, edited by Richard McKeon. New York: Random House, 1941.

———. *Politics*, in *The Basic Works of Aristotle*, edited by Richard McKeon. New York: Random House, 1941.

Arrupe, Pedro. "Men for Others: Education for Social Justice and Social Action Today." Paper delivered at Tenth International Congress of Jesuit Alumni of Europe, Valencia, July 1973. http://onlineministries.creighton.edu/CollaborativeMinistry/men-for-others.html.

Arum, Richard, and Josipa Roksa. *Academically Adrift: Limited Learning on College Campuses.* Chicago: University of Chicago Press, 2011.

Bakewell, Sarah. *How to Live, or, A Life of Montaigne: In One Question and Twenty Attempts at an Answer.* New York: Other Press, 2010.

Bangert, William V., and Thomas M. McCoog, *Jerome Nadal, SJ, 1507–1580: Tracking the First Generation of Jesuits.* Chicago: Loyola University Press, 1992.

Barber, Noel. "Education: A Reflection of Social Change? Durkheim on Jesuit Education." *Studies* 76 (1987): 216–26.

Barthes, Roland. *Sade, Fourier, Loyola,* translated by Richard Miller. Berkeley: University of California Press, 1989.

Becker, Kenneth L. *Unlikely Companions: C. G. Jung on the Spiritual Exercises of Ignatius of Loyola—An Exposition and Critique Based on Jung's Lectures and Writings.* Leominster, UK: Gracewing, 2001.

Beirne, Charles J. *Jesuit Education and Social Change in El Salvador.* New York: Garland, 1996.

Bellah, Robert N. "Confronting Modernity: Maruyama Masao, Jürgen Habermas, and Charles Taylor." In *Varieties of Secularism in a Secular Age,* edited by Michael Warner, Jonathan VanAntwerpen, and Craig Calhoun, 32–53. Cambridge, MA: Harvard University Press, 2010.

———. "Education for Justice and the Common Good." *Conversations on Jesuit Higher Education* 25 (2004): 28–37.

Bergman, Roger. *Catholic Social Learning: Educating the Faith That Does Justice.* New York: Fordham University Press, 2010.

Bernstein, Richard J. "The Secular/Religious Divide: Kant's Legacy." *Social Research: An International Quarterly of the Social Sciences* 76, no. 4 (2009): 1035–48.

Bilgrami, Akeel. "What Is Enchantment?" In *Varieties of Secularism in a Secular Age,* edited by Michael Warner, Jonathan VanAntwerpen, and Craig Calhoun, 145–65. Cambridge, MA: Harvard University Press, 2010.

Bingham, Charles. "Before Recognition, and After: The Educational Critique." *Educational Theory* 56, no. 3 (2006): 325–44.

Bloom, Allan. *The Closing of the American Mind.* New York: Simon & Schuster, 1987.

Blum, Lawrence. "Recognition and Multiculturalism in Education." *Journal of Philosophy of Education* 35, no. 4 (2001): 539–59.

———. "Review of *Common Schools, Uncommon Identities: National Unity and Cultural Difference,* by Walter Feinberg." *Teachers College Record* 103, no. 1 (2001): 99–112.

Blum, Richard Paul, ed. *Philosophers of the Renaissance,* translated by Brian McNeil. Washington, DC: Catholic University of America Press, 2010.

Bok, Derek. *Beyond the Ivory Tower: Social Responsibilities of the Modern University.* Cambridge, MA: Harvard University Press, 1982.

Bonnett, Michael. "Environmental Concern and the Metaphysics of Education." *Journal of the Philosophy of Education* 34, no. 4 (2000): 591–602.

———. "Environmental Education and Beyond." *Journal of Philosophy of Education* 31, no. 2 (1997): 249–66.

Bowen, John R. "Secularism: Conceptual Genealogy or Political Dilemma." *Comparative Studies in Society and History* 52, no. 3 (2010): 680–94.

Brackley, Dean. *The Call to Discernment in Troubled Times: New Perspectives on the Transformative Wisdom of Ignatius Loyola*. New York: Crossroad, 2004.

———. "Higher Standards for Higher Education: The Christian University and Solidarity." Commemorative address delivered at Creighton University, Omaha, November 1999.

Braman, Brian J. *Meaning and Authenticity: Bernard Lonergan and Charles Taylor on the Drama of Authentic Human Existence*. Toronto: University of Toronto Press, 2008.

Brighouse, Harry. *On Education: Thinking in Action*. New York: Routledge, 2006.

Brown, Wendy. "The Sacred, the Secular, and the Profane: Charles Taylor and Karl Marx." In *Varieties of Secularism in a Secular Age*, edited by Michael Warner, Jonathan VanAntwerpen, and Craig Calhoun, 83–104. Cambridge, MA: Harvard University Press, 2010.

Bruni, Leonardo. *De Studiis et Litteris Liber ad Baptistam de Malatestis*. In *Humanist Educational Treatises*, edited and translated by Craig W. Kallendorf, 92–125. Cambridge, MA: Harvard University Press, 2002.

Buckley, Michael J. *The Catholic University as Promise and Project: Reflections in a Jesuit Idiom*. Washington, DC: Georgetown University Press, 1998.

Buijs, Joseph. "Teaching: Profession or Vocation?" *Catholic Education: A Journal of Inquiry and Practice* 8, no. 3 (2005): 326–45.

Bullough, Robert V., Jr., Clifford T. Mayes, and Robert S. Patterson. "Teaching as Prophecy." *Curriculum Inquiry* 32, no. 3 (2002): 311–29.

———. "Wanted: A Prophetic Pedagogy: A Response to Our Critics." *Curriculum Inquiry* 32, no. 3 (2002): 341–47.

Burtchaell, James Tunstead. *The Dying of the Light: The Disengagement of Colleges and Universities from Their Christian Churches*. Grand Rapids: William B. Eerdmans, 1998.

Burtonwood, Neil. "Social Cohesion, Autonomy and the Liberal Defense of Faith Schools." *Journal of the Philosophy of Education* 37, no. 3 (2003): 415–25.

Butler, Jon. "Disquieted History in *A Secular Age*." In *Varieties of Secularism in a Secular Age*, edited by Michael Warner, Jonathan VanAntwerpen, and Craig Calhoun, 193–216. Cambridge, MA: Harvard University Press, 2010.

Butler, Judith. "Is Judaism Zionism?" In *The Power of Religion in the Public Sphere*, edited by Eduardo Mendieta and Jonathan VanAntwerpen, 70–91. New York: Columbia University Press, 2011.

Cadet, Félix, ed. *Port-Royal Education: A Sketch of Its History with Extracts from Its Leading Authors*. Syracuse: C. W. Bardeen, 1899.

Caldecott, Stratford. *Beauty of Truth's Sake: On the Re-enchantment of Education*. Grand Rapids: Brazos Press, 2009.

Calhoun, Craig. "Imagining Solidarity: Cosmopolitanism, Constitutional Patriotism, and the Public Square." *Public Culture* 14, no. 1 (2003): 147–71.

———. "Introduction." In *Knowledge Matters: The Public Mission of the Research University*, edited by Diana Rhoten and Craig Calhoun, 1–33. New York: Columbia University Press, 2011.

———. "Morality, Identity, and Historical Explanation: Charles Taylor on the Sources of the Self." *Sociological Theory* 9, no. 2 (1991): 232–63.

———. "Rethinking Secularism." *Hedgehog Review: Critical Reflections on Contemporary Culture* 12, no. 3 (Fall 2010).

Calhoun, Craig, Mark Juergensmeyer, and Jonathan VanAntwerpen, eds. *Rethinking Secularism*. Oxford: Oxford University Press, 2011.

Califano, Joseph A., Jr. "Memories of a Jesuit Education." *America* 174, 18 (1996): 10–17.

Carmody, Denise Lerner. "The Catholicity of the Catholic University." *Conversations on Jesuit Higher Education* 22 (2002): 4–9.

Casanova, José. "A Secular Age: Dawn or Twilight?" In *Varieties of Secularism in a Secular Age*, edited by Michael Warner, Jonathan VanAntwerpen, and Craig Calhoun, 265–81. Cambridge, MA: Harvard University Press, 2010.

———. "The Secular and Secularisms." *Social Research: An International Quarterly of the Social Sciences* 76, no. 4 (2009): 1049–66.

Cassirer, Ernst. *The Individual and the Cosmos in Renaissance Philosophy*, translated by Mario Domandi. Chicago: University of Chicago Press, 1963.

Cassirer, Ernst, Paul Oskar Kristeller, and John Herman Randall Jr., eds. *The Renaissance Philosophy of Man: Petrarca, Valla, Ficino, Pico, Pomponazzi, Vives*. Chicago: University of Chicago Press, 1948.

Castoriadis, Cornelius. *The Imaginary Institution of Society*, translated by Kathleen Blamey. Cambridge, MA: MIT Press, 1987.

Cervantes, Fernando. "*Phronèsis* vs. Scepticism." *New Blackfriars* 91, no. 1036 (November 2010): 680–94.

Chatterjee, Partha. "A Response to Taylor's 'Modes of Civil Society'." *Public Culture* 3, no. 1 (1990): 119–32.

Codina, Gabriel. "El 'Modus Parisiensis.'" *Gregorianum* 85 (2004): 43–64.

———. "Modus Parisiensis." In *The Jesuit Ratio Studiorum: 400th Anniversary Perspectives*, edited by Vincent J. Duminuco, 28–49. New York: Fordham University Press, 2000.

Coghlan, David. "Authenticity as First-Person Practice: An Exploration Based on Bernard Lonergan." *Action Research* 6, no. 3 (2008): 351–66.

Cole, Jonathan R. *The Great American University: Its Rise to Preeminence, Its Indispensable National Role, Why It Must Be Protected*. New York: PublicAffairs, 2009.

Connolly, William E. "Belief, Spirituality, and Time." In *Varieties of Secularism in a Secular Age*, edited by Michael Warner, Jonathan VanAntwerpen, and Craig Calhoun, 126–44. Cambridge, MA: Harvard University Press, 2010.

———. "Catholicism and Philosophy: A Nontheistic Appreciation." In *Charles Taylor*, edited by Ruth Abbey, 166–86. Cambridge: Cambridge University Press, 2004.

———. "The Human Predicament." *Social Research: An International Quarterly of the Social Sciences* 76, no. 4 (2009): 1121–40.

———. "Shock Therapy, Dramatization, and Practical Wisdom." In *The Joy of Secularism: 11 Essays for How We Live Now*, edited by George Levine, 95–114. Princeton, NJ: Princeton University Press, 2011.

Costa, Paolo. "A Secular Wonder." In *The Joy of Secularism: 11 Essays for How We Live Now*, edited by George Levine, 134–54. Princeton, NJ: Princeton University Press, 2011.

Cronin, Vincent. *A Pearl to India: The Life of Roberto de Nobili*. New York: E. P. Dutton, 1959.

Crowe, Frederick. *Method in Theology: An Organon for Our Time*. Milwaukee: Marquette University Press, 1980.

Crowley, Paul. "The Jesuit University and the Search for Transcendence." *Conversations on Jesuit Higher Education* 22 (2002): 10–15.

Cuypers, Stefaan E. "The Ideal of a Catholic Education in a Secularized Society." *Catholic Education: A Journal of Inquiry and Practice* 7, no. 4 (2004): 426–45.

Daoust, Joseph. "Of Kingfishers and Dragonflies: Faith and Justice at the Core of Jesuit Education." *Conversations on Jesuit Higher Education* 19 (2001): 13–20.

de Dalmases, Cándido. *Ignatius of Loyola: Founder of the Jesuits*, translated by Jerome Aixalá. Saint Louis: Institute of Jesuit Sources, 1985.

DeGioia, John J. "Regional Challenges Jesuit Higher Education Faces in North America." Paper presented at Global Jesuit Higher Education Conference, Universidad Iberoamericana, Mexico City, April 2010.

de Guibert, Joseph. *The Jesuits: Their Spiritual Doctrine and Practice—A Historical Study*, edited by George E. Ganss, SJ, and translated by William J. Young, SJ. Saint Louis: Institute of Jesuit Sources, 1986.

de Loyola, Ignatius. *The Autobiography* in *Ignatius of Loyola: Spiritual Exercises and Selected Works*, edited by George E. Ganss, SJ, and translated by Parmananda R. Divarkar, SJ, 65–112. New York: Paulist Press, 1991.

———. *The Constitutions of the Society of Jesus and Their Complementary Norms: A Complete Translation of the Official Latin Texts*. Saint Louis: Institute of Jesuit Sources, 1996.

———. *The Spiritual Exercises of Saint Ignatius: A Literal Translation and a Contemporary Reading*, edited by David L. Fleming. Saint Louis: Institute of Jesuit Sources, 1991.

de Montaigne, Michel. *Michel de Montaigne: The Complete Essays*, translated by M. A. Screech. London: Penguin Classics, 1991.

———. *Michel de Montaigne: The Complete Works—Essay, Travel Journal, Letters*, translated by Donald M. Frame. New York: Everyman's Library, 2003.

———. "Of Cannibals." In *Michel de Montaigne: The Complete Essays*, translated by M. A. Screech, 150–59. London: Penguin Classics, 1991.

———. "Of Experience." In *The Complete Essays of Montaigne*, translated by Donald M. Frame, 815–57. Palo Alto, CA: Stanford University Press, 1948.

———. "Of the Inconsistency of Our Actions." In *The Complete Essays of Montaigne*, translated by Donald M. Frame, 239–44. Palo Alto, CA: Stanford University Press, 1948.

———. "Of Practice." In *The Essays of Michel de Montaigne*, translated by M. A. Screech, 416–27. New York: Penguin, 1991.

———. "Of Repentance." In *The Complete Works of Montaigne: The Complete Essays of Montaigne*, translated by Donald M. Frame, 610–21. Palo Alto, CA: Stanford University Press, 1948.

———. "On Educating Children." In *The Essays: A Selection*, translated by M. A. Screech, 37–73. New York: Penguin, 2004.

Denig, Stephen. "What Would Newman Do? John Cardinal Newman and *Ex Cord Ecclesiae*." *Catholic Education: A Journal of Inquiry and Practice* 8, no. 2 (2004): 162–74.

Deutscher, Max. "Introduction." In *Michéle Le Dœuff: Operative Philosophy and Imaginary Practice*, edited by Max Deutscher, 9–29. Amherst, NY: Humanity Books, 2000.

———, ed. *Michéle Le Dœuff: Operative Philosophy and Imaginary Practice*. Amherst, NY: Humanity Books, 2000.

Deutscher, Penelope. "At Home in Philosophy: Le Dœuff's Gritty Vignettes." In *Michéle Le Dœuff: Operative Philosophy and Imaginary Practice*, edited by Max Deutscher, 199–219. Amherst, NY: Humanity Books, 2000.

de Waal, Frans B. M. "Prehuman Foundations of Morality." In *The Joy of Secularism: 11 Essays for How We Live Now*, edited by George Levine, 155–67. Princeton, NJ: Princeton University Press, 2011.

Dewhurst, David. "Education and Passion." *Educational Theory* 47, no. 4 (1997): 477–88.

Diggins, John Patrick. "The Godless Delusion" (Review of *A Secular Age*, by Charles Taylor). *New York Times Book Review*, December 16, 2007.

Dolan, Jay P. *In Search of an American Catholicism: A History of Religion and Culture in Tension.* Oxford: Oxford University Press, 2002.

Dreyfus, Hubert, and Sean Dorrance Kelly. *All Things Shining: Reading the Western Classics to Find Meaning in a Secular Age.* New York: Free Press, 2011.

———. "Saving the Sacred from the Axial Revolution." *Inquiry* 54, no. 2 (April 2011): 195–203.

Duminuco, Vincent J., ed. *The Jesuit Ratio Studiorum: 400th Anniversary Perspectives.* New York: Fordham University Press, 2000.

———. "A New *Ratio* for a New Millennium?" In *The Jesuit Ratio Studiorum: 400th Anniversary Perspectives,* edited by Vincent J. Duminuco, 145–61. New York: Fordham University Press, 2000.

Dupré, Louis. *The Quest of the Absolute: Birth and Decline of European Romanticism.* Notre Dame, IN: University of Notre Dame Press, 2013.

During, Simon. "Completing Secularism: The Mundane in the Neoliberal Era." In *Varieties of Secularism in a Secular Age,* edited by Michael Warner, Jonathan VanAntwerpen, and Craig Calhoun, 105–25. Cambridge, MA: Harvard University Press, 2010.

Ellacuría, Ignacio. "Is a Different Kind of University Possible?" translated by Phillip Berryman. In *Towards a Society That Serves Its People: The Intellectual Contribution of El Salvador's Murdered Jesuits,* 177–207, edited by John Hasset and Hugh Lacey Washington, 1–15. Washington, DC: Georgetown University Press, 1991.

———. "The Task of a Christian University." Convocation address, University of Santa Clara, Santa Clara, CA, June 12, 1982. http://www.scu.edu/Jesuits/ellacuria.html.

———. "The Challenge of the Poor Majority," translated by Phillip Berryman. In *Towards a Society That Serves Its People: The Intellectual Contribution of El Salvador's Murdered Jesuits,* edited by John Hassett and Hugh Lacey, 171–76. Washington, DC: Georgetown University Press, 1991.

Ellacuría, Ignacio, Ignacio Martín-Baró, and Jon Sobrino. *A Different Kind of University: Ignatian Voices from El Salvador,* edited by O. Morgan and F. Homer. Scranton, PA: Center for Mission Reflection, 1996.

Ellis, John Tracy. "American Catholics and the Intellectual Life." *Thought* 30 (Autumn 1955): 351–88.

Endean, Philip. "The Spiritual Exercises." In *The Cambridge Companion to the Jesuits,* edited by Thomas Worcester, 52–67. Cambridge: Cambridge University Press, 2008.

Erasmus, Desiderius. *De Ratione Studii (Upon the Right Method of Instruction).* In *Desiderius Erasmus Concerning the Aim and Method of Education,* edited by William Harrison Woodward, 162–79. New York: Bureau of Publication of Teachers College, Columbia University, 1964.

———. *The Praise of Folly,* translated by Clarence H. Miller. New Haven, CT: Yale University Press, 2003.

Fahey, Johannah, and Jane Kenway. "The Power of Imagining and Imagining Power." *Globalisation, Societies and Education* 4, no. 2 (2006): 161–66.

Fallis, George. *Multiversities, Ideas, and Democracy.* Toronto: University of Toronto Press, 2007.

Farrell, Allan P. *The Jesuit Code of Liberal Education: Development and Scope of the Ratio Studiorum.* Milwaukee: Bruce, 1939.

Feeney, Joseph. "The Core of Jesuit Undergraduate Education as Catholic: Some Issues for Faculties." *Conversations on Jesuit Higher Education* 15 (1999): 31–34.

Feldman, Noah. "Religion and the Earthly City." *Social Research: An International Quarterly of the Social Sciences* 76, no. 4 (2009): 989–1000.

Ferruolo, Stephen. *The Origins of the University: The Schools of Paris and their Critics, 1100–1215.* Palo Alto, CA: Stanford University Press, 1985.

Fisher, Mark. *Capitalist Realism: Is There No Alternative?* Winchester, UK: Zero Books, 2009.

Flanagan, Joseph. "The Jesuit University as a Counter-Culture." *Method* 10 (1999): 127–45.

Flanagan, Kieran. "*A Secular Age*: An Exercise in Breach-Mending." *New Blackfriars* 91, no. 1036 (November 2010): 699–721.

Frame, Donald. *Montaigne: A Biography.* New York: Harcourt, Brace, and World, 1965.

Gadamer, Hans-Georg. *Truth and Method*, translated by Joel Weinsheimer and Donald G. Marshall. New York: Continuum, 1975.

Gallagher, Michael Paul. *Faith Maps: Ten Religious Explorers from Newman to Joseph Ratzinger.* New York: Paulist Press, 2010.

Gallin, Alice, ed. *American Catholic Higher Education: Essential Documents, 1967–1990.* Notre Dame, IN: University of Notre Dame Press, 1992.

Ganss, George E., ed. *Ignatius of Loyola: Spiritual Exercises and Selected Works.* New York: Paulist Press, 1991.

———. *Saint Ignatius' Idea of a Jesuit University: A Study in the History of Catholic Higher Education.* Milwaukee: Marquette University Press, 1956.

Gleason, Philip. *Contending with Modernity: Catholic Higher Education in the Twentieth Century.* Oxford: Oxford University Press, 1995.

———. "The First Century of Jesuit Higher Education in America." *US Catholic Historian* 25 (2007): 37–52.

———. "Vehicle of Great Tradition: Saint Louis University and Catholic Higher Education." *Theology Digest* 43 (1996): 134–50.

Göle, Nilüfer. "The Civilization, Spatial, and Sexual Powers of the Secular." In *Varieties of Secularism in a Secular Age*, edited by Michael Warner, Jonathan VanAntwerpen, and Craig Calhoun, 243–64. Cambridge, MA: Harvard University Press, 2010.

Gordon, Peter E. "Must the Sacred be Transcendent?" *Inquiry* 54, no. 2 (April 2011): 126–39.

———. "The Place of the Sacred in the Absence of God" (Review of *A Secular Age*, by Charles Taylor). *Journal of the History of Ideas* 69, no. 4 (2008): 647–73.

Gosine, C. Jane, and Erik Oland. "Docere, Delectare, Movere: Marc-Antoine Charpentier and Jesuit Spirituality." *Early Music*, November 2004, 511–40.

Gourgouris, Stathis. "Detranscendentalizing the Secular." *Public Culture* 20, no. 3 (2008): 437–45.

Gray, Howard. "The Experience of Ignatius Loyola: Background to Jesuit Education." In *The Jesuit Ratio Studiorum: 400th Anniversary Perspectives*, edited by Vincent J. Duminuco, 1–21. New York: Fordham University Press, 2000.

Guarinus, Baptista. *Ad Maffeum Gambaram Brixianum Adulescentem Generosum Discipulum Suum, De Ordine Docendi et Studendi.* In *Humanist Educational Treatises*, edited and translated by Craig W. Kallendorf, 260–309. Cambridge, MA: Harvard University Press, 2002.

Gutmann, Amy, ed. *Multiculturalism: Examining the Politics of Recognition.* Princeton, NJ: Princeton University Press, 1994.

Habermas, Jürgen. "'The Political': The Rational Meaning of a Questionable Inheritance of Political Theology." In *The Power of Religion in the Public Sphere*, edited by Eduardo Mendieta and Jonathan VanAntwerpen, 15–33. New York: Columbia University Press, 2011.

Habermas, Jürgen, and John R. Blazek. "The Idea of the University: Learning Processes." *New German Critique* 41 (1987): 3–22.

Hacker, Andrew, and Claudia Dreifus. *Higher Education: How Colleges and Universities Are Wasting Our Money and Failing Our Kids—And What We Can Do About It.* New York: Times Books, 2010.

Hadot, Pierre. *Philosophy as a Way of Life*, edited by Arnold I. Davidson. Oxford: Blackwell, 2008.

———. *The Present Alone Is Our Happiness: Conversations with Jeannie Carlier and Arnold I. Davidson*, translated by Marc Djaballah. Palo Alto, CA: Stanford University Press, 2009.

———. *What Is Ancient Philosophy?* translated by Michael Chase. Cambridge, MA: Belknap Press of Harvard University Press, 2004.

Hamilton, David. "When Does a 'House of Studies' Become a 'School'? A Comment on the Jesuits and the Beginning of Modern Schooling." Cambridge: History of Education Society, 2003.

Hammond, N. G. L., and H. H. Scullard, eds. *The Oxford Classical Dictionary, Second Edition.* Oxford: Clarendon Press, 1970.

Hansen, David T. *The Teacher and the World: A Study of Cosmopolitanism as Education.* New York: Routledge, 2011.

Hassett, J., and H. Lacey, eds. *Towards a Society That Serves Its People: The Intellectual Contribution of El Salvador's Murdered Jesuits.* Washington, DC: Georgetown University Press, 1991.

Hassett, J., and H. Lacey. "Introduction." In *Towards a Society That Serves Its People: The Intellectual Contribution of El Salvador's Murdered Jesuits*, edited by John Hassett and Hugh Lacey, 1–15. Washington, DC: Georgetown University Press, 1991.

Haughey, John C. "Enhancing the Traditions." *Conversations on Jesuit Higher Education* 22 (2002): 32–34.

———. *Where Is Knowing Going? The Horizons of the Knowing Society.* Washington, DC: Georgetown University Press, 2009.

Hector, Kevin. "Grappling with Charles Taylor's *A Secular Age*: Kevin Hector and Theology and Philosophy of Religion." *Journal of Religion* 90, no. 3 (July 2010): 373–77.

Heft, James L., ed. *Believing Scholars: Ten Catholic Intellectuals.* New York: Fordham University Press, 2005.

Henry, Douglas V., and Michael D. Beaty, eds. *Christianity and the Soul of the University: Faith as a Foundation for Intellectual Community.* Grand Rapids: Baker Academic, 2006.

Higgins, Chris. "Teaching and the Good Life: A Critique of the Ascetic Ideal in Education." *Educational Theory* 53, no. 2 (2003): 131–54.

Himes, Michael J., and Stephen J. Pope, eds. *Finding God in All Things: Essays in Honor of Michael J. Buckley, SJ.* New York: Herder & Herder, 1996.

Hollenbach, David. "The Catholic Intellectual Tradition, Social Justice, and the University." *Conversations on Jesuit Higher Education* 36 (Fall 2009): 20–22.

———. "Is Tolerance Enough? The Catholic University and the Common Good." *Conversations on Jesuit Higher Education* 13 (Spring 1998): 5–15.

Holston, James, and Arjun Appadurai. "Cities and Citizenship." *Public Culture* 8, no. 2 (1996): 187–204.

Höpfl, Harro. *Jesuit Political Thought: The Society of Jesus and the State, c. 1540–1640—Ideas in Context.* New York: Cambridge University Press, 2004.

Hostetler, Karl. "The Common Good and Public Education." *Educational Theory* 53, no. 3 (2003): 347–61.

Hsia, R. Po-Chia. *A Jesuit in the Forbidden City: Mateo Ricci, 1552–1610.* Oxford: Oxford University Press, 2010.

Hutchins, Robert Maynard. *Education for Freedom.* Baton Rouge: Louisiana State University Press, 1947.

———. *The Higher Learning in America.* Westport, CT: Greenwood Press, 1979.

———. *The University of Utopia.* Chicago: University of Chicago Press, 1953.

Hyma, Albert. *The Christian Renaissance: A History of the "Devotio Moderna."* Hamden, CT: Archon Books, 1965.

Idígoras, José Ignacio Tellechea. *Ignatius of Loyola: The Pilgrim Saint,* edited and translated by Cornelius Michael Buckley. Chicago: Loyola University Press, 1994.

Institute of Jesuit Sources. *Documents of the 31st and 32nd General Congregations of the Society of Jesus.* Saint Louis: Institute of Jesuit Sources, 1977.

———. *Documents of the Thirty-Fourth General Congregation of the Society of Jesus.* Saint Louis: Institute of Jesuit Sources, 1995.

Ivens, Michael. *Understanding the Spiritual Exercises.* Leominster, UK: Gracewing, 1998.

Jaeger, Werner. *Early Christianity and the Greek Paideia.* Cambridge, MA: Harvard University Press, 1965.

———. *Paideia: The Ideals of Greek Culture, Volume I: Archaic Greece, the Mind of Athens,* translated by Gilbert Highet. Oxford: Oxford University Press, 1945.

———. *Paideia: The Ideals of Greek Culture, Volume II: In Search of the Divine Center,* translated by Gilbert Highet. Oxford: Oxford University Press, 1945.

———. *Paideia: The Ideals of Greek Culture, Volume III: The Conflict of Cultural Ideals in the Age of Plato,* translated by Gilbert Highet. Oxford: Oxford University Press, 1963.

Jager, Colin. "This Detail, This History: Charles Taylor's Romanticism." In *Varieties of Secularism in a Secular Age,* edited by Michael Warner, Jonathan VanAntwerpen, and Craig Calhoun, 166–192. Cambridge, MA: Harvard University Press, 2010.

Jaspers, Karl. *The Idea of the University,* edited by Karl W. Deutsch. Boston: Beacon Press, 1959.

Joldersma, Clarence W. "How Can Science Help Us Care for Nature? Hermeneutics, Fragility, and Responsibility for the Earth." *Educational Theory* 59, no. 4 (2009): 465–83.

Jones, Peter. "Equality, Recognition and Difference." *Critical Review of International Social and Political Philosophy* 9, no. 1 (2006): 23–46.

Kallendorf, Craig W., ed. and trans. *Humanist Educational Treatises.* Cambridge, MA: Harvard University Press, 2002.

Kant, Immanuel. *The Conflict of the Faculties,* translated by Mary J. Gregor. New York: Abaris Books, 1979.

———. *Critique of Judgement,* translated by James Creed Meredith and edited by Nicholas Walker. Oxford: Oxford University Press, 2007.

———. *Doctrine of Virtue: Part II of the Metaphysics of Morals,* translated by Mary J. Gregor. Philadelphia: University of Pennsylvania Press, 1971.

Kateb, George. "Locke and the Political Origins of Secularism." *Social Research: An International Quarterly of the Social Sciences* 76, no. 4 (2009): 1001–34.

Kerr, Clark. "Introduction." *Mission of the University,* by José Ortega y Gasset, edited and translated by Howard Lee Nostrand, ix–xxvi. New Brunswick, NJ: Transaction, 1991.

———. *The Uses of the University.* Cambridge, MA: Harvard University Press, 2001.

Kimball, Bruce A. *Orators and Philosophers: A History of the Idea of Liberal Education.* New York: College Entrance Examination Board, 1995.

Kitcher, Philip. "Challenges for Secularism." In *The Joy of Secularism: 11 Essays for How We Live Now*, edited by George Levine, 24–56. Princeton, NJ: Princeton University Press, 2011.

Kolvenbach, Peter-Hans. "A Universidade Jesuíta a Luz do Carisma Inaciano." *Brotéria* 153 (2001): 723–41.

———. "The Service of Faith and the Promotion of Justice in American Jesuit Higher Education." Conference address, Commitment Justice in Jesuit Higher Education Conference, Santa Clara University, Santa Clara, CA, October 2000. www.loyola.edu/yotc/father _kolvenbach.html#txxv.

Koppleman, Andrew. "Naked Strong Evaluation" (Review of *A Secular Age*, by Charles Taylor). *Dissent* 56, no. 1 (2009): 105–9.

Kristeller, Paul Oskar. *Renaissance Thought and Its Sources*, edited by Michael Mooney. New York: Columbia University Press, 1979.

Kronman, Anthony. *Education's End: Why Our Colleges and Universities Have Given Up on the Meaning of Life*. New Haven, CT: Yale University Press, 2007.

La Caze, Marguerite. "Analytic Imaginary." In *Michéle Le Dœuff: Operative Philosophy and Imaginary Practice*, edited by Max Deutscher, 61–79. Amherst, NY: Humanity Books, 2000.

Lacey, Michael. "The Backwardness of American Catholicism." *Conversations on Jesuit Higher Education*, 8 (1995): 4–13.

Lackner, Michael. "'The Other Is Manifold': A Jesuit's Comparative Approach to China, Japan, and India (1583)." In *Den Jadestein Erlangen (Festschrift für Harro von Senger)*, 121–139. Frankfurt: Verlag Otto Lembeck, 2009.

Lacouture, Jean. *Jesuits: A Multibiography*, translated by Jeremy Leggatt. Washington, DC: Counterpoint, 1995.

Lakies, Chad. "Challenging the Cultural Imaginary: Pieper on How Life Might Live." *New Blackfriars* 91, no. 1035 (August 2010): 499–510.

Larrimore, Mark. "Introduction: Religious Selves, Secular Selves." *Social Research: An International Quarterly of the Social Sciences* 76, no. 4 (2009): 1069–71.

Leahy, William P. *Adapting to America: Catholics, Jesuits, and Higher Education in the Twentieth Century*. Washington, DC: Georgetown University Press, 1991.

Lécrivain, Philippe. *Paris in the Time of Ignatius of Loyola (1528–1535)*, translated by Ralph C. Renner. Saint Louis: Institute of Jesuit Sources, 2011.

Le Dœuff, Michéle. *The Philosophical Imaginary*, translated by Colin Gordon. Stanford, CA: Stanford University Press, 1989.

Lehman, Glen. "Perspectives on Charles Taylor's Reconciled Society: Community, Difference and Nature." *Philosophy and Social Criticism* 32, no. 3 (2006): 347–76.

Letson, Douglas, and Michael Higgins. *The Jesuit Mystique*. Chicago: Jesuit Way, 1995.

Levine, Donald N. *Powers of the Mind: The Reinvention of Liberal Learning in America*. Chicago: University of Chicago Press, 2006.

Levine, George. "Introduction." In *The Joy of Secularism: 11 Essays for How We Live Now*, edited by George Levine, 1–23. Princeton, NJ: Princeton University Press, 2011.

———, ed. *The Joy of Secularism: 11 Essays for How We Live Now*. Princeton, NJ: Princeton University Press, 2011.

Levine, Lawrence W. *The Opening of the American Mind: Canons, Culture, and History*. Boston: Beacon Press: 1996.

Lloyd, Genevieve. "Feminism in History of Philosophy: Approaching the Past." In *The Cambridge Companion to Feminism in Philosophy*, edited by Miranda Fricker and Jennifer Hornsby, 245–63. Cambridge: Cambridge University Press, 2000.

————. "Le Dœuff and History of Philosophy." In *Michéle Le Dœuff: Operative Philosophy and Imaginary Practice*, edited by Max Deutscher, 33–43. Amherst, NY: Humanity Books, 2000.

Loach, Jodi. "Revolutionary Pedagogues? How Jesuits Used Education to Change Society." In *The Jesuits II: Cultures, Sciences, and the Arts 1540–1773*, edited by John W. O'Malley, Gauvin Alexander Bailey, Steven J. Harris, and T. Frank Kennedy, 66–85. Toronto: University of Toronto Press, 2002.

Lonergan, Bernard. "Cognitional Structure." In *Collected Works of Bernard Lonergan: Volume 4, Collection*, edited by Robert M. Doran and Frederick E. Crowe, 205–21. Toronto: University of Toronto Press, 1988.

————. "The Response of the Jesuit, as Priest and Apostle, in the Modern World." *Studies in the Spirituality of Jesuits* 2, no. 3 (September 1970): 89–110.

————. "Topics in Education: The Cincinnati Lectures of 1959 in the Philosophy of Education." In *The Collected Writing of Bernard Lonergan: Volume 10, Topics in Education*, edited by Robert M. Doran and Frederick E. Crowe. Toronto: University of Toronto Press, 2005.

Lucas, Christopher J. *American Higher Education: A History*. New York: Palgrave Macmillan, 2006.

Lukas, Ladislaus. "A History of the Jesuit *Ratio Studiorum*." In *Church, Culture, and Curriculum*, 17–46. Philadelphia: St. Joseph's University Press, 1999.

Lyon, David. "Being Post-Secular in the Social Sciences." *New Blackfriars* 91, no. 1036 (November 2010): 648–62.

MacIntyre, Alasdair. *God, Philosophy, Universities: A Selective History of the Catholic Philosophical Tradition*. New York: Rowman & Littlefield, 2009.

Mackler, Stephanie. *Learning for Meaning's Sake: Toward the Hermeneutic University*. Rotterdam: Sense, 2009.

Mahmood, Saba. "Can Secularism Be Otherwise?" In *Varieties of Secularism in a Secular Age*, edited by Michael Warner, Jonathan VanAntwerpen, and Craig Calhoun, 282–99. Cambridge, MA: Harvard University Press, 2010.

————. "Secular Imperatives?" *Public Culture* 20, no. 3 (2008): 461–65.

Mahoney, Kathleen A. *Catholic Higher Education in Protestant America: The Jesuits and Harvard in the Age of the University*. Baltimore: Johns Hopkins University Press, 2003.

Maritain, Jacques. *Education at the Crossroads*. New Haven, CT: Yale University Press, 1943.

Marsden, George M. *The Outrageous Idea of Christian Scholarship*. Oxford: Oxford University Press, 1997.

————. *The Soul of the American University: From Protestant Establishment to Established Nonbelief*. Oxford: Oxford University Press, 1994.

Marsden, George M., and Bradley J. Longfield, eds. *The Secularization of the Academy*. Oxford: Oxford University Press, 1992.

Marsh, James L. "A Response: What Is Jesuit Higher Education—The Service of Faith and the Promotion of Justice?" In *Jesuit Education 21: Conference Proceedings on the Future of Jesuit Higher Education*, edited by Martin R. Tripole, 45–54. Philadelphia: St. Joseph's University Press, 2000.

Marty, Martin E. "Review of *A Secular Age*, by Charles Taylor." *Church History* 77, no. 3 (2008): 773–75.

Mason, Mark. "The Ethics of Integrity: Educational Values Beyond Postmodern Ethics." *Journal of Philosophy of Education* 35, no. 1 (2001): 47–69.

———. "Teachers as Critical Mediators of Knowledge." *Journal of Philosophy of Education* 34, no. 2 (2000): 343–52.

May, Collin. "Review of *A Secular Age*, by Charles Taylor." *Society* 46 (2009): 199–203.

McConnell, Michael W. "Reclaiming the Secular and the Religious: The Primacy of Religious Autonomy." *Social Research: An International Quarterly of the Social Sciences* 76, no. 4 (2009): 1333–44.

McClintock, Robert. *Homeless in the House of the Intellect: Formative Justice and Education as an Academic Study.* New York: Laboratory for Liberal Learning, 2005.

———. "Toward a Place for Study in a World of Instruction." *Teachers College Record* 73, 2 (1971): 161–206.

McDade, John. "The Jesuit Mission and Dialogue with Culture." In *Jesuit Education 21: Conference Proceedings on the Future of Jesuit Higher Education*, edited by Martin R. Tripole, 56–66. Philadelphia: St. Joseph's University Press, 2000.

McDonough, Peter. *Men Astutely Trained: A History of the Jesuits in the American Century.* New York: Free Press, 1992.

McKevitt, Gerald. "The Great Principle of Unity? Is the Shifting History of Philosophy and Theology in the Jesuit Curriculum?" *Conversations on Jesuit Higher Education*, 32 (2008): 12–15.

———. "Jesuit Higher Education in the United States." *Mid-America* 73 (1991): 209–26.

———. "Jesuit Schools in the USA, 1814–c. 1970." In *The Cambridge Companion to the Jesuits*, edited by Thomas Worcester, 278–97. Cambridge: Cambridge University Press, 2008.

McLennan, Gregor. "Uplifting Belief." *New Blackfriars* 91, no. 1036 (November 2010): 627–45.

McManamon, John M. *Pierpaolo Vergerio the Elder: The Humanist as Orator.* Medieval and Renaissance Texts and Studies, vol. 163. Tempe: Arizona State University Press, 1996.

Meiklejohn, Alexander. *Education Between Two Worlds.* New York: Atherton Press, 1966.

———. *The Experimental College*, edited by John Walker Powell. Washington, DC: Seven Locks Press, 1981.

———. *The Liberal College.* New York: Arno Press, 1969.

Melloni, Javier. *The Exercises of St. Ignatius Loyola in the Western Tradition.* Leominster, UK: Gracewing, 2000.

Menand, Louis. *The Market Place of Ideas.* New York: W. W. Norton, 2010.

Mendieta, Eduardo, and Jonathan VanAntwerpen, eds. *The Power of Religion in the Public Sphere.* New York: Columbia University Press, 2011.

Milbank, John. "A Closer Walk on the Wild Side." In *Varieties of Secularism in a Secular Age*, edited by Michael Warner, Jonathan VanAntwerpen, and Craig Calhoun, 54–82. Cambridge, MA: Harvard University Press, 2010.

Mill, John Stuart. *Autobiography.* New York: Penguin Classics, 1989.

———. *Inaugural Address: Delivered to the University Students of St. Andrews.* Memphis: General Book, 2010.

Modras, Ronald. *Ignatian Humanism: A Dynamic Spirituality for the 21st Century.* Chicago: Loyola University Press, 2004.

———. "Rooted in the Renaissance." *Conversations on Jesuit Higher Education* 18 (2000): 31.

Morelli, Mark D., and Elizabeth A. Morelli, eds. *The Lonergan Reader.* Toronto: University of Toronto Press, 2002.

Morey, Melanie, M., and John J. Piderit. *Catholic Education: A Culture in Crisis.* Oxford: Oxford University Press, 2006.

Morgan, Michael L. "Review of *A Secular Age*, by Charles Taylor." *Philosophical Reviews* (2008). http://ndpr.nd.edu/review.cfm?id=13905.

Morris, Charles R. *American Catholic: The Saints and Sinners Who Built America's Most Powerful Church*. New York: Vintage Books, 1998.

Moseley, Nicholas. "Pius Aeneas." *Classical Journal* 20, no. 7 (1925): 387–400.

Moss, Pamela A. "Understanding the Other / Understanding Ourselves: Toward a Constructive Dialogue about 'Principles' in Educational Research." *Educational Theory* 55, no. 3 (2005): 263–83.

Nelles, Paul. "Historia Magistra Antiquitatis: Cicero and Jesuit History Teaching." *Renaissance Studies* 13 (1999): 130–72.

Newfield, Christopher. *Unmaking the Public University: The Forty-Year Assault on the Middle Class*. Cambridge, MA: Harvard University Press, 2008.

Newman, John Henry. *The Idea of a University*, edited by Frank Turner. New Haven, CT: Yale University Press, 1996.

Nicolás, Adolfo. "Challenges to Jesuit Higher Education Today: Remarks for Networking Jesuit Higher Education—Shaping the Future for a Human, Just, Sustainable Globe." *Conversations on Jesuit Higher Education* 40 (2011): 6–9.

———. "Depth, Universality, and Learned Ministry: Challenges to Jesuit Higher Education Today." Conference address, Universidad Iberoamricana, Mexico City, April 23, 2010. www.loyola.edu/Justice/commitment/NicolasSJ.JHE.April23.2010[1].pdf.

Nussbaum, Martha C. *Creating Capabilities: The Human Development Approach*. Cambridge, MA: Belknap Press of Harvard University Press, 2011.

———. *Cultivating Humanity: A Classical Defense of Reform in Liberal Education*. Cambridge, MA: Harvard University Press, 1997.

———. *Not for Profit: Why Democracy Needs the Humanities*. Princeton, NJ: Princeton University Press, 2010.

Nygren, Anders. *Agape and Eros*, translated by Philip S. Watson. London: SPCK, 1957.

Oakeshott, Michael. *The Voice of Liberal Learning*. Indianapolis: Liberty Fund, 2001.

Obirek, Stanisław. "Jesuits in Poland and Eastern Europe." In *The Cambridge Companion to the Jesuits*, edited by Thomas Worcester, 136–50. Cambridge: Cambridge University Press, 2008.

O'Brien, David J. *From the Heart of the American Church: Catholic Higher Education and American Culture*. Maryknoll, NY: Orbis Books, 1994.

O'Brien, William J., ed. *For That I Came: Virtues and Ideals of Jesuit Education*. Washington, DC: Georgetown University Press, 1997.

———, ed. *Let Justice Roll Down Like Waters: Jesuit Education and Faith That Does Justice*. Washington, DC: Georgetown University Press, 1993.

O'Malley, John W. *The First Jesuits*. Cambridge, MA: Harvard University Press, 1993.

———. *Four Cultures of the West*. Cambridge, MA: Belknap Press of Harvard University Press, 2004.

———. "From the 1599 *Ratio Studiorum* to the Present: A Humanist Tradition?" In *The Jesuit Ratio Studiorum: 400th Anniversary Perspectives*, edited by Vincent J. Duminuco, 127–44. New York: Fordham University Press, 2000.

———. "How the First Jesuits Became Involved in Education." In *The Jesuit Ratio Studiorum: 400th Anniversary Perspectives*, edited by Vincent J. Duminuco, 56–74. New York: Fordham University Press, 2000.

————. "How Humanist Is the Jesuit Tradition? From the 1599 *Ratio Studiorum* to Now." In *Jesuit Education 21: Conference Proceedings on the Future of Jesuit Higher Education*, edited by Martin R. Tripole, 189–201. Philadelphia: St. Joseph's University Press, 2000.

Ortega y Gasset, José. *Mission of the University*, edited and translated by Howard Lee Nostrand. New Brunswick, NJ: Transaction, 1991.

Outka, Gene. *Agape: An Ethical Analysis*. New Haven, CT: Yale University Press, 1972.

Padberg, John W. "Development of the *Ratio Studiorum*." In *The Jesuit Ratio Studiorum: 400th Anniversary Perspectives*, edited by Vincent J. Duminuco, 80–100. New York: Fordham University Press, 2000.

————, ed. *Ignatius of Loyola: Letters and Instructions*. Saint Louis: Institute of Jesuit Sources, 2006.

————, ed. *Jesuit Life and Mission Today: The Decrees and Accompanying Documents of the 31st–35th General Congregations of the Society of Jesus*. Saint Louis: Institute of Jesuit Sources, 2009.

Paffenroth, Kim, and Kevin L. Hughes, eds. *Augustine and Liberal Education*. Lanham, MD: Lexington Books, 2008.

Palmer, Parker. *The Courage to Teach*. San Francisco: Jossey-Bass, 2007.

————. *The Promise of Paradox*. San Francisco: Jossey-Bass, 2008.

————. *To Know as We Are Known*. San Francisco: HarperCollins, 1993.

Palmer, Parker, and Arthur Zajonc. *The Heart of Higher Education: A Call to Renewal*. San Francisco: Jossey-Bass, 2010.

Papastephanou, Marianna. "Arrows Not Yet Fired: Cultivating Cosmopolitanism through Education." *Journal of Philosophy of Education* 36, no. 1 (2002): 69–86.

Pavur, Claude. "The Curriculum Carries the Mission: The *Ratio Studiorum*, the Making of Jesuit Education, and the Making of the Society of Jesus." *New Jesuit Review* 2, no. 5 (2010). www.newjesuitreview.org/newjesuitreview/Home.html.

————. "The Curriculum Carries the Mission: Why We Still Need the *Ratio Studiorum*, Especially Today." *Conversations on Jesuit Higher Education*, 34 (2008): 30–33.

————. "Jesuit Spirituality and Catholic Higher Education." *Review for Religious* 52 (1993): 875–85.

————, trans. *The Ratio Studiorum: The Official Plan for Jesuit Education*. Saint Louis: Institute of Jesuit Sources, 2005.

Pelikan, Jaroslav. *The Idea of the University: A Reexamination*. New Haven, CT: Yale University Press, 1992.

Phillips, Adam. "Freud's Helplessness." In *The Joy of Secularism: 11 Essays for How We Live Now*, edited by George Levine, 115–33. Princeton, NJ: Princeton University Press, 2011.

Pickstock, Catherine. "Liturgy, Art and Politics." *Modern Theology* 16, no. 2 (2000): 159–80.

Pico della Mirandola, Giovanni. *Oration on the Dignity of Man*, translated by Elizabeth Livermoore Forbes. In *The Renaissance Philosophy of Man: Petrarca, Valla, Ficino Pico, Pomponazzi, Vives*, edited by Ernst Cassirer, Paul Oskar Kristeller, and John Herman Randall Jr. Chicago: University of Chicago Press, 1948.

Piccolomini, Aenas Silvius. *De Liberorum Educatione*. In *Humanist Educational Treatises*, edited and translated by Craig W. Kallendorf, 126–259. Cambridge, MA: Harvard University Press, 2002.

Pinkard, Terry. "Taylor, 'History,' and the History of Philosophy." In *Charles Taylor*, edited by Ruth Abbey, 187–214. Cambridge: Cambridge University Press, 2004.

Post, R. R. *The Modern Devotion: Confrontation with Reformation and Humanism*. Leiden: E. J. Brill, 1968.

Proctor, Robert E. *Defining the Humanities: How Rediscovering a Tradition Can Improve Our Schools—With a Curriculum for Today's Students*. Bloomington: Indiana University Press, 1998.

———. *Education's Great Amnesia: Reconsidering the Humanities from Petrarch to Freud—With a Curriculum for Today's Students*. Bloomington: Indiana University Press, 1988.

Putnam, Robert D. *Bowling Alone: The Collapse and Revival of American Community*. New York: Simon & Shuster, 2000.

Rashdall, Hastings. *Universities of Europe in the Middle Ages, Volume I: Salerno, Bologna, Paris*. Cambridge: Cambridge University Press, 2010.

———. *Universities of Europe in the Middle Ages, Volume II, Part I: Italy, Spain, France, Germany, Scotland, Etc*. Cambridge: Cambridge University Press, 2010.

———. *Universities of Europe in the Middle Ages, Volume II, Part II: English Universities, Student Life*. Cambridge: Cambridge University Press, 2010.

Rausch, Thomas P. *Educating for Faith and Justice: Catholic Higher Education Today*. Collegeville, MN: Liturgical Press, 2010.

Resnik, Julia. "Contextualizing Recognition, Absence of Recognition, and Misrecognition: The Case of Migrant Workers' Children in Daycares in Israel." *Journal of Curriculum Studies* 41, no. 5 (2009): 625–49.

Reuben, Julie A. *The Making of the Modern University: An Intellectual Transformation and the Marginalization of Morality*. Chicago: University of Chicago Press, 1996.

Richards, Robert J. "Darwinian Enchantment." In *The Joy of Secularism: 11 Essays for How We Live Now*, edited by George Levine, 185–204. Princeton, NJ: Princeton University Press, 2011.

Rizvi, Fazal. "Imagination and the Globalization of Educational Policy Research." *Globalisation, Societies and Education* 4, no. 2 (2006): 193–205.

Robbins, Bruce. "Disenchanted" (Review of *A Secular Age*, by Charles Taylor). *Notre Dame Philosophical Reviews*, 2008. http://ndpr.nd.edu/review.cfm?id=13905.

———. "Enchantment? No, Thank You!" In *The Joy of Secularism: 11 Essays for How We Live Now*, edited by George Levine, 74–94. Princeton, NJ: Princeton University Press, 2011.

Roberts, Jon H., and James Turner. *The Sacred and the Secular University*. Princeton, NJ: Princeton University Press, 2010.

Rogers, Daniel T. *Age of Fracture*. Cambridge, MA: Belknap Press of Harvard University Press, 2011.

Rossi, Philip. "Review of *A Secular Age* by Charles Taylor." *Theological Studies* 69, no. 4 (2008): 953–54.

Scaglione, Aldo. *Essays on the Arts of Discourse: Linguistics, Rhetoric, Poetics*, edited by Paolo Cherchi, Stephen Murphy, Allen Mandelbaum, and Giuseppe Velli. New York: Peter Lang, 1998.

———. *The Liberal Arts and the Jesuit College System*. Philadelphia: John Benjamins, 1986.

Schervish, Paul. "Finding God in Some Things: Unintended Consequences for the Academy of the Faith That Does Justice." *Conversations on Jesuit Higher Education* 19 (2001): 21–27.

Schweiker, William. "Grappling with Charles Taylor's *A Secular Age*: William Scheiker and Theological Ethics." *Journal of Religion* 90, no. 3 (July 2010): 367–73.

———. "Humanizing Religion." *Journal of Religion* 89, no. 2 (April 2009): 214–35.

Seligman, Adam B. "Ritual, the Self, and Sincerity." *Social Research: An International Quarterly of the Social Sciences* 76, no. 4 (2009): 1073–96.

Sheehan, Jonathan. "When Was Disenchantment? History and the Secular Age." In *Varieties of Secularism in a Secular Age*, edited by Michael Warner, Jonathan VanAntwerpen, and Craig Calhoun, 217–42. Cambridge, MA: Harvard University Press, 2010.

Shuman, Samuel. *Seeing the Light: Religious Colleges in the Twenty-First Century*. Baltimore: Johns Hopkins University Press, 2010.

Smeyers, Paul, and Nicholas C. Burbules. "Education as Initiation into Practices." *Educational Theory* 56, no. 4 (2006): 439–49.

Smeyers, Paul, and Nicholas C. Burbules. "The Changing Practices and Social Relations of Education." *Educational Theory* 56, no. 4 (2006): 363–69.

Smith, Nicholas H. *Charles Taylor: Meaning, Morals and Modernity*. New York: Blackwell, 2002.

Smith, Steven D. *The Disenchantment of Secular Discourse*. Cambridge, MA: Harvard University Press, 2010.

Spohn, William C. "Developing a Moral Conscience in Jesuit Higher Education." In *Jesuit Education 21: Conference Proceedings on the Future of Jesuit Higher Education*, edited by Martin R. Tripole, 389–404. Philadelphia: St. Joseph's University Press, 2000.

———. "The University That Does Justice." *Conversations on Jesuit Higher Education* 19 (2001): 4–12.

Starrett, Gregory. "The Varieties of Secular Experience." *Comparative Studies in Society and History* 52, no. 3 (2010): 626–51.

Steinfels, Peter. "Modernity and Belief" (Review of *A Secular Age*, by Charles Taylor). *Commonweal* 135, no. 9 (2008): 14–21.

Stott, Rebecca. "The Wetfooted Understory: Darwinian Immersions." In *The Joy of Secularism: 11 Essays for How We Live Now*, edited by George Levine, 205–24. Princeton, NJ: Princeton University Press, 2011.

Taylor, Charles. "Apologia pro Libro suo." In *Varieties of Secularism in a Secular Age*, edited by Michael Warner, Jonathan VanAntwerpen, and Craig Calhoun, 300–324. Cambridge, MA: Harvard University Press, 2010.

———. "A Catholic Modernity?" In *A Catholic Modernity? Charles Taylor's Marianist Award Lecture, with Responses by William M. Shea, Rosemary Luling Haughton, George Marsden, and Jean Bethke Elshtain*, edited by James L. Heft, 13–38. Oxford: Oxford University Press, 1999.

———. "Cross-Purposes: The Liberal/Communitarian Debate." In *Philosophical Arguments*, 181–203. Cambridge, MA: Harvard University Press, 1995.

———. "Cultures of Democracy and Citizen Efficacy." *Public Culture* 19, no. 1 (2007): 117–50.

———. *Dilemmas and Connections: Selected Essays*. Cambridge, MA: Belknap Press of Harvard University Press, 2011.

———. *The Ethics of Authenticity*. Cambridge, MA: Harvard University Press, 1991.

———. "Foundationalism and the Inner/Outer Distinction." In *Reading McDowell: On Mind and World*, 106–19. New York: Routledge, 2002.

———. *Hegel*. Cambridge: Cambridge University Press, 1975.

———. *Human Agency and Language: Philosophical Papers, Volume 1*. Cambridge: Cambridge University Press, 1985.

———. *The Language Animal: The Full Shape of the Human Linguistic Capacity*. Cambridge, MA: Belknap Press of Harvard University Press: 2016.

———. "The Meaning of Secularism." *Hedgehog Review: Critical Reflections on Contemporary Culture* 12, no. 3 (Fall 2010): 23–34.

———. "Modern Social Imaginaries." *Public Culture* 14, no. 1 (2002): 91–124.

———. "Modes of Civility." *Public Culture* 3, no. 1 (2002): 95–118.

———. *Philosophical Arguments.* Cambridge, MA: Harvard University Press, 1995.

———. *Philosophy and the Human Sciences: Philosophical Papers, Volume 2.* Cambridge: Cambridge University Press, 1985.

———. "The Politics of Recognition." In *Multiculturalism: Examining the Politics of Recognition,* edited by Amy Gutmann, 25–74. Princeton, NJ: Princeton University Press, 1994.

———. "The Polysemy of the Secular." *Social Research: An International Quarterly of the Social Sciences* 76, no. 4 (2009): 1143–66.

———. "Reason, Faith, and Meaning." *Faith and Philosophy* 28, no. 1 (January 2011): 5–18.

———. "Recovering the Sacred." *Inquiry* 54, no. 2 (April 2011): 113–25.

———. *A Secular Age.* Cambridge, MA: Belknap Press of Harvard University Press, 2007.

———. *Sources of the Self: The Making of the Modern Identity.* Cambridge, MA: Harvard University Press, 1989.

———. "Statement Upon Reception of the Templeton Prize," press release, March 14, 2007. www.templetonprize.org/ct_statement.html.

———. "Taylor Replies to Keith Tester's 'Multiculturalism, Catholicism and Us.'" *New Blackfriars* 91, no. 1036 (November 2010): 677–79.

———. "Taylor Replies to Kieran Flanagan's '*A Secular Age*: An Exercise in Breach-Mending.'" *New Blackfriars* 91, no. 1036 (November 2010): 721–24.

———. "Understanding the Other: A Gadamerian View on Conceptual Schemes." In *Gadamer's Century: Essays in Honor of Hans-Georg Gadamer,* edited by Jeff Malpas, Ulrich Arnswald, and Jens Kertscher, 279–98. Cambridge, MA: MIT Press, 2002.

———. *Varieties of Religion Today: William James Revisited.* Cambridge, MA: Harvard University Press, 2002.

———. "Western Secularity." In *Rethinking Secularism,* edited by Craig Calhoun, Mark Juergensmeyer, and Jonathan VanAntwerpen. Oxford: Oxford University Press, 2011.

———. "What Exactly Is Reason?" Paper presented at Faith and Reason Conference, Fordham University, New York, June 16, 2009.

———. "Why We Need a Radical Redefinition of Secularism." In *The Power of Religion in the Public Sphere.* Edited by Eduardo Mendieta and Jonathan VanAntwerpen, 34–59. New York: Columbia University Press, 2011.

Taylor, Charles, and Jocelyn Maclure. *Secularism and Freedom of Conscience,* translated by Jane Marie Todd. Cambridge, MA: Harvard University Press, 2011.

Tester, Keith. "Multiculturalism, Catholicism and Us." *New Blackfriars* 91, no. 1036 (November 2010): 665–76.

Theobald, Paul. "A Case for Inserting Community into the Public School Curriculum." *American Journal of Education* 112 (May 2006): 315–34.

Thomson, Ian. "Transcendence and the Problem of Otherworldly Nihilism." *Inquiry* 54, no. 2 (April 2011): 140–59.

Toulmin, Stephen. *Cosmopolis: The Hidden Agenda of Modernity.* Chicago: University of Chicago Press, 1992.

Traub, George W. *A Jesuit Education Reader.* Chicago: Loyola University Press, 2008.

Tripole, Martin R., ed. *Jesuit Education 21: Conference Proceedings on the Future of Jesuit Higher Education.* Philadelphia: St. Joseph's University Press, 2000.

van der Veer, Peter. "Spirituality in Modern Society." *Social Research: An International Quarterly of the Social Sciences* 76, no. 4 (2009): 1097–1120.

Verene, Donald Phillip. *The Art of Humane Education*. Ithaca, NY: Cornell University Press, 2002.

Vergerio, Pier Paolo. *De Ingenius Moribus et Liberalibus Studiis*. In *Humanist Educational Treatises*, edited and translated by Craig W. Kallendorf, 2–91. Cambridge, MA: Harvard University Press, 2002.

Warner, Michael, Jonathan VanAntwerpen, and Craig Calhoun. "Editor's Introduction." In *Varieties of Secularism in a Secular Age*, edited by Michael Warner, Jonathan VanAntwerpen, and Craig Calhoun, 243–64. Cambridge, MA: Harvard University Press, 2010.

Warner, Michael, Jonathan VanAntwerpen, and Craig Calhoun, eds. *Varieties of Secularism in a Secular Age*. Cambridge, MA: Harvard University Press, 2010.

Watson, Philip S. "Translator's Preface." In *Agape and Eros*, by Anders Nygren, translated by Philip S. Watson. London: SPCK, 1957.

West, Cornel. "Prophetic Religion and the Future of Capitalist Civilization." In *The Power of Religion in the Public Sphere*, edited by Eduardo Mendieta and Jonathan VanAntwerpen, 92–100. New York: Columbia University Press, 2011.

Westphal, Merold. "A Midrash of (and for) Hope." *Conversations on Jesuit Higher Education* 18 (2000): 16–24.

Whitehead, Alfred North. *The Aims of Education*. New York: Free Press, 1967.

Whitehead, Kenneth D., ed. *The Idea of the Catholic University: Proceedings from the 30th Annual Convention of the Fellowship of Catholic Scholars*. Chicago: University of Chicago Press, 2009.

Whitfield, Teresa. *Paying the Price: Ignacio Ellacuría and the Murdered Jesuits of El Salvador*. Philadelphia: Temple University Press, 1994.

Wildavsky, Ben. *The Great Brain Race*. Princeton, NJ: Princeton University Press, 2010.

Wilson, David Sloan. "The Truth Is Sacred." In *The Joy of Secularism: 11 Essays for How We Live Now*, edited by George Levine, 168–84. Princeton, NJ: Princeton University Press, 2011.

Wood, James. "Is That All There Is? Secularism and Its Discontents." *New Yorker*, August 15, 2011: 87–92.

Worcester, Thomas, ed. *The Cambridge Companion to the Jesuits*. Cambridge: Cambridge University Press, 2008.

Wright, Jonathan. *God's Soldiers: Adventure, Politics, Intrigue, and Power—A History of the Jesuits*. New York: Doubleday, 2004.

———. "The Suppression and Restoration." In *The Cambridge Companion to the Jesuits*, edited by Thomas Worcester, 263–77. Cambridge: Cambridge University Press, 2008.

# INDEX